Dear Gillian,

Thank you for all your support in my first few years at the U of C.

Warmly,
Pallavi

The Opportunity Trap

*High-Skilled Workers, Indian Families, and
the Failures of the Dependent Visa Program*

Pallavi Banerjee

NEW YORK UNIVERSITY PRESS
New York

NEW YORK UNIVERSITY PRESS
New York
www.nyupress.org

References to Internet websites (URLs) were accurate at the time of writing. Neither the author nor New York University Press is responsible for URLs that may have expired or changed since the manuscript was prepared.

Library of Congress Cataloging-in-Publication Data
Names: Banerjee, Pallavi, author.
Title: The opportunity trap : high-skilled workers, Indian families, and the failures of the dependent visa program / Pallavi Banerjee.
Description: New York : New York University Press, [2022] | Includes bibliographical references and index.
Identifiers: LCCN 2021024174 | ISBN 9781479852918 (hardback ; alk. paper) | ISBN 9781479841042 (paperback ; alk. paper) | ISBN 9781479825158 (ebook) | ISBN 9781479860821 (ebook other)
Subjects: LCSH: Foreign workers, East Indian—United States. | Professional employees—United States. | Skilled labor—United States. | East Indians—United States—Social conditions. | Visas—United States. | United States—Emigration and immigration—Government policy.
Classification: LCC HD8081.E3 B36 2022 | DDC 331.6/254073—dc23
LC record available at https://lccn.loc.gov/2021024174

New York University Press books are printed on acid-free paper, and their binding materials are chosen for strength and durability. We strive to use environmentally responsible suppliers and materials to the greatest extent possible in publishing our books.

Manufactured in the United States of America

10 9 8 7 6 5 4 3 2 1

Also available as an ebook

For Pratim, Chulbul, Jhumama, and Harubaba

CONTENTS

Introduction

The Anatomy of State-Imposed Dependence

We're a nation of immigrants, but we are also a nation of laws.
—George W. Bush (2006)

Even as we are a nation of immigrants, we're also a nation of laws.
—Barack Obama (2014)

The year was 1998, the second year of my undergraduate education in India. A member of my extended family, Trina—quite a few years older than I and recently married—was leaving for the United States on what she called a "dependent visa" (officially, an H-4 visa). This was the first I had heard of this visa; I did not want to see her leave. I looked up to Trina, a smart, dynamic young woman who lived in the city of Bangalore, India's then technological capital. She had an MBA from one of India's top universities and was working as a consultant for a Mumbai-based multinational firm. She met her future husband on one of her business projects. He worked in a large Indian information technology (IT) company, which was also a so-called body-shopping agency, supplying Indian IT workers to corporations across the world. Four months after their marriage, he received a promotion, an offshore assignment to work for a US financial firm as a tech developer for three to six years. He left for America, and soon after Trina followed her new husband on an H-4 "dependent" visa sponsored and paid for by her husband's company. The decision to move to the United States wasn't easy for Trina. She was giving up a prestigious job in a bustling Indian city to be with her husband in rural Washington State. But her friends and family assured her that with her qualifications she need not worry about finding appropriate work as soon as she landed in America—the land of opportunities. While she knew that her type of visa prohibited the holder from obtaining lawful (and paid) employment, she was not entirely aware of the extent of the barriers she would face in finding a job in an organization that was willing or able to sponsor her for a work visa (of which there are many categories).

Trina left India with mixed emotions—both excitement and trepidation. But she was determined to make something of her life in the United States. However, as the years passed without finding a job under worker-visa sponsorship, her hope and determination waned. She shared with me how her family life had become a gendered regimen of unpaid housework, child care (after she had a child), household labor,[1] and support for her husband's long, intense hours as a computer programmer in the IT division of a large financial firm. Her emotional life and selfhood became defined by a sense of loss, a decline in self-worth, and the onset of severe depression. She described her situation as "the effacement and invisibility of the person" that she had once been. After spending six years on a dependent visa and making many failed attempts to escape her dependent status, she returned to India with her two-year-old daughter. She went through a difficult divorce and remained chronically depressed for years. In one of our many conversations after her return, she told me: "Never go to that country on someone else's visa. Only go if you have and can get your visa, or you will become a basket case like me." When I sought her permission to share her story in my book, she offered a note of caution and advice:

> Let me know if the women you talk to feel as helpless as I did, or if it was just me. It was so hard to express why I was so unhappy—I did not have an abusive husband or a bad life or anything. I just couldn't take being no one and nothing beyond being the spouse of so-and-so, and in my unhappiness, I made him miserable. The whole thing was a train wreck, and clearly the trauma has not left me yet. I just want to find out if it was just me.

Trina now lives with her daughter in Bangalore, works in a bank as a financial analyst, and still blames her broken marriage on the US government and the visa system.

* * *

The Opportunity Trap is a comparative study focusing on the experiences of Indian professional migrant families that are led by men (high-tech workers in IT) versus families that are led by women (nurses in the medical field). In particular, the book unravels the implications of visa laws on Indian professional families where the working professionals—men and women—come to the United States on skilled-worker visas and bring their spouse (and children) on the popular dependent visa (H-4). Specifically, I ask several questions. How do visas, as a tool of control and a structure of dominance, play out in the everyday lives of visa holders? What are the gendered implications of a visa system that forces migrant workers' spouses to be dependents? What can we learn about the global mobility of labor and the reconfiguration of families when we frame immigrant visas as tools for controlling paid and unpaid labor? In answering these questions, this book spotlights the disenfranchised lives of temporary workers and their families in the United States who are asked to contribute their labor while being denied political and social rights. The book invites readers to reflect on how both immigration and visa laws function as a government apparatus of control and leave indelible imprints on the existence of those who lives these laws encumber.

The book is inspired by my personal and academic investment in understanding how immigration and visa laws affect immigrant families and how gendered patterns of migration further complicate their experiences. I am an Indian woman who immigrated to the United States and who knows several people subject to immigration and visa laws. This quest led to a six-year journey looking at the lives of Indian nurses and tech workers who come to the United States (as temporary workers) with their conjugal families (dependents).

* * *

Houston, Texas. The year was 2009, a balmy late afternoon in October. I was knee-deep in fieldwork for what would become the soul of *The Opportunity Trap*. On this particular afternoon, I was sitting in a hotel lobby with an Indian immigrant couple, talking about their migration history. As in Trina's situation, the woman in this couple, Maira, migrated to the United States in 2004 on a skilled-worker's visa as a nurse, and her husband, Mat, followed from India with their children in 2006 on an H-4 dependent visa.

The lobby was bustling with Indian nurses and their families, attending the biennial conference of the National Association for Indian Nurses of America. The atmosphere was festive, with children running around, food being carted in by hotel staff, Indian nurses (all women) wearing sarees and sporting flowers in their hair, and men wearing colorful *kurtas*[2] (formal suits). It was the last day of the conference, and everyone was gearing up for that evening's grand banquet and cultural show. Maira, a Houston resident, was at the conference to give a presentation on the challenges of being an immigrant nurse in the United States. While Maira and Mat's children were getting dressed up to perform in the cultural show, I had a window of 30 minutes to talk with them together; I would later speak with each individually as well.

When Maira was 25, she left her job in a large hospital in Bangalore to take a position in Qatar—her first job as a nurse outside India. While she worked in Qatar, her newlywed husband stayed in India. Their transnational relationship resulted in two children who also stayed with their father in India after they were born—because immigrant nurses were not allowed to bring families to Qatar for the first three years. Mat was a middle-school teacher in the village in India where he had grown up and where he lived with his extended family and the children.

Maira summed up her experience in Qatar as follows: "The money in Qatar was good, the work was hard and excruciating, and I experience a lot of indignity. All I wanted was to move to the United States or some other place where my family could join me." Maira's wish to move was fulfilled a few years later, when she found a job in the United States. Mat and the children were able to join her there after two years of separation. As they recounted the story of their immigration to the United States, I could not help but notice how little Mat spoke. All he said was: "I am here on a dependent visa"; and all my efforts as an experienced interviewer to get him to share more failed miserably. Before we came to the question of his life in the United States, he had eloquently and at length laid out his life as a working single father living with the extended family in India during Maira's stint in Qatar. But he clammed up on the question of migration to the United States even though that move on Maira's part was orchestrated so the family could reunite.

Maira, in contrast, spoke openly about her work, talked about the hurdles she had to overcome as an immigrant health care worker, and shared extensively the challenges she faced every day as a working mother and wife. She, too, not even once raised the issue of her husband's dependent status during our conversations. However, she did describe the bureaucracy of the migration process, the many documents and papers she had to gather to bring her family to the United States, the many lawyers she consulted in the United States and India to figure out whether her husband could come on a worker's visa—and how she had failed in the process. As she was describing this experience, a suddenly animated Mat interjected to explain how nightmarish and humiliating it was for him to go for his visa interview at the US embassy in Chennai, in India, where he was the only man coming on a dependent visa (the rest of the dependent visa applicants present that day were women, as per his observation). While Maira looked on sheepishly, her husband spoke with sharpness in his voice about his experience at the consulate. He recounted how the visa officer pointedly told him that he could not look for work while on the visa. "Yes, sir, your country, your rules, I said to the officer," was the slightly sarcastic retort Mat described making. We had talked for about 45 minutes when it was time to walk to the banquet hall. I attempted to lighten the mood by asking Maira what her children planned on performing. "I am not quite sure; I was working two shifts for the past month—Mat would know," she responded.

* * *

Trina's experience as a dependent visa holder in the United States resonates with the many stories of women participants in this study whose lives are marked by the dependency forced on them due to their visa status. Maira and Mat's story also resembles in many ways the lived experiences of Indian families of nurses who come to the United States with men (husbands) as dependents. These two opening vignettes provide an introduction to four arguments that are central to this book, explained below.

First, I make the overarching argument that, in comparing the experiences of the families of high-tech workers and nurses, the book focuses on how gendered migration—in conjunction with the visa laws that nonimmigrant[3] workers arrive on—shapes migration experiences and histories. Visas are not simply state-endorsed documents that allow people to move across international borders. Visas are sociologically and legally relevant in that they form a gendered and racialized regime that controls the day-to-day experiences of migrating populations.

Second, the book questions the gender neutrality of visa laws. Both men and women are eligible for the same visas, yet some visa laws translate to heavily gendered interactions, expressions, and experiences in the everyday lives of migrants. This is especially relevant in the household division of labor and in parenting, as the book demonstrates.

Third, the book develops the concept of the "visa regime" as a key analytic framework with which to understand the experiences of professional Indian immigrant families in the United States. By illustrating the deep and enduring processual effects that the legal visa status has on the public discourse on visa holders; on the self of the visa holder; on gendered and racialized work lives; and gendered familial and parenting labor of the visa holders, I establish the systemic impact of the visa regime on every aspect of the lives of the participants in this book. I see the visa regime as a technique that controls the lives and subjectivities of immigrant workers and families through the reconstruction of the self as gendered and racialized beginning, on the day of their arrival. Analysis through this lens of a gendered and racialized visa regime punctures the myth that *highly skilled migrant/temporary workers* and their families (who are considered more privileged than other types of migrant workers) have unfettered access to *flexible* and *cultural* citizenship through which to carve out their life course in the host country. As my analysis will show, the individuals in this study struggled with various kinds of disenfranchisement in both the public and the private spheres because of visa structures.

Fourth, *The Opportunity Trap* explores how Indian migrants grapple with the identities of being workers and being people. I examine the dissonance between the state's perceptions of the needs of immigrant families and the challenges that immigrant workers and their families face when negotiating the contradictory expectations of being ideal migrants/workers/families without full or even partial citizenship. After the immigration reforms of 1965, Asian immigrants in the United States were pigeonholed as model minorities while reinforcing their otherness and foreigner status. This "model minority" label is loaded with the expectations that Asian immigrants will be "ideal workers" and will create traditional family systems as economic migrants to the United States.

The visa regime often structures both the work conditions and the family dynamics of professional migrants to fit the model-minority groove. And yet the women respondents who hold dependent visas contemptuously refer to their visas as "vegetable visas" (visas that make them vegetate) and "prison visas," indicating the stifling effect that H-4 visas have on their lives. Dependent visas strip women and men of rights within the home and in civil society by creating a gendered structure of dependence comprising the state, work organizations, transnational global processes, and migrant workers and their families. Visa policies that are ostensibly gender-blind and race-neutral have intersectional ramifications[4] for visa holders and their spouses, making the visa policy structure a conduit for creating what I call a "gendered and racialized visa regime."

Asian Indian Skilled Workers in the United States: Historical Context

The word "visa" derives from the French *visé*, which means "having been seen."[5] A technique of state domination that regulates mobility of populations, the "visa" is defined as "(1) the authorization given by a consul to enter or to pass through a country, and (2) the stamp placed on the passport when the holder enter[s] or [leaves] a foreign country."[6]

In contemporary times, visa approval also requires the "prescreening of travelers and represents a prima facie case for admission."[7] Discrimination is an inherent characteristic of the visa itself. Relevant policies and laws categorize the internationally mobile population as temporally usable entities that should be jettisoned when the receiving states deem fit; this population includes international students, temporary nonimmigrant workers (skilled, semi-skilled and low wage), dependent migrants, refugees, visitors, and tourists. Visa policies often racialize the global population by dividing the global economy into a supply-chain assemblage of racialized workers, the Global South being both the supplier of labor and consumer of products and the Global North being the importer of labor and producer of consumption needs. This assemblage is cultivated and maintained through specific immigration policies based on visa laws instituted by neoliberal states in most cases.

The technology boom of the 1990s and the Immigration Act of 1990 introduced the distinctive category of the nonimmigrant H-1B visa and other H-type visas. This opened the floodgates to migration by highly skilled tech workers (computer engineers and programmers) to the United States from all over the world. Indian and Chinese workers were the top recipients of H-1B visas.[8] According to a 2019 report by the Peterson Institute for International Economics,[9] Indian skilled workers and their spouses were the top recipients of highly skilled H-1B temporary visas and H-4 temporary visas and were the second-largest group of international students in the United States.

Immigration reforms in 1990 made it possible for skilled workers to bring their spouses and children on what was called the "dependent visa." Since 1990, there has been a steady flow of Indian tech workers, and men have dominated this migration. The migration of skilled high-tech workers from India has become a part of the public discourse.[10] What has garnered less attention is the influx of Indian nurses as a result of nursing shortages in the United States.[11] Indian nurses—almost exclusively women—were also recipients of the nonimmigrant H visa system and have been arriving in the United States on H-1B and sometimes H1-C visas.[12]

These professional men and women workers subsequently bring their spouses and children to the United States on dependent visas or H-4 visas. The dependent visa places a range of restrictions on the spouses of skilled workers. It does not permit dependent visa holders (H-4 visa holders) to work for pay until the lead migrant (the H-1B or -C visa holder) has gained permanent residency in the United States, a process that can take anywhere upward of six to twenty years. But most of all, as this book unravels, it strips dependent visa holders of their human dignity and worth.

Only a handful of sociological studies have examined how immigration laws and visa policies affect migrant families and individual visa holders. While studies indicate that women and children are the majority of H-4 dependent visa holders,[13] the migration of nurses as the lead migrant means that some husbands are also migrating to the United States as dependents. While there are a handful of studies examining the lives of dependent wives,[14] the last study to comprehensively examine the lives of dependent spouses who are men was Sheba George in

2005. There is no research comparing men- and women-led migration particularly in the context of how gendered migration interacts with visa policies to affect the families' lives and structures to theorize how the same visas may have different gendered outcomes in families led by men versus women.

Visa Regimes: Structures of Power and Control

The structure that regulates the rights and access to resources as a "foreign national" or "resident alien" (as described by US Citizenship and Immigration Services, or USCIS, previously known as Immigration and Naturalization Services) for my participants is the superincumbent apparatus of visa status. Sociologists have rarely critically examined visa status as a structural force that, co-constitutively with gender, race, sexuality, and class, shapes—even constrains—the material conditions of migrant workers and their families. In my search for such scholarship, I have found very few sociological studies that engage with the question of power and inequality in the day-to-day lives of these visa holders, engendered by what some political theorists have called "visa regimes."

Political theorists[15] have critiqued the technologies of international mobility as "global mobility regimes of passports [and] visas" that organize an international population within a paradoxical framework, one in which mobile bodies understand themselves to be free and international and yet remain controlled and constrained by the biopolitics of surveillance, documentation, biometrics, and confessional imperatives.[16] However, political scientists have not studied the use of visas as tools of state control and how these affect the everyday social lives of individuals involved. Foucault's 1977/78 concept of governmentality contends that technologies of power used by the state ensnare the self to exercise control over its own subjectivity. I use Foucault's theory of governmentality to understand how visas work as mechanisms of power in the lives of the individuals and families in my study.

Governmentality involves tactics used by government and its agencies that allow for "the continual definition and redefinition of what is within the competence of the state and what is not, the public versus the private."[17] This ability to extend the jurisdiction of state power into both public and private spheres is dependent on a range of techniques developed by the state that systematically and pragmatically regulate the everyday actions and material lives of private individuals.[18] Governmentality functions through the smooth, simultaneous, and symbiotic relationship of the dual overlapping techniques of domination and techniques of the self.[19] These *techniques of domination* are characterized by systematized, stabilized, and regulated power relations in which the subordinated persons have little or no room to maneuver, given that their "margin of liberty is extremely limited."[20] Thus, techniques of domination, which coerce people into certain actions or behaviors, need to be coupled with "techniques of the self," through which people's selves are constructed and disciplined optimally to shape their social and cognitive behaviors through consensus and dominant political and economic ideologies. "Techniques of the self" become enforceable where they are integrated into the structure of coercion and punishment.[21] This raises questions of individual freedom and agency, given that modern democratic neoliberal governments and policy makers use the ideological crutches of individual choice and free markets to assert that migration and mobility among people is aspirational and incentivized through a drive for a better life. However, we know that aspirations are often manufactured, and individual choice does not preclude the action of forces of state securitization and surveillance on people.

The concept of governmentality, especially in the context of legal migration, provides a framework to understand the global migration of labor as predicated in techniques of regulation enforced through the state's border security apparatus in the service of multinational corporate assemblages. As a technology of power, visas severely regulate the rights and freedoms of foreign nationals and their families. But because these are presented as the terms of migration, the oppressive structures of visa power remain unquestioned and become normalized. Accepting the terms of a visa thus becomes an individual economic and life choice made by the immigrant and her family. For instance, my participants often said that it was *their choice* to be in the United States on dependent visas and that therefore they had to endure the consequences of that choice (see chapter 2).

The sociologist Cecelia Menjívar[22] offers the concept of liminal legality and legal violence[23]—concepts that underscore the mechanisms of Foucault's governmentality to capture the experiences of legal and undocumented immigrants in the United States. Menjívar contends that some legal immigrants are often forced to straddle an in-between space of uncertain legality while waiting to gain full citizenship rights in the United States. This state of legal limbo affects their own and their families' immediate social and cultural lives as well as future full membership in the US citizenry. Immigration laws have such a hold on the lives of immigrants that people whose lives are constrained by legal ambiguity constantly adjust their lives to conform to the law. Within the frame of governmentality, this is the "technique of the self." But technique of the self happens under the shadow of domination or coercion that Menjívar and Leisy Abrego label "legal violence"—a type of violence that normalizes coercion and cumulatively obstructs immigrants from effective incorporation into the United States because of oppressive immigration laws. The experiences of the participants in this study live between legal violence and liminal legality. They experience these through their gender, class, and racialization, creating several structures of dependence that they are then forced to navigate and negotiate.

At the core of this book lies the unveiling of such hidden and yet obvious complex structures of legal dependence. These structures propel the state—in this case, the United States—to work hand in hand with corporations to ensure a steady supply of racialized and gendered labor force for its tech sector (and what it defines as the "highly skilled" economic sector) through its visa policies. Governmentality in conjunction with Menjívar's concepts of liminal legality and legal violence frames the analysis of how visa policies act as regimes of control to co-construct the legal, familial, and material realities of the people who experience them.

In the first two chapters of this book, I analyze how the legal techniques of governmentality within visa structures co-construct the material realities of people who experience them. Subsequent chapters trouble the gender and race neutrality of the visa laws by showing how deeply gendered and racialized the consequences of these visa-driven lives are for those who are bounded by them.

One of the key critiques of governmentality as a theory has been the seeming dismissal of agency that subjects may exercise when negotiating state power.[24] Disruptive actions of resistance by some of the participants in this research challenge the notion of the all-encompassing power of governmentality, illustrating that agentic maneuvers are possible even in the face of ubiquitous and supposedly totalizing power structures. It therefore becomes imperative to explore in depth the effects of visa policies, particularly dependent visa policy—a policy that presents a complex story of governmentality mediated through a façade of individual choice and heteropatriarchal family relations. Gendered, heterosexist assumptions around the migration of skilled temporary workers of color and their families, as built into visa policies, regulate their subjectivities in relation to their immigration statuses in the context of transnational global migration of labor. Through a critical analysis of this process, I invite the field of international migration to recognize the pervasiveness and all-encompassing influence of visa policies on the lives of migrants. I urge policy makers to incorporate a sociological understanding of the dialectics between visa structures on the one hand and immigrant subjectivities and material realities on the other so as to design fairer visa policies for nonimmigrant workers. Through the study of the category of the dependent visa and the skilled-worker visa, I explore how the temporality of the visa status regulates and controls the co-constructed positionality and subsequent experiences[25] of the visa holder. This visa holder is simultaneously and relationally a temporary migrant, a gendered employee beholden to their visa status, an internationally mobile body, a dependent wife or dependent husband, a parent, and a racial minority labeled a "model minority" in the United States. The dependent visa status is so central to the life of the immigrant that the state is able to control the life of the immigrant through an intersectional regime of power and control created by the visa and associated policies.

Visa Regime: Governmentality of Gendered-Racialized Immigration Policies

Gender theorists[26] in sociology who conceptualize gender to be a regime, a structure, or an institution that stratifies society provide a lens through which to view gender as a principle that organizes our social, sexual, political, and economic lives. Dependent visas exemplify the migration processes as embedded in gender disparity and, by default, a heteronormative migration regime that frames engagement with compulsory heterosexuality[27] as the only path to legal migration for conjugal partners across genders and sexualities.[28] Raewyn Connell contends that gender is institutionalized within the (heterosexual) family, the state, and the street such that "the patterning of gender relations in these institutions . . . provides the structural context of particular relationships and individual practices."[29] This provides the structural context of particular relationships and individual practices. Connell offers two important frames: First, relationships are gendered and heterosexist within the family's power structures and divisions of labor; and second, within the state's control, authority, force, and violence are organized along gender lines such that the state becomes a hegemonically masculinist institution of power that organizes production and consumption, including the gendering of work and occupations and the privileging of paid work over domestic work. This framework of the gender regime allows for an analysis of the visa regime as a gender regime insofar as it shows how visa laws have gendered consequences in the familial, economic, and other relational spheres. However, the framework of the gender regime focuses on the structures outside of the self, within which the gendered self is embedded. It does not fully uncover how internalized gendered cultural scripts can manipulate or reify gender in the family, in governance, and on the street—a phenomenon very much present in the lives of the participants in this research as they negotiated their own state-imposed dependencies.

Barbara Risman's[30] integrative theory of gender contends that, in order to better analyze and possibly reduce gender inequality, one needs to conceptualize gender itself as a structure "deeply embedded in society."[31] This premise is based on a dynamic, dialectical process in which structures shape individuals and individual agency shapes and reshapes structures at multiple levels of analysis—the levels or dimensions being *individual* (internalized gender), *interactional* (gendered performance in social and cultural realms), and *institutional* (organizational practices organized to privilege gendered distribution of resources). My book adds to Risman's theory by showing the intersectional processes at the various levels of inquiry while also explicating not only the constitutive nature but also the overlapping nature of a multilevel inquiry.

A combination of Risman's and Connell's theorizations of gender help me contend that we can gain new sociological insights by analyzing visas as regimes of control that are intersectional and that operate at multiple levels. Visas are techniques of legal control at the institutional level, which structures not only employment and residential opportunities for migrants but also everyday interactions. Two empirical questions emerge. The first asks whether visas are so powerful that they can shape the selves and subjectivities of their holders. The second asks whether acts of resistance by visa holders can cause the state to change or revise visa policies.

Visa laws are gendered as well as racialized. They facilitate labor migration from the Global South to the Global North as an inherently racialized process, as they create the "racially other" category of the immigrant/transnational "alien worker."[32] Evelyn Nakano Glenn points out in her 2009 book *Unequal Freedom* that US immigration laws and citizenship criteria have historically been determined by the race and gender of the migrants. Glenn contends that being male (gender), white (race), and productive in the paid labor force defined full US citizenship, excluding those who did not meet those criteria at various historical moments. These criteria relegate my participants on dependent visas to second-class citizenship status, as they are not considered as productive (employed in the public sphere and working for pay) in the labor force. Further, the visa policies that facilitate family migration are based on a gendered and racialized assumption that families in the Global South almost always have a patriarchal structure with women as dependents and men as providers.[33]

Nation-states in the Global North use their legal apparatus and statist discourse to discipline the subjectivities of women from the Global South. Euro-American states, Chandra Mohanty[34] contends, are masculine, racialized, and capitalist systems that organize power relations by regulating gender and sexual relations through immigration, fiscal, and nationality policies that control the family, the provision of child care, the population, the labor force, housing, and gendered and (hetero)sexual behaviors and expressions. These configurations make the state machinery of the Global North gendered and racialized regimes. In Mohanty's words:

> [T]he fact that notions of sexuality (morality of women), gender (familial configurations), and race ("Oriental") are implicitly written into these laws indicates the reason why this particular aspect of the contemporary state is a crucial context for Third World women's feminist struggles and

provides a method of feminist analysis that is located at the intersections of systemic gender, race, class and sexual paradigms as they are regulated by the liberal state.[35]

She further contends that Western political and academic discourse constructs "Third-World women" as a monolithic universal dependent category by "colonizing the material experiences and historical heterogeneities of the lives of women."[36] The implicit assumption in this cultural discourse that women are an "already constituted and coherent group with identical interests and desires, regardless of class, ethnic or racial location, implies a notion of gender or sexual difference or even patriarchy which can be applied universally and cross-culturally."[37]

I use gender structure as an organizing theoretical tool and Mohanty's concept of gender and racial regimes as the backbone for understanding the experience of state-imposed dependence among the participants in this research. Risman aids my analysis of the dynamics in the families of migrant women and men breadwinners as shaped by gender at the individual and interactional levels. Mohanty provides the tools to better deconstruct the impact of US visa policies on Third World family migrants and the transnational processes of labor and family migration more broadly.

I find Mohanty's discussion of Third World women as "universal dependents" particularly useful in framing my research. The category of the dependent visa emerges from a globalized gender and race structure that defines Third World women as a dependent category, such that institutionalization of their "dependence" through visa law appears normalized and almost invisible. Paradoxically, however, the women in my study are highly qualified women, educated in a anglicized education system, many working in high-paying jobs, and leading an independent life prior to migration. The second category of women, the Indian nurses, who arrive on work visas as the main migrants and breadwinners, also challenge the discourse of dependence around Third World women of color. Despite the gendered assumption underlying the creation of the visa regime, an outcome of the dependent visa policy is the category of "dependent men," refuting the notion of Third World women as universally dependent. And yet, despite the perceived gender neutrality of the visa laws, only a few men use dependent visas for migration.

According to US Department of Labor statistics, the majority of those who come to the United States on these visas are women. Dependent visas are also given to dependent children, the official language being "visa for dependent spouse and children," which speaks to the paternalistic and patriarchal political tendency of grouping women and children as one category. I contend that the category H-4 visa is a system derived from the ideal of a heterosexist family structure that privileges the underlying premise of the gendered division of labor.

Several empirical studies show how the immigration and emigration policies of the state operate as a gendered and racialized regime.[38] For instance, research on Central American documented and undocumented immigrants shows how legal regulations on immigrants constitute acts of racialized and gendered violence that control the work and family lives of immigrants.[39] Studies on family reunification laws in Asian families show the gendered and racialized impact of these laws on the families.[40] And the work on labor-brokering in the Philippines and creation of the "great Filipino worker"[41] offers strong critiques of gendered and racialized migration systems. And yet much of the literature does not address the complex and systemic impact of immigration and visa policies on families in an oppressive migration regime. The migration of Indian temporary skilled workers and their families to the United States on "special occupation" visas—and the specifics of the conditions of their legal status—becomes an important site for the excavation of how the US migration regime and its visa regulations shape the gendered migration of a racialized group of potential permanent immigrants.

Visa Regimes in the Context of Migration of Indian Highly Skilled Workers: Tech Workers and Nurses

When I began research for this book, one of my worries was finding enough immigrant professionals from India without having to travel across the United States. My fears, as I discovered, were unfounded. India has emerged as one of the largest exporters of highly skilled workers to the global markets. Since about 1990, India has produced the largest number of well-trained computer engineers and programmers in the world.[42] Since 2000, India has also produced the largest number of women engineers, computer programmers, and health care workers. Indian professionals, mostly men but also women, have joined the national and global high-tech and health care labor markets in unprecedented numbers since the 1990s.[43] The demand for immigrant Indian professionals in the Global North is fueled by the perception of Indians as skilled, flexible, and cheap workers.[44] However, Indians in the diaspora use the perception of privileged minorities based on their class, educational, and cultural backgrounds to mobilize their resources to counter the racial othering they experience as professional workers in US workplaces.[45] Since the late 2010s, some sociologists have specifically focused on the racialization and gendering of migrant information technology workers, especially those possessing skilled worker visas (H-1B).

To examine the different kinds of racialization of skilled workers, it was important to understand the immigration and visa policies of the United States.[46] As the research unfolded, this insight became an imperative. Payal Banerjee contends that, because visa policies "have . . . been about the racial designation of immigrant and migrant workers as an exploitable workforce for the benefit of capital,[47] the interplay between flexible hiring and visa policies makes Indian IT workers a vulnerable and marginalized group. Migrant tech workers are subcontracted and body-shopped rendering them fireable at any time. The insecurity of their employment status is compounded by the fact that IT workers rely on visa-sponsoring employers for legal immigration status in the United States; if fired, they lose legal status in the United States. The need to remain employed and legal drives H-1B employees to accept severely exploitative work conditions including wage cuts, deduction of commissions from hourly wages, lack of benefits, and frequent relocations.

While I did not find many Indian women H-1B visa holders in the IT industry, Payal Banerjee[48] had a small number of women IT workers in her sample, and she found that the terms of employment and visa restrictions severely disadvantaged women, more so than men. Indian immigrant men outnumber Indian immigrant women massively in the IT industry in the United States because it is more difficult for women, especially women with families, to relocate frequently and work for extended hours. Payal Banerjee's study found that the relatively few Indian women who work in the industry struggled, finding themselves often to be the only women engineer from India on a given project, not being accepted as legitimate experts in their field, or having to constantly "fight for [their] entitlements."[49] This ensured that immigrant women were pushed out of the IT industry, which then became largely the domain of men immigrant workers of color with legally dependent wives in tow. US immigration policies depend on the racialization and gendering of immigration for labor exploitation in order to "sustain the exigencies of late capital."[50]

Indian medical workers, especially nurses, are the other stream of highly skilled immigrant workers to the United States who experience simultaneous gendering and racialization because of their legal status and working conditions there. Nursing, a historically feminized profession across the world, became racialized en masse as immigrant women from the Global South were employed to overcome nursing shortages in the United Kingdom and the United States. Since the 1970s, immigrant Filipina and Indian nurses (primarily from Kerala and of the Christian faith) have filled these positions in the United States. As documented in several studies, immigrant nurses of color experience racism and gendering at work from patients as well as coworkers, doctors, and administrators. Indian nurses in the United States also have the particular experience of feeling pressured to maintain transnational cultural expectations of being subordinated to their husbands at home and at church despite being the main breadwinner.[51] Simultaneously, they have to navigate the trope of the Third World as a ready-made docile and dexterous workforce eager to work for lower pay[52] as well as their legal status as temporary workers with a stay-at-home husband.

Late capitalism, coupled with global assemblages of production and consumption, has created a demand in the economies of the Global North for cheap, amenable workers[53] in the technology and health care sectors. This demand fashions structures through which states in the Global North innovate techniques in the form of visa regimes to fulfill corporate demand for a particular kind of labor force, while the knowledge industry of the Global South in tandem produces a surplus of technology and professional workers to send overseas. These workers then become the main export of countries in the Global South, such as India, and constitute that temporary, ideal worker who is termed "highly skilled" in the host country. They also become aspiring neoliberal subjects of migrations, with desires and dreams of material gain that a migration to the West can afford them in both host and home countries.[54]

The story of Indian highly skilled professional migrant workers in the United States is not complete without examining the consequences of applying for permanent residency with very long wait periods while still possessing an H-1B visa and being beholden to employers as a result. Immigrants in this study often described it as a "carrot-and-stick story" in which they had to endure exploitive conditions until they received permanent residency, which took about two decades for many. The anthropologist Paula Chakravartty's[55] work on tech workers holding H-1B visas who had applied for permanent residency corroborates the existence of multilevel structural inequalities faced by visa-bound Indian tech workers in the United States. These tech workers—mostly men and a few women—all experienced the glass ceiling in terms of promotion and pay when compared to American counterparts; they also experienced isolation and segregation at work, including being given work spaces separated from American colleagues. Her study shows that women experienced more isolation and segregation not only because they were fewer in number in a predominantly male occupation but also because they felt rejected by Indian male colleagues as equals and coworkers. Meanwhile, the Indian men tech professionals married to highly qualified women on dependent visas described their legally dependent spouses as "frustrated housewives" but generally remained in their jobs until they could apply for permanent residency or received the same. In contrast, in the few cases where the woman was a tech worker and the breadwinner and had a husband on a dependent visa, she was ready to relocate anywhere within or outside the United States where her husband might find a job, even at the cost of her own. These sets of experiences underscore how the desire for permanent residency becomes the trope that holds temporary workers hostage to their workplaces, perpetuating the gendered exploitation both at the workplace and at home, as clearly articulated by the participants in subsequent chapters.

The handful of studies of the "frustrated housewives" in Chakravartty's study demonstrates the oppressive nature of the H-4 dependent visas for women. In an article on women H-4 dependent visa holders, lawyer and now councilwoman Shivali Shah[56] illustrates how H-4 visas created situations of domestic abuse for women in transnational households in the United States. The skilled migration regime's dependence on the unpaid work done by the Indian dependent spouses is explored by Bhatt.[57] Bhatt's exploration of the affects of visa laws on dependent women also corroborated my previous finding that this regime of skilled migration depended on the unpaid work of Indian dependent wives to support the labor of their husbands. For another set of Indian Tamil immigrant women who had come to the United States on dependent visas, their inability to work legally made it difficult to attain a desired standard of living in the United States.[58] In a different context, the dependent wives of Korean international students on F-2 visas (which allows dependents of F-1 student visa holders to move to the United States) were forced to perform unpaid care work and were relegated to housewifery positions, thereby reproducing "gender unequal relations."[59] The women were considered subordinate in the family yet important enough for their husbands' professional success. Dependent visas in all cases legitimize a deep-rooted patriarchal ideology within the family and substantively reduce the citizenship status of dependent wives with the result that their own career ambitions are deprioritized for the sake of husbands' careers.[60]

The dependent visa is unique because it shows very specific ways in which the global migration of labor and families is gendered and racialized. The structure that regulates the rights and access to resources of a "foreign national" or "resident alien" (the terms used by USCIS) for the participants in this study is the visa, with its ubiquitously powerful force, on which they enter the United States. This book unearths how *visa techniques*, as an institutional form of domination, shape the lived experiences of transnational populations from the Global South. An analysis of dominant public discourse on dependent visas and the actual lived experiences of those whose lives are affected by this visa category reveals how *structures of dependence* are put in place to control and manipulate the global migration of labor and the everyday lives of the migrating populations.

The Research Process

This book is based on five years of qualitative data collection in two phases including in-depth life-course interviews, ethnography, and archival research. I entered the field in the summer of 2009 and collected data through the summer of 2011. I reentered the field a few years later to conduct follow-up interviews with some of the participants and pursued additional interviews about changes in the visa laws and new activism surrounding dependent visa policies from 2015 to 2018. Primarily, fieldwork involved conducting ethnography and in-depth interviews in communities of Indian professionals (tech workers and nurses) in the greater Chicagoland area, other parts of the Midwest, Silicon Valley, and Houston, as well as with a handful of activists on the East Coast.

The tech workers on H-1B visas, all of whom were men, and their dependent wives on H-4 visas were mostly near Chicago; some were in a few smaller cities in the Midwest and in Silicon Valley. The Indian immigrant nurses interviewed for this study—all of them women who were the lead migrants and main wage earners in their families—and their husbands on dependent visas, were based in the suburbs of Chicago and Houston.

The first round of interviews consisted of life-course interviews with couples, exploring their lives prior to migration, experiences with the migration process, understandings of their own visas, and their descriptions of everyday family lives, including parenting and caregiving after migration. Each spouse in a couple was interviewed separately, after which both were interviewed together. The tech workers were mostly from northern parts of India and were mostly of Hindu faith, with a few exceptions. Almost half of these families lived in gentrified urban neighborhoods, while the other half lived in suburban communities for reasons of access to better public schools. All of the nurses and their husbands were from one state and region in India—the southern state of Kerala—and all the families identified with the Christian faith. The nurses and their families usually lived in suburban communities close to their ethnic churches.

The first round included interviews with 20 couples in families of tech workers and 25 couples in the families of nurses. In the second round, along with doing follow-up interviews about the continuing impact of the visa laws on the previously interviewed participants, I also interviewed some new families. Five additional tech workers (men) on H-1B visas and their wives, as well as five nurses and their husbands, were included in the interviews; in each case the spouses had received work authorization after the Obama-era ruling that allowed spouses of those migrants who had filed for lawful permanent residency and received the first round of approval to apply for employment authorization documents (EADs). A total of 55 couples (110 individuals) were interviewed: 25 high-tech workers and their wives, and 30 nurses and their husbands (see appendix A and appendix B for details). I also conducted nine additional interviews with women on H-4 visas waiting for EADs, as well as six nurses and their husbands who had recently gained permanent residency in the United States, for a total of 125 interviews (see table 1.1 in chapter 1 for a breakdown) with lead migrants and their spouses.

All the women in the sample in both types of family had at least a college degree, and most had 16-plus years of education. The men tech workers all had professional college degrees, and most of the husbands of the nurses had some college education. The average income was about $65,000 in the families of the nurses and about $75,000 in the families of the tech workers. Most tech-worker families self-identified as middle-class in the United States and as belonging to upper-middle-class families in India. The nurses identified as middle-class both in the United States and in their families of origin in India.

I also interviewed 10 immigration experts, including lawyers, activists, and policy makers, to understand their views on visa policies and the immigration of highly skilled workers during the course of the study. A total of 135 individuals were interviewed for the project.

In addition to in-depth interviews, I conducted more than 500 hours of ethnographic observations over two years at various community and public events to observe family and gender dynamics. These events and spaces included religious services, parties, religious and cultural festivals, potlucks, and children's birthday parties. I also attended gender-segregated events such as tech workers' amateur weekly cricket games or church activities run solely by husbands of nurses, as well as women-only gatherings and events attended by nurses and by wives of tech workers. In these settings, I observed families' division of labor, the discussions that men and women had about their work and family lives, and interactions between spouses.

To gain a deeper understanding of specific visa laws and how and why they had changed over the years, I conducted archival research and analysis of discourse by politicians on visa policies. In the archival research, I examined congressional committee reports concerning highly skilled migration and public reports from congressional hearings and public hearings about the passing of the relevant visa laws from the 1990s to the present day. For the critical discourse analysis, I reviewed speeches and comments made by political figures about the relevant visa program. I also discursively engaged with media content between 2008 and 2018 at various inflection points when the issue of dependent visas was under the media microscope either because of a policy debate or policy change. Further, I analyzed social media content by an activist social media group founded in 2013 by an Indian H-4 visa holder to raise awareness about dependent visas. Throughout the study design and my fieldwork, I remained deeply aware of and shaped by my own standpoints and social locations. And I realized in the process that standpoint research at its core gives rise to moral consternations and dilemmas within and without, perhaps making the research process more honest by situating it in social, cultural, and political contexts of the researcher, discussed in the next section.

Standpoint Dilemmas

It was a cold, snowy morning in February 2005. I stood at the long, winding immigration queue at a Chicago airport with my luggage and a bunch of immigration forms. I knew the drill, as I had been travelling to the United States for work for a few years. It was slightly different this time. I was excited to begin graduate school in the fall of that year. But given that my partner lived in Chicago and went to graduate school at Northwestern University, I was living in the city during the year I applied to PhD programs in the US. I was on a dependent visa (F-2) designed for spouses of students, as it was too early to process my student visa (F-1).

As I went to the immigration officer's booth, I extended my passport with a polite smile, expecting the regular questions about where I was coming from and what I was here for. The immigration officer looked at my passport, looked at me, fingerprinted me, and then, without looking at me again, asked a volley of questions that had little to do with me. He asked for my "husband's" name, his address, and what he did.

The officer then reminded me, still without looking at me, that as the dependent spouse of an international student, I was not allowed to work legally in this country. He then said: "Welcome to America—hope you have a good stay." Despite my own strong feminist identity and given that my real purpose for being in the United States was to attend gradu-ate school, the humiliation I felt at that moment, and for the months I was on dependent F2 visa, remains a powerful and haunting memory. In fact, as I write my experience here, I still have a strong sense memory of my affective state at the time: the overwhelming feeling of invisibility and shame I felt during that period connects me to the participants of this study in deeply visceral and emotional ways.

As a feminist researcher, it is as important to locate my research in the larger social and political context as it is to locate it within a theo-retical context, as urged by critical feminist epistemologists.[61] As an Indian woman in the United States who has experienced being on a dependent visa status for a brief period, I share an "insider" status with some of my participants, especially the women dependent visa holders. The women often told me that I was among the very few people who understood their plight and acknowledged their pain. At the end of my interview, one of the women said to me: "This was like a therapy session. Who else would be so patient and understanding, listening to my sad story?" Perhaps paradoxically, the tech workers and the nurses also felt camaraderie with me, given their status as immigrant workers in the United States. They saw me as a researcher and also believed that I would understand their lived experiences as immigrant workers on temporary visas.

And yet, while this insider status provided me with cultural access and a nuanced understanding of the experiences of my participants, my gender was an impediment in connecting with some of my men par-ticipants, who sometimes perceived me as a feminist researcher on a mission to show that they oppressed their wives. Furthermore, my status as a North Indian, Hindu, upper-caste, non-Christian, non–Malayalee speaking woman made me an outsider in the communities of nurses. Indians in the United States are not a monolithic category, and being Indian (the national identity) did not warrant me automatic insiderness to all regional groups, particularly the Malayalee-Christian community in my case. Malayalam is a completely different language from Hindi or Bengali (Indian languages I speak).[62] Malayalee-Christians also are a small minority religious group, a minority even in Kerala. Therefore, I was as much an outsider to this community as I would be if I were studying a non-Indian South Asian population.

Factors such as professional/class status, education, gender, marital status, and religious and cultural histories separate the researcher from the participants and "shape participants' perceptions of them as dissimilar."[63] These identities probably make the researcher an "outsider within"—a status that accommodates the fluidity of the multiple identities that a researcher such as myself traverses vis-à-vis the research participants and even the research settings.

However, once trust was established, I became more than a researcher to my participants. During the interviews, I often found myself offering to engage with the women participants with issues of self-worth, loneliness, and exploring volunteering and educational opportunities that might be available to them while on dependent visas. I saw this as a form of reciprocity for their involvement in the project. At the same time, this also illuminated my outsider position and, to a certain extent, my position of privilege, given the social location that granted me more social and cultural resources compared to the participants. Feminist scholars have demonstrated that such relationships become more complex when the researchers share racial and ethnic identities with the research subjects.[64]

In each community, my experience varied. In the community of nurses, they joked that my not being from the community reduced the risk of me "gossiping." One of the nurses told me that it was easier to talk to me because she knew I would not judge her in the same way as some members of her community might. The middle-class status of the participants also made them less vulnerable in their interactions with me, the researcher.

My standpoint as an Indian woman who had undergone the experience of being on a dependent visa, even if temporarily and briefly, provided a unique understanding of the experiences of the women and, to an extent, the men on dependent visas. As a feminist sociologist studying gender and immigration, and as an Indian woman who grew up in a semiurban, traditionally heterosexual, middle-class, patriarchal household, my awareness of the way gender is performed in a typical Indian household helped provide a nuanced understanding of the lives of the participants. Marjorie DeVault[65] contends that the insights of the insider are instrumental to interpretive and standpoint research. I argue that, along with insider status, my outsider-within status in relation to the participants created a balance of power between us. It also placed me in a unique position to decipher the finer cultural and familial nuances and examine them through a critical sociological lens—all this yielding deep theoretical introspection.

One such introspective moment experienced while writing this book—a moment that evoked a deeper standpoint dilemma than the outsider-within status—was difficult to resolve and was in fact partly a moral issue that I had to reconcile with my conscience before I could submit the final version of this manuscript. I feel compelled to articulate this dilemma given my epistemological stance. As a standpoint sociologist, it is imperative to address how larger power structures bleed into intellectual work. This reveal is part of that endeavor.

This dilemma emerged primarily from two prominent political shifts: one in the United States, and one in India. In 2014, India elected Prime Minister Narendra Modi, a populist, majoritarian Hindu nationalist party member; both Modi and his party were reelected in a landslide victory in 2019. And in 2016, the United States elected Donald Trump as president. These events had a profound impact on this research and my intellectual consciousness. Modi commands overwhelming support among Indian upper-caste Hindus residing in North America, despite his anti-Muslim, antipoor, anti-proletariat, anti-Dalit, antiwoman policies and politics. During both his presidential campaigns, Trump appealed to Indians in the United States, repurposing Modi's campaign slogan for his own campaign to woo Hindu Indian American voters.[66]

As mentioned earlier, most of the families of tech workers in this study were upper-caste Hindus and enjoyed privileged social-class status in India. While most participants expressed worry about Trump's election, the issue of Hindu nationalism in India did not come up during interviews in discussing their political leanings in the context of India. What is noteworthy is that most of my Hindu participants talked about various political and social issues with me but refrained from problematizing the landslide victory of an openly Hindu supremacist prime minister in India. Regardless of participants' political beliefs, the fact remains that most possessed class and caste capital in India. This form of class and caste capital does not wholly translate into privilege in the United States, given the racial structure and the immigration regime that subsumes migrants of color. However, we know from sociological research that legacies of privilege find translations in various ways. For instance, legal Indian migrants in the United States are likely to have more social and cultural capital compared to undocumented migrants of color in the United States, owing to the social and financial capital available to them. For example, I was born into an upper-caste Hindu family, and even though I have identified as an atheist all my adult life, my last name still signifies my upper-caste status in India, which often offers me opportunities and licenses unasked and unbeknownst. Given this shared history I have with half of the participants, I have experienced deep conflict in writing this book, particularly because the data and analysis are oriented toward unraveling the dependency structures that the visa regime created for the participants and not delving into the caste and religious privileges they enjoyed in India and how those privileges might be reflected in the migration process. The empirical evidence collected for this research does not afford me the grounding to unpack the privileges that the participants might have because of their premigration caste and class location, despite the oppressive conditions in which they find themselves in the United States because of the visa regime. This is, in my view, a huge shortcoming of this research. That being said, I have not been able to resolve that dilemma in this book. I'll leave that to a future project. In *The Opportunity Trap*, I am merely acknowledging it, and wherever possible throughout my analysis, I spotlight the ramifications of privilege in the ways some participants understood their experiences with the visa regime.

Plan of the Book

It was difficult to decide how to arrange this book given the various paths it could have taken. I could have arranged it by groups of participants or the visa statuses they held. But in order to capture the facets of oppression resulting from the visa regime, I organized the chapters to reflect the imprints of the visa regime on the different parts of participants' lives. In chapter 1, however, I must lay out the history of Asian migration to the United States, with a particular focus on Indians. I analyze the social, economic, and cultural forces in India that lead to the out-migration of tech workers and nurses. I trace the mechanisms of global export of the highly skilled labor force from Indian multinational corporations—mechanisms of export that facilitate the steady flow of professional workers to the Global North. I also provide a description of the process of recruitment of tech workers by US companies, the procedures these companies go through to procure H-1B visas, and the legal entailments of each the types of visas.

The gender story that is hidden in the migration trajectories of these professional workers and their families and that unfolds in chapter 1 lays the foundation for the claim that visa laws are not really gender-neutral and have serious gendered and raced consequences for migrant families. The remaining chapters examine how the policies translate to the lived experiences of the immigrants and their families.

In chapter 2, I analyze the narratives of the participants specific to H-4 dependent visas (particularly the women) and argue that the visa laws levy *penalties* on the public interactions and private selfhood of visa holders. Two major themes explored in this chapter are the "invisibility" and "devaluation" that dependent visa holders experience within their selfhood and in their public interactions. Building on the concept of the governmentality of the visa regime, I argue that the effectiveness of global labor migration is predicated on the seamless disciplining of individuals to become model migrants and ideal workers. The underlying coercive power of the state dictates this disciplining of self. As individuals negotiate their new identity as dependent spouses, the mechanisms through which dependence is created and sustained eventually render the structures of the oppressive visa regime invisible. Most of the dependent women, unlike the dependent men, had the consciousness and the language to unravel the structural oppression of the visa order. But in the final analysis, the dependent women tended to readjust their selves to conform within the structure, training themselves to live with trauma and alienation, whereas the dependent men resigned themselves to humiliation but refused to talk about it for fear of acknowledging the emasculation they experienced. And yet, both men and women on dependent visas resisted becoming the "vegetables" that the visas seemed to require them to be.

In chapter 3, I investigate the ways in which the workplace and the family lives of the migrant workers were intertwined and heavily tied to the visas they hold. The visa regimes that shape these immigrants' lives create a legally liminal status for migrants and their families. Because both work and dependent visas are tied to the employment of the main migrant and therefore control the ability of these families to reside in the United States, losing the job would mean losing residential rights as well as financial resources. This puts migrant workers and their spouses in an in-between status of legality that makes them beholden to their employers through the visa regime. This status of what I call "legal liminality" building on Menjívar, is extended indefinitely when their employers sponsor the immigrant workers to qualify as lawful permanent residents (LPRs). Quitting one's job means killing any chance of gaining residency in the United States, which is what many participants called the "carrot-and-stick condition," as mentioned earlier. This legal liminality intersects with the racialization and gendering of the workers to produce a complex web of dependence for the families. Chapter 3 is an exploration of that particular structure of dependence embedded in the visa regime.

In chapter 4, I analyze how visa laws reshape the gendered behavior of individuals and alter interactions between spouses within the homes of the participants. Here, I also explore how class intersects with gender within families to complicate the understanding that participants developed regarding state-imposed dependence. In families where men were the main breadwinners, traditional gendered patterns remained intact, as women performed gendered femininities even while they resisted the housewife status forced on them. The men in these families also struggled to reorient themselves to their wives' new status as housewives, forced into doing what they call "crappy domestic work." In families where women were the breadwinners and men were dependents, the gender-neutral visa category did not alter the traditional gendered division of labor, except in the context of child care. The type of gendered interaction varied by the class and regional backgrounds of the migrant families, but expectations about household work remained largely gendered.

In chapter 5, I look closely at how the visa regime shaped parenting discourses and action in the families of participants with children. The analysis in chapter 5 reveals that dependent spouses who had children spent a disproportionate amount of time on rearing children because of their dependent status. In this chapter, I focus on what parenting means for dependent spouses. I examine whether and to what extent dominant theories of class-based parenting—juxtaposed with approaches to parenting in middle-class Black families in the United States and immigrant transnational families—work in the context of Indian immigrant middle-class families in which one parent holds a professional job and the other parent stays home because of visa restrictions. I show that the way these families parented aligned more with notions of racialization and transnationalism in parenting that intersected with gendered intensive mothering because of the visa regime, rather than the prevalent explanations of class-based parenting in the United States. I call this form of parenting "transcultural cultivation."

In the conclusion, I present evidence of participants' struggles as they resist their dependent visa status. Through what I call "acts of disruption," individuals push back against the power of the visa regime. I highlight the periodic collective efforts by some women on H-4 visas to end their invisibility and bring their situation before the public eye. Through acts of disruption, dependent visa holders and their families actively resisted dependence and challenged the intent and purpose of laws purported to ensure "stable families" for migrant workers. These examples of active resistance highlight the failures of dependent visa policy. I present the anxieties of the Trump era while also offering specific policy recommendations to dismantle the dependence created by visa regimes. I also argue that there is an urgent need to establish more structured support groups and information-disseminating groups for dependent visa holders in the United States and in India so that immigrant families coming to the United States on work and dependent visas understand the full import of the visa laws for their futures in the United States, especially futures that could resemble the recent terrifying Trumpian times.

1

The Visa Regime

Indian Migration and the Interplay of Race and Gender

Getting to America is a process; it's a story, a full feature film.
—Aniket, research participant

One of the most hotly debated issues in US immigration is the migration of highly skilled workers, especially those on temporary (H-1B) visas. President Barack Obama's immigration agenda featured the issue of highly skilled migration. He sought to empower spouses of H-1B workers in an attempt to attract more such workers to the United States.[1] Characteristically, Donald Trump—starting in his presidential campaign and continuing well into his term as president—frequently changed his stance on skilled migration, sometimes embracing it, but often using intensely anti-immigrant rhetoric. For instance, in a quote from his 2016 presidential campaign on highly skilled immigrants, he said: "I'm changing. I'm changing. We need highly skilled people in this country. If we can't do it, we will get them in. And we do need in Silicon Valley, we absolutely have to have. So, we do need highly skilled."[2] But during the four years of his presidency, Trump intensified surveillance and scrutiny on temporary workers who were already in the United States, suspending the issuance of temporary work visas in response to the COVID-19 pandemic, even as he encouraged highly skilled migration in his speeches. However, Trump's contradictory posturing is not an aberration in the history of highly skilled migration to the United States but is in fact an amplification of trends that have been persistent in the history of US immigration policy,[3] which I explain later in this chapter. Here I simply want to orient the reader toward the fact that government ambivalence toward Asian and Asian Indian migration has been a persistent historical fact in the

United States, and this historicity is carried forward both at the policy level and in the lived experiences of immigrants.

The current scenario of dependent visas first became a legislative reality when the family reunification clause of the Immigration Act of 1965 proposed the creation of visas for dependents of the "H"-type work visas—spouses and children of temporary workers—as well as for dependents of "F"-type student visas. However, it was much later when H-4 visas came into existence. The Immigration Act of 1990 created the H-4 visa category as an ancillary to the H-category visas (H-1B, H-1C, H-2, and H-3). Temporary workers on H-1B visas could bring dependent spouses and children on H-4 visas with restrictions on their ability to work for pay. The creation of the H-4 visa category, as I explain later in this chapter, was a means of placating the populist notion that admitting the spouses of foreign skilled workers would burden the American economy and impinge on employment opportunities available to US citizens. With the creation of H-4 visas, the migration of temporary skilled workers, particularly from India and China, increased exponentially in the years after the Immigration Act of the 1990. The top-two immigrant-sending countries to the United States after Mexico are India and China.[4] According to the US Department of Homeland Security, more than a third of all foreign-born Indians in the United States came here in 2000 or later.[5]

As Indians from abroad began to succeed economically and educationally, they began to be categorized as "model minorities"[6] in the United States. Nevertheless, as the migration of foreign nationals from India and other parts of the world increased, the government instituted different regulatory visa categories and laws for the migration of temporary workers, permanent workers, and their families over the years. These visa regulations were meant to monitor, surveil, and control Indian and other Asian migrations. The regulations became a covert mechanism to create a racialized visa regime and that began resembling pre-1965, overtly racist immigration policy. In the remainder of this chapter, I show how Indian migrants have been historically racialized in the United States, then explain why I call the participants in this study "immigrants and migrants" instead of "temporary workers." Finally, I unpack the visa categories and their legal consequences, along with the recruitment process of visa holders.

The Racialization of Asian and Asian-Indian Migrations

The migration of Asian Indians to the United States is continuous and growing. Both the receiving and sending states appear to be benefactors of this process, as well as immigrants themselves who purport to want a "better life" when they decide to migrate.[7] However, the realities of the migration process are different depending on which groups they are part of. Migrating individuals from the Global South historically have been viewed by the US government as a monolithic category: temporary workforce/guest workforce. While these supposedly temporary workers are called "nonresident aliens," foreign nationals who have residency in the United States were called "aliens" by the Department of Homeland Security,[8] which could change (at the time of writing, the Joe Biden administration proposed to change the nomenclature).[9]

Historian Lisa Lowe[10] contends that this is emblematic of a state that has historically benefited from racializing Asian immigrant groups as the "Other" and the "foreigner" while simultaneously burdening them with the expectation of behaving as a so-called model minority. For the state, immigrants serve a paradoxical function: As aliens, they help define Americanness; as workers, they meet the demand for cheap, exploitable labor. Immigrants are both solicited economically and "othered" ideologically. The state simultaneously includes and excludes immigrants while producing racialized labor forces to further its own economic and political interests.[11]

Lowe also contends that immigrants can use their cultural resources to form local alliances and push back against exploitation: "The contradictions through which immigration brings national institutions into crisis produces immigrant cultures as oppositional and contestatory, and these contradictions, critically politicized in cultural forms and practices, can be utilized in the formation of alternative social practices."[12] However, while hybridity, heterogeneity, and plurality can provide tools for resistance through the creation of local and transnational alliances, they are also byproducts of globalization and can be used to promote further disenfranchisement of currently minoritized populations.

A historical analysis of citizenship as a racialized project in the United States clarifies the construction of immigrants of color as the other. The 1924 Johnson Reed Act established numerical limits on immigration for the first time. The act assigned numerical quotas to European nationalities, disadvantaging some European citizens more than others, while excluding *all* Asians from immigration on the ground that they were ineligible for naturalized citizenship, with the explicit agenda of preventing Asians as a race from entering the United States. This legislation further solidified racial categories in the law and established a global racial and national hierarchy that favored white immigrants over immigrants of color.[13]

Indian migration has its own distinct racialized history in the United States. According to the 2009 proceedings of the Indian History Congress,[14] and the work of early migration scholars,[15] the first Indian migration to the United States can be traced to the turn of the nineteenth century when a few thousand people came to the United States when India was still a British colony. Many of these migrants came as agriculturalists, or as merchants on the East Coast, or as railroad workers on the West Coast. These immigrants were primarily farmers without any formal education, hailing from rural areas of Punjab Province in India, who arrived as single men or as married men who had left their families behind.[16] Among the more elite migrants, some were Hindu religious and spiritual leaders and missionaries. Others came as students, mostly with ties to the Indian Freedom movement and many of whom had joined the Gadhar movement of 1913 (*Gadhar* means "mutiny"; this movement was ultimately unsuccessful) organized by Indian exiles in the United States to overthrow the rule of the British Raj. This first phase of Indian migration, comprising mostly Sikhs and some Hindus and Muslims, made enough of a ripple that it spurred the Asiatic Exclusion League and American Association of Labor to refer to Indian migrants as the "tide of the turbans," "rag heads," and a "distinct menace."[17] As Indian migration grew, several measures were taken and laws passed by the United States and Canada to restrict the immigration of Indians, particularly poor Indians.

The timeline represented in figure 1.1 shows the history and the movement of US immigration from blatantly racist policies that restricted or banned the entry of immigrants of color, especially from Asia, to the slow dismantling of those policies in favor of seemingly less exclusionary policies. As shown, while some of the laws—such as the Naturalization Law of 1790, the Chinese Exclusion Act of 1882, and the Gentleman's

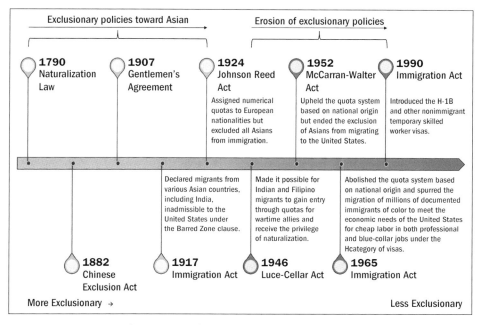

Figure 1.1. History of immigration laws and Asian migration to the United States.

Agreement—targeted East Asian migration, the Immigration Act of 1917 declared migrants from various Asian countries, including India, inadmissible to the United States under the Barred Zone clause. The 1924 Johnson Reed Act, which excluded all Asians from migrating to the United States and followed the 1917 act, remained in place until 1946, when it was replaced by the Luce-Cellar Act, which made it possible for Indian and Filipino migrants to gain entry through quotas for wartime allies and receive the privilege of naturalization. The partition of India after its independence from the British Empire in 1947 spurred some Indians to migrate to the United States, but in the period between 1946 and 1965, only about 7,000 Indians migrated there, 6,000 of whom came as part of family reunification. This period constituted the second wave of Indian migration to the United States.[18] Historians often see the McCarran-Walter Act of 1952 and the Immigration Act of 1965 as enabling the third wave of Indian migration. The 1952 act upheld the quota system based on national origin but ended the exclusion of Asians from migrating to the United States. It also introduced a system of quotas and preferences based on skill sets desired in the United States, as well as family reunification, and introduced the H categories of visas for skilled and unskilled workers and their families.[19] The Immigration Act of 1965 abolished the quota system based on national origin and spurred the migration of millions of documented immigrants of color to meet the economic needs of the United States for cheap labor in professional and blue-collar jobs under the H category of visas.

The Immigration Act of 1990—the first comprehensive immigration reform in twenty-five years—was key in charting the course of Indian migration to the United States in the following two decades and can be considered to have launched a fourth phase in the migration history of Indians.[20] In 1989, the Immigration Nursing Relief Act reorganized the H-1 category of visas for skilled workers, placing nurses within the H-1A visa group for five years to expedite their migration and ameliorate a nursing shortage. The remaining H-1 visa recipients were reclassified as H-1B. The 1990 act capped the annual number of new H-1B visas at 65,000 and included a pathway to permanent residency if the employers of the H-1B workers were agreeable to sponsoring them for permanent residency.

Very little history is available on the formulation of the H-4 family/dependent visa. While the family/dependent visa has existed since 1952, it can be assumed that the H-4 visa in its current form can also be traced to the legislation passed in the 1990s since it is ancillary to the H categories of visas. Congressional hearings in the 1990s indicate that the restrictions on work for dependent spouses and other restrictions on H-1 visas were a response to union concerns about nonimmigrant workers taking jobs from qualified Americans. The legacy of dependent (or "derived" visas, as they were called in 1952) can be traced to the coverture principle of the mid-nineteenth century "under which a married woman's legal rights were merged into those of her husband."[21] The coverture laws were extended to immigrant women in the 1890s when a court ruled that immigrant men were entitled to bring their wife and children to the United States with them because "[t]he company of the one, and the care and custody of the other, are his by natural right; and he ought not to be deprived of either."[22]

While principles of coverture were eliminated in domestic law, the institutionalization of the derived visa laws or the dependent visa laws in their current form in the 1990s can be traced back to the 1890 ruling, given that the majority of H-4 dependent visa holders are women. As Sabrina Balgamwalla notes: "The present-day Immigration and Nationality Act specifically states that the status of qualifying relatives, such as spouses and children, 'derives' from the person with the visa, in a sense, 'covering' the spouse with the visa holder's lawful status."[23] Folding H-4 visas into H-1B visas contributes to their insignificance in the eyes of the state. For instance, the travel website of the United States government (travel.state.gov) does not even list the H-4 visa as a category of visa to be obtained for travel to the United States, symbolizing its irrelevance outside its relationship to work visas in the H categories. The interviews I conducted with legislators demonstrate how this insignificance transfers to the person who is the recipient of the visas. Of the seven legislators I interviewed (in 2010), six had an extensive understanding of and strong opinions about the H-1B visa category, whereas only two knew that the H-4 visa category even existed. When a legal category is made invisible by the state, this inevitably has lasting consequences for the personhood of those placed within that legal category; this makes the H-4 visa category and its recipients important analytically.

The Racialized [and Gendered] History of Indian Tech Workers

The United States Congress has both restricted and relaxed (mostly relaxed) the cap on the number of H-1B visas (and, consequently, H-4 visas) many times since 1990, depending on political and economic discourse and labor needs at various times. As is well documented, nonimmigrant H-1B visas have propelled the migration of "temporary" skilled workers, mostly in science, engineering, technology, and math (so-called STEM fields), especially from India. India displaced Canada as the largest recipient of such visas in the 1990s. Asian immigrants, especially from India, fill the demand for what the United States considers skilled workers (those trained in specialized professional skills), particularly tech professionals and health care workers.[24]

While visa allocations are no longer based on national origin or racial classification in the United States, because the majority of H-1B recipients come from the Global South (specifically from South Asia and East Asia), the category of skilled immigrants has become re-racialized.

Indians, who mostly arrive on nonimmigrant visas, have been hired by technology firms as rote computer programmers and hardware engineers in large numbers. Some H-1B visa holders are sent to the United States on work visas by their home companies in India, often as "body-shopped labor."[25] Body-shopping is a uniquely Indian phenomenon whereby Indian tech professionals are recruited by a firm in India that then shops them out to international clients for a particular project for a set period of time, even if the recruiting firm is not involved with the project. Recruiting agencies play a key role in the process of body-shopping; they negotiate salaries on behalf of the workers, process temporary visas, and even arrange for accommodations.[26] While body-shopping has led to a flexible international labor supply and has created a highly mobile global tech labor force as part of global capitalism, it has also facilitated intense labor exploitation. The body-shopped workers are usually low-paid, as the real profit for their labor goes to their recruiting firms in India; their jobs are tedious and monotonous, requiring "only body and no brain."[27] Additionally, they lack job security as temporary workers, and recruiting agencies can retrench them at any time at the whim of the international client.

Most body-shopped skilled workers migrate on temporary work visas that can be extended up to six years.[28] Many US-based firms apply for permanent residency for their migrant workers after three years, but in most cases, it takes upward of fifteen years for Indian migrants to obtain permanent residency.[29] Body-shopped workers often move to other companies before the expiration of their visa term so that they are not at the mercy of the parent company and the client, where they need to be re-sponsored for a H-1B visa by the new employer. If a permanent residency application was in process at the behest of the previous employer, it gets nullified with the job change.[30] The restrictions built into the design of visa laws have created a racially stratified workforce, much as Glenn describes in her 2002 book *Unequal Freedom*. Glenn demonstrates that when the state restricts citizenship rights for certain racial/ethnic groups, allowing employers to limit their authority and autonomy,[31] it results in the racial concentration of workers in systematically unequal jobs, making them vulnerable to capitalistic exploitation. Similarly, in large tech firms, racialized immigrant workers—primarily men from India—take on the bulk of contract-based back-end coding work,[32] which makes them expendable and beholden to their visas and their hiring companies to maintain legal status in the United States. Gender-typing of jobs can therefore be an exploitative force that constructs the trope of docile and dexterous workers.[33] Applied in the context of tech work, where many Indian H-1B workers are concentrated, the cadres of men from the Global South form a secondary workforce with labor conditions unlike those of US workers. The insight on this form of gendered worker[34] helps to conceptualize a racialized and gendered metonymy of an "idealized worker" who is efficient and uncomplaining but also expendable and unassimilable to the American social and economic fabric.

The Racialized [and Gendered] History of Indian Nurse Migration

Predominantly male tech work force from India are not the only gendered migration category of docile and skilled labor to the United States. Gendered migration includes the women who have come to join their husbands on dependent visas via the family reunification clause, as well as the Indian women nurses who have been migrating to the United States since the 1970s.[35] Eleonore Kofman and Parvati Raghuram,[36] writing out of the United Kingdom, point out that the literature on international migration of skilled workers in male-centered occupations has excluded the experiences of skilled women, who are often the lead migrants on H-1B visas in the United States. The authors have attempted to correct that by centering the experiences of skilled women migrants to the United Kingdom and Europe in their work[37] on the East-West migration of Asian women, which spotlights the skilling and deskilling of women immigrants as they move from Southeast Asia and East Asia to the West. Rochelle Ball's research on the migration of skilled nurses from the Philippines to the United States and Saudi Arabia shows how both locations produced a racialized hierarchy of feminized labor resulting in the deskilling of a skilled work force.[38] Research exploring Asian women's migration has, however, barely scratched the surface of how visa laws intersect with a racialized and feminized labor market structure to design a particularly oppressive system that creates a continuum of workplace inequities and gendered hierarchies at home. While the literature on East Asian and Asian Pacific migration of women to the United States has pioneered the discussion of women as lead migrants, the literature on South Asian migration has given less space to the discussion of women as skilled and lead migrants. Beyond the theoretical and empirical depth that a comparison between the families of immigrant tech workers (men) and nurses (women) adds, this book attempts to fortify the literature on women-led skilled migration of South Asians to the United States by including Indian immigrant nurses, who have consistently migrated as a skilled group to the United States. They have reshaped the landscape of paid and unpaid work in South Asian families as they juggle paid health care work, unpaid care, and reproductive work at home while straddling legal statuses.[39]

Immigrant nurses have historically been the pioneers of women skilled worker migration to the United States. In the Immigration Act of 1990, nurses were returned to the H-1B visa category after temporarily being assigned to the H-1A category, and in 1997 a new category (H-1C) was created for nurse migration under the Health Professions Shortage Area Nursing Release Act, which assigned this temporary visa category to nurses to expedite the process of permanent residency for nurses on H visas.[40] Indian nurses, especially those from the southern Indian state of Kerala, have been migrating to various parts of the world, including the United States, since the 1970s as a response to nursing shortages in the Global North.[41] Migration numbers increased considerably after 1990 and then plummeted after 9/11 because of increased scrutiny. And yet Indian nurses have continued to migrate to the United States, as evidenced by the increase in the percentage of Indian nurse candidates for the licensure examination since 2001. In 2005–06, Indians held the second rank in the United States, with 3,800 nurses qualifying for the licensure exam.[42]

Much like the tech workers, the experiences of Indian nurses in the United States are shaped by the positionality of being racialized and gendered care workers who are bound to their jobs through their legal status,[43] as this book discusses in later chapters. In addition, family migration, which is dependent on the legal status of the lead migrants, as in the case of H-4 visa holders, takes on a gendered and racialized life of its own when women are the main breadwinners. It reconfigures familial and filial exchanges and produces complex gendered interactions within families. Because women are now often the drivers of labor migration, feminist scholars have begun to pay attention to globalization as a gendered capitalist project with differential outcomes for women and men of the Global South vis-à-vis the Global North.

Linkages between Globalization, Gender, and the Immigration/Visa Regime

Any attempt to discuss the impacts of immigration and visa policies on economic migrants is incomplete without looking at globalization and its gendered and racialized consequences. Globalization in its current form began at the end of the nineteenth century as the process of economic integration among sovereign countries via increased and less restricted flows of goods, services, capital, and labor across nation-states.[44] Joseph Stiglitz argued that, with appropriate regulation of big financial institutions and banks and the mitigation of power of international organizations such as the International Monetary Fund, globalization could be a positive force in the world. However, given the lack of regulations, developing countries have been harmed by the forces of globalization as it fostered neoliberalization of economies in the Global South, leading to increased privatization and the decimation of social safety nets. Scholars[45] critical of globalization describe it as a highly complex and contradictory process run by powerful and undefined sets of social relations and institutions, marked by "flow of goods, services, ideas, technologies, cultural forms, and people across national boundaries via a global networked society."[46] This means that the migration of global labor is a key mechanism of globalization. As such, many critical migration scholars see labor migration as a neoliberal tool of globalization that the Global North uses to import (racialized) labor from the Global South to serve the capitalist agenda of the Northern elite in the global capitalist market, all the while touting migration as an individual choice.[47] Further, migration policies in the Global North direct migration flows and determine the division of both paid and unpaid labor in global and domestic contexts.[48] Bandana Purkayastha[49] urges us to apply a human-security approach to conceptualize the movement of people across global as well as local boundaries to unpack the global structures "that affect migrants as well as their ability to build economically/politically/socially/culturally secure lives." A human security approach builds on a human rights approach but departs from the repertoire of actual laws and conventions to recognize that, despite having legal status and legal protections, migrants often encounter marginalizing conditions because of social and economic constraints and legal binds.

Feminist and postcolonial theorists further critique globalization by exposing its gendered, racialized, and imperialist aspects. In a globalized era, gender and race have taken on new significance with the massive incorporation of Third World women into a cheap labor force in global markets and factories.[50] Globalization has largely exploited the labor of poor women of color and supported growing inequities within economies and families transnationally.[51] The feminization of low-paying jobs in the global economy has caused a disproportionate transnational labor migration of women to fill these jobs. The work of critical feminist scholars[52] has decentered men as drivers of global labor migration, disrupting the notion that global spaces and formal economies are traversed by men and the masculine, while local spaces and the informal are women's realms—that is to say, so-called Third World women are outside globalization.

Feminist critiques of globalization belie the master image of globalization in media and policy circles as one of "hypermobility, communication, the neutralization of place and distance, and the highly educated, human-capital-intensive worker."[53] This discourse privileges nonhuman aspects of globalization such as global information sharing, global mobility, and transnational corporate cultures over material support, workers, immigrant labor, and the feminized low-wage labor force that make the economic structures of globalization tick. These are the human and material resources that keep the machinery of globalization running in the shadow economy and that Saskia Sassen calls "alternative global circuits,"[54] arguing that invisible feminine labor exported from the Global South, such as nurses, maids, sex workers, and brides, are a key part of such global circuits. She urges researchers to pay attention to alternative global circuits because that will help in understanding how gender and racialization allow for the "formation and viability"[55] of the global economy. In another essay, Sassen[56] contends that globalization is a process whereby the Global North's economic and political hegemony over international financial institutions weakens the economies of the Global South. The instability of their economies pushes struggling nations to sustain them through strategic gendered and racialized emigration.

Other scholars of gender and globalization remind us how feminist ideas can be and have been co-opted by global economic institutions to further the exploitation of women as global labor.[57] Global capitalist organizations in the United States have used the feminist idea of women's economic independence to channel poor women of color into the global workforce as docile labor in jobs such as assembly-line workers in factories.[58]

The migration of highly skilled tech workers and nurses from India to the United States on temporary work and family visas, I contend, crystallizes a mechanism of global capitalism that is both racialized and gendered. In the case of the participants in my research, migration is propelled by a global capitalist corporate structure, facilitated by the neoliberal visa policies of the sending and receiving countries (India and the United States), and that is contested and reconfigured by the migrants who are affected by such policies and structures. The restructuring of the global economy and the tech revolution in the post-1990 world have created an unprecedented demand and supply chain of highly skilled workers from the Global South to the Global North, ensuring a flow of labor, capital, and products. While labor and products can flow freely, as Sara Ahmed[59] puts it, the *motility of the bodies* (the ease with which bodies can move through spaces) of the people producing the labor and the products is impeded, interrupted, controlled, and shaped by visa laws—especially for temporary guest workers. Visa laws for temporary workers are a conduit for the nation-states of the Global North to control the movement of bodies by creating a contingent group of people who contribute to the nation-state through their migrant labor but are bereft of the full social and political benefits available to citizens and other immigrants.[60] The visa laws determine who can come to the United States, in what capacity, for how long, whether they are able to work or not, and whether they can stay on permanently in their new country. And as this book will show in coming chapters, these laws lead to gendered and racialized outcomes for migrants, at every stage in their lives, from the moment they start to apply for a visa.

Nomenclature: "Temporary Skilled Workers" Versus "Migrants" and "Immigrants"

In this book, I refer to the participants in my study as "immigrants" and "migrants" interchangeably. I rarely refer to them as "aliens/non-immigrant aliens" or "temporary workers," which is the legal nomenclature assigned by the Department of Homeland Security to workers who come to the United States via the H category of visas for skilled workers. H-4 visas are referred to in official documents as "visas for the dependent families of H visa holders." However, my participants on H-4 visas called it simply the "dependent visa," which is the phrase I use. My reasons for rejecting the state-anointed terminology are political and epistemological. The nomenclature "resident alien" and "temporary worker" is emblematic of a state engaged in undermining the humanism and security of a group whose labor it seeks even as it constructs them as permanent outsiders. However, the participants in this study continually resisted being cast as outsiders. As a scholar deploying critical feminist epistemology, I am committed to respecting and upholding the voices of my participants, all of whom labeled themselves "immigrants" and not "temporary workers." In most cases, this was because all the nurses and their spouses, as well as most tech workers and their spouses, had been sponsored for a green card, or permanent residency, by their employers and intended to stay in the United States permanently. The extended wait periods (upward of 20 years) for green-card approvals put most of the participants in a liminal legal position, where they straddled a dual legal status: temporary worker and an imminent permanent resident. However, given the embeddedness that most of my participants felt in the social and economic life of the United States, they found the labels "resident alien" and "temporary worker" to be hurtful and alienating. Arif, a tech worker, poignantly summed up the sentiments of all participants when I asked him why he insisted on calling himself an immigrant and not a temporary worker, which is the assigned legal status. He said:

> Why this constant reminder that we are temporary or aliens—*aliens* for god's sake!—Yes, Indians are from Mars! It is like a dagger to the heart. We live here, we have our lives here, we pay taxes, we care for this country.

What happens here politically affects us as much as any citizen here, and we are still *aliens*. They want to take everything from us and deny us even the dignity of calling us immigrants. I refuse to be denied that dignity.

My use of the terminology of immigrants throughout this book is therefore an attempt to honor the self-identification of the participants, especially because for them it was an affective pronouncement of dignity.

I still must explain the seeming conflation of immigrants and migrants. As defined broadly in the sociological literature, *migrants* are people who move, domestically or internationally, usually voluntarily, to live or work, either temporarily or permanently in the new place. In the context of the United States, the Department of Homeland Security defines *immigrants* as follows:

> Lawful permanent residents (LPRs), also known as "green card" holders, are non-citizens who are lawfully authorized to live permanently within the United States. LPRs may accept an offer of employment without special restrictions, own property, receive financial assistance at public colleges and universities, and join the Armed Forces. They also may apply to become U.S. citizens if they meet certain eligibility requirements.[61]

The Internal Revenue Service calls LPRs "resident aliens"[62] for tax purposes, according immigrants the position of permanent outsiders. The participants in this study inhabited a space between migrants and immigrants. They arrived in the United States as migrants (temporary workers) and held a status between that of a nonimmigrant migrant and an immigrant permanent resident, which resulted in the seeming interchangeability of terminologies in this book. This intentional fusing of migrants and immigrants when referring to the participants is important because it captures the liminal positionality of the participants within the rubric of legal migration.

Unpacking the Visa Categories

Most of my participants arrived in the United States on one of four visa categories: the temporary-worker non–immigrant visa (H-1B); the dependent visa (H-4); the employment-based immigrant visa (EB-3);

TABLE 1.1. Number of participants in each visa category

Visa categories	High-tech workers	Wives of high-tech workers	Nurses	Husbands of nurses	Total
H1-B Skilled workers temporary nonimmigrant visa	24	N/A	14 + 6 (in follow-up) = 20	N/A	44
H-4 Dependent nonimmigrant visa	N/A	24 + 9 (in follow-up) = 33	N/A	14*	47
EB-3 Employment-based immigrant visa	N/A	N/A	7	N/A	7
E34 Employment-based immigrant dependent visa	N/A	N/A	N/A	7	7
Green Card Permanent residency/ citizens	1**	1**	9**	9**	20**
Total	25	34	36	30	**125**

*Only 3 of the 15 husbands on H-4 visas primarily lived in India with a transnational family arrangement at the time of the interview.
**Participants on green cards or lawful permanent residency transitioned from H-1B and H-4 visa to become permanent residents during the course of this study.

or the family visa for spouses and children of EB-3 holders (E34). Some nurse participants who married men who were US citizens or permanent residents arrived on green cards as permanent residents using the family reunification clause. Table 1.1 shows the number of participants on each of these visa statuses.

In the following section, I provide basic information on each type of visa. A detailed description with sources for each of the visa laws can be found in appendix B.

H-1B Visas

The H-1B is a nonimmigrant temporary visa issued to foreign professional workers who fill a specialized knowledge position in the United States. Basic eligibility for H-1B status requires that the job the worker requests be a "specialty occupation," meaning that it requires at least a bachelor's degree in the field. Fields may include but are not limited to architecture, engineering, mathematics, physical sciences, social sciences, medicine and health, education, law, accounting, business specialties, theology, and the arts. Table 1.2 shows the demographic details of the top-five categories of H-1B visa recipients between 2007 and 2017. India sent the largest group of H-1B workers to the United States during this period, with 25–34 years as the most common age category and computer-related jobs as the top job category; the median compensation was $50,000–$79,000; 44 percent had bachelor's degrees, and 42 percent had master's degrees. According to the Department of Homeland Security's Non–Immigrant Admission[63] database for 2019 (the last available data), 54.5 percent of 601,594 H-1B visas issued that year went to Indian temporary workers, followed by Canada at 11.7 percent and China at 11.2 percent; the remainder was divided among 187 other countries. Not surprisingly, 68 percent of all H-4 visas went to dependents (spouses and children) of Indians within all H categories of visas. In 2017, Indians were the top recipients of H-1B temporary visas for skilled workers and were the second-largest group of international students in the United States.

The alignment of degree and job became more flexible over the years. For instance, one did not have to have a computer science degree to be a software engineer—a mechanical engineer with experience in software development could potentially get an H-1B visa to work in the United States. However, in 2017, under the "Buy American, Hire American" policy, the Trump administration mandated that jobs need to align strictly with educational degrees, which resulted in a spike of denial rates for H-1B visas. For the first time ever, the rate of denials of H-1B applications rose from 10 percent in 2016 to 24 percent in 2019.[64]

The H-1B visa usually has a three-year term and can be extended another three years, after which the H-1B holder is required to leave the United States for one year before being eligible for H-1B status again. The H-1B is a non–immigrant visa but has a pathway to immigration via the permanent residency program. All the tech workers in my study held H-1B status, and about ten of the nurses who had a bachelor's in nursing held H-1B status, and, all except two tech workers had been sponsored for permanent residency by their employers.

TABLE 1.2. Top categories of H-1B receipts

FY 2007–FY 2017

	2007	2008	2009	2010	2011	2012	2013	2014	2015	2016	2017	Total	% of total receipts
Receipts	314,621	285,475	246,126	248,272	268,412	308,242	299,690	325,971	368,852	399,349	336,107	3,401,117	(100.00%)
Country													
India	166,575	157,608	122,475	135,931	155,791	197,940	201,114	227,172	269,677	300,902	247,927	2,183,112	(64.19%)
China	26,370	24,434	22,411	21,119	23,227	22,528	23,924	27,733	32,485	35,720	36,362	296,313	(8.71%)
Philippines	12,230	10,713	10,407	8,887	9,098	9,400	7,399	6,772	4,147	3,704	3,161	85,918	(2.53%)
South Korea	10,730	10,277	10,704	8,721	7,480	7,204	5,576	4,897	4,298	4,269	3,203	77,359	(2.27%)
Canada	8,562	7,111	7,871	7,342	6,761	6,688	5,478	5,267	5,050	4,547	3,551	68,228	(2.01%)
25 to 34	205,353	188,772	162,468	168,686	187,822	220,472	214,291	233,452	262,417	276,597	226,195	2,346,525	(68.99%)
35 to 44	68,281	58,225	53,047	53,314	54,942	58,716	60,084	67,563	81,831	96,955	84,193	737,151	(21.67%)
Computer-related	158,078	144,550	107,525	120,257	134,817	182,695	184,944	210,396	253,003	281,017	231,033	2,008,315	(59.05%)
Architecture, engineering, and surveying	33,965	30,631	27,349	24,431	29,602	29,038	27,496	29,301	28,902	29,822	28,133	318,670	(9.37%)
Occupations in education	29,827	29,159	26,330	24,364	22,380	21,057	19,571	18,961	19,351	19,253	14,355	244,608	(7.19%)
Occupations in administrative specialization	27,749	23,689	24,041	21,330	22,015	21,636	19,399	20,047	21,140	22,786	21,472	245,304	(7.21%)
Medicine and health	18,602	18,044	20,304	19,089	17,822	17,386	16,342	15,195	14,957	15,196	12,113	185,050	(5.44%)
25,000 to 49,999	75,047	59,642	51,630	41,772	36,361	34,103	26,813	23,797	20,524	17,855	12,321	399,865	(11.76%)
50,000 to 74,999	135,727	128,802	102,781	105,306	111,649	140,780	128,858	132,372	142,865	142,847	105,827	1,377,814	(40.51%)
75,000 to 99,999	60,765	55,384	50,044	55,298	65,225	71,703	74,269	87,998	105,383	117,529	99,326	842,924	(24.78%)
100,000 to 124,999	23,511	22,620	20,477	24,341	29,118	33,584	38,974	45,443	55,288	64,982	59,988	418,326	(12.30%)
Bachelor's degree	143,937	122,941	104,511	109,478	112,334	146,174	136,453	146,368	170,865	180,077	139,055	1,512,193	(44.46%)
Master's degree	121,987	116,561	97,703	96,163	113,284	122,325	125,052	141,470	159,828	180,961	165,830	1,441,164	(42.37%)
Professional degree	14,677	13,353	13,225	13,387	13,279	12,625	12,206	12,001	11,812	11,880	9,863	138,308	(4.07%)

H-4 "Dependent" Visas

The family reunification clause of the Immigration Act of 1965 facilitated "dependent visa" status for the spouses and children of temporary skilled workers; this clause was revised to its current form, and included the spouses of foreign students, in the Immigration Act of 1990.[65] The H-4 dependent visa—which most of the spouses in my study held—allows the dependent spouse and children of any principal H-class visa holder to enter the United States.[66] According to United States Citizenship and Immigration Services, nonimmigrant temporary visa dependents on H-4 visas are not permitted to be employed or receive compensation from any US source. If they are offered a paid position, dependents may apply for a change of status to a visa that does allow employment. These opportunities are rare however, and conditions dictated by the visa type must be met before a status change is approved. In addition, employment may not commence until USCIS approves the change, which can take up to six months. The data on H-4 recipients is not disaggregated by gender, but according to the Department of Homeland Security, the majority of dependent H-4 visas since 2010 have been issued to women, followed (in terms of numbers) by children; only a small percentage of dependent visas go to men. In 2015, the Obama administration ruled that spouses in H-1B families that had cleared the first step in permanent residency application processing would receive work authorization, which would reduce the length of unemployment for H-4 spouses. A 2018 Congressional Research Services report by Jill Wilson indicated that 93 percent of "granted applications for employment authorization" were issued to women, with only 7 percent going to men. According to the same report: "Ninety-three percent of approved applications for H-4 employment authorization were issued to individuals born in India, and 5 percent were issued to individuals born in China. Individuals born in all other countries combined make up the remaining two percent of approved applications." These numbers confirm that most recipients of H-4 visas are women from India. Among my participants, all the wives of tech workers held H-4 visas, and about 10 of the husbands of nurses held H-4 visas, as indicated in table 1.1.

EB-3 Visas for Nurses and Their Dependents

As with tech workers, nurses can hold H-1B status because they fall into the "specialty occupation" category. However, because of the shortage of nurses in the United States, they can bypass the H-1B nonimmigrant visa process and apply for an employment-based immigrant visa, or EB-3. The EB-3 opens up a direct pathway to permanent residency for the immigrant worker, meaning they can enter the United States as an LPR. To be eligible for an EB-3 visa, a nurse or a health care worker must have worked for at least three years in their area of expertise at an accredited and government-recognized health institution in the country of origin. Spouses of EB-3 visa holders may be admitted to the United States in the E34 category (spouse of a "skilled worker" or "professional") and can apply for a work permit. Once the work permit is issued, which can take up to three years, the spouse of the worker can seek employment. About nine of the nurses in my study held EB-3 status and their husbands E34.

Employment-Based Lawful Permanent Residency "Green Card"

Green cards are employment-based immigrant residency permits available to qualified applicants from all national origins under the provisions of US immigration law. Spouses and children in certain preferred categories are allowed to accompany employment-based immigrants or join them later. Several of the H-1B holders in my study had petitioned for permanent residency through their employers and were waiting for approval. About eight of the nurses in my study and their spouses, who had arrived on EB-3 and E34 visas respectively, held permanent residency or had become naturalized citizens.

Tech Workers: Recruitment and Visa Process

My explanation of the recruitment and visa processes is based on Biao Xiang's[67] work, on my archival research, and on the interviews I conducted. Most of the tech-worker participants followed the route Xiang describes, whereby tech firms that hire workers in India facilitate the offshore recruitment of tech workers. As noted earlier, body-shopping firms in India earn revenue by lending tech employees (their bodies and

TABLE 1.3. Summary of H-1B, H-4, and EB-3 visa characteristics

Visa categories	H-1B visa or skilled workers temporary nonimmigrant visa	H-4 visa or dependent non-immigrant visa for family members	EB-3 employment-based immigration visa
Purpose of the visa	Visa for professionals in "Specialty Occupation" (SO) with at least a bachelor's degree.	Spouse and children of any of the H (1, 2, and 3) visa holders can apply for an H-4 dependent visa	Offered to foreign nationals with specialized training that US labor markets have shortage of such as nurses, health care workers, and skilled factory workers
Employment eligibility	Includes: accountants, computer professionals, engineers, financial analysts, doctors, scientists, architects, and lawyers.	H-4 visa holder may not hold any kind of employment in the United States until receiving a work permit or H-4 EAD after being approved for permanent residency, which can take six to ten years.	Must either demonstrate two years of work experience in related field before migration or job requires at least a US baccalaureate degree or a foreign equivalent and must be members of the profession
Duration of the visa	Issued for three years and extendable for another three years	The term of the visa aligns with the term of the employed spouse	Three years before LPR is processed; no option for extension if LPR is not processed
Legal expectation from visa holder	H-1B workers are expected to make valuable contribution to American society	H-4 visa holders are not allowed to obtain Social Security card or any kind of government-issued identification	Fulfill shortage of health care workers and make valuable contribution to American society
Possibilities of legal permanent residency (LPR)	Employer can choose to apply for LPR or not	The H-4 visa holders obtain LPR when their spouses obtain it and are permitted to work once the first step of LPR is fulfilled, which takes between three to five years after arrival	Employer must process the first step of LPR for the migrant worker before arrival; opens a straight path to LPR for both worker and spouse

labor representing "products") to companies around the world. One participant described the process in these words: "We, the tech workers, become international products that can be sold from project to project. How do you think these giant companies make money? By renting us out, selling our skills!"

Most of the large body-shopping firms liaise with the consulates of different countries and obtain a certain number of visas that they hold for their workers. Body-shopping agencies compete to secure visas for employees, which guarantees a set number of workers who they can export every year. The larger and more powerful the firm, the stronger its networks with international clients in countries such as the United States and United Kingdom. Some firms work only with US companies to supply tech workers. Every year, Indian firms send up to 65,000[68] tech workers to the United States. Employees are selected for offshore recruitment based on criteria such as: the expertise of the employee relevant to a given project; the experience the employee already has working with off-site and international clients; the client's request for a particular employee; and the overall performance of the employee. Offshore recruitment is viewed as a promotion by the employee selected.

Tech firms in India are structured so that the promotion of employees depends on an offshore assignment. Employees in entry-level positions start out in the position of junior coder, then are promoted to senior coder. The promotion after that is to the position of offshore programmer. Almost everyone who is hired at a tech firm or body-shopping agency receives an offshore appointment and thus a promotion. Employees who do not receive an offshore promotion or choose not to accept one for family or other reasons usually remain in the senior coder position, with little increase in their pay. Even when they change jobs, they do not achieve significant gains in pay and promotions. The higher-profile and higher-salaried jobs in the tech industry usually go to tech workers who have returned to India after their time at an offshore location. The most coveted offshore locations for body-shopping agencies and their employees are the United States and United Kingdom. An offshore promotion in either country means more revenue for the company, relatively higher pay for the employee (as least compared to offshore recruitments in countries such as Singapore or South Africa or in Latin America), and the possibility of permanent immigration, particularly to the United States. As mentioned earlier, the United States does offer the option for H-1B holders to apply for employment-based permanent residency, which the United Kingdom and European Union countries do not. Therefore, Indian tech firms tout the United States to their employees as the most desirable offshore position, fostering competition among employees for a US appointment. This is common practice in almost all body-shopping firms in India.[69]

After internal selection of employees for offshore projects is complete, the international client interviews the selected candidates. According to participants, most employees selected for offshore projects "sail through client interviews." Once a firm in the United States has agreed to hire a certain number of employees from a body-shopping agency, the firm's legal office sends out contract letters to companies stating the pay and fringe benefits offered to the employee. The employee usually does not have the leeway to negotiate pay or benefits; the body-shopping agency decides all terms on behalf of the employee. The agency receives monthly revenue for each employee it sends to international clients. Once the paperwork is processed by a hiring agency in the United States, the legal division of the Indian firm prepares letters of support for the employee to apply for an H-1B visa and sets up dates for visa interviews at the US consulate in a city closest to the place of employment.[70] Interview dates are available only three months prior to travel dates. The documents required for an H-1B visa include the employee's Indian passport, visa fees paid by the company, visa forms completed by the applicant, a sponsorship letter from the US firm, letters of support from the Indian parent company, the employee's educational certificates, the employee's CV, current pay stubs, and a description of the project for which the employee is being hired. Since 2000, after reforms to the H-1B laws, H-1B workers are no longer required to prove intent to return to the home country during the visa interviews.

The employee appears at the consulate on the day and time set for the interview with the relevant documents. The employee's company pays for travel costs to the consulate. The employee has a face-to-face interview (or interviews) with a visa officer, who typically asks all employees about: their current employment firm in India; the recruiting firm in the United States; the project they will be working on; and the location they will be staying in the United States. If the visa is granted, the consulate retains the passport to add the visa stamp; the passport is available for pick-up after 48 hours or is sent to the employee's company via a courier service. If the visa is rejected, the passport is returned on the spot. One of the tech-worker participants, Arif, described the experience to me. He said:

> It's nerve-racking. You are in this building made of steel with policemen carrying heavy weapons. The visa officer stands behind the bulletproof-glass window and shoots all these questions. Most people are granted a visa, but it is always a 50/50 chance, and you are always nervous. People are always so happy once they are granted a visa and so sad when they are not. It's hard to face your colleagues if you are denied a visa. It is as if you are a loser![71]

Arif's description of his experience of the visa interview process is emblematic of how the United States constructs inequitable status for those (legally) migrating for labor at every step. The heavily armed security personnel and bulletproof glass windows at US consulates in many other countries symbolize an imperial state that insists on creating physical and other barriers for the noncitizens who are seeking permission to enter. Arif's depiction of the emotional toll of the visa process indicates an added neoliberal irony: those applying for a work visa do so at the behest of the company that wants to hire them. And yet, the granting or denial of the visa seemingly becomes a marker of personal success or failure for the individual applicant, beginning a saga in which the applicant assumes personal responsibility for structural inequities and trains the self in the governmentality of the visa regime.

After the visa is granted, the employee prepares to leave the country. The company covers travel costs to the offshore location. The Indian firm also assumes responsibility for employees during travel including any misconduct at work during their tenure at the US-based firm. If an employee is married or has children, the company also applies for a dependent visa for the spouse and children of the H-1B worker. This process is described in the next section. While on the surface this seems like a fair process, it has deeply troubling ramifications for the familial lives of the visa holders as explored in the subsequent chapters.

A minority of participants who were not tech workers but worked at US companies on H-1B visas as financial analysts or research scientists mostly held graduate degrees from American universities and were able to apply for jobs in the United States upon graduation. In such situations, the employer petitions USCIS for an H-1B visa on the employee's behalf. Once the visa petition is approved, employees must return to India or go to a consulate outside the United States to get the visa stamped on their passport, then go through the interview process there (just as the tech workers did) to be able to travel and return to the United States. Once their visa is stamped and issued, they can return to the United States to continue their employment.

Indian Nurses: Recruitment and Visa Process

One would logically assume that the recruitment process for similar categories of visas would be analogous. As I discovered through this study, that is not the case. The nurses go through somewhat of a different set of processes that produces its own gendered and racialized outcomes as they enter the visa regime through the stages of recruitment and the visa application.

A third of the nurse participants arrived in the United States with a green card, having married a man with permanent US residency or citizenship. The majority of respondents came to the United States on a nonimmigrant H-1B visa or on an EB-3 employment-based immigrant visa. Because of the shortage of nationally trained nurses in the United States and increased demand for registered nurses, there is mounting pressure by commercial recruiters and employers to ease restrictions on nurses' immigration.[72] The nurses arrive mainly on two types of visas: immigrant visas called EB-3 given to specially trained skilled workers who fill an acute labor shortage in the United States; or a nonimmigrant skilled worker visa (H-1A or H-1B), in fewer numbers.[73] In some instances, nurses arrives on H-1C visas, which are given to foreign health care workers migrating to areas (usually rural) with an acute nurse shortage. I did not have any nurses on H-1C visas among my participants because most of the interviews conducted were in metropolitan, not rural, areas.

In their critical exposé of the recruitment process of foreign nurses in the United States, Khadria[74] and Patricia Pittman and her colleagues[75] provide a thorough depiction of how nurses are recruited to work in the

American health care industry. These studies, along with experiences participants shared during interviews, form my sketch of nursing recruitment in India and the processes they followed to obtain a visa. According to Khadria, the high emigration rate of Indian nurses resulted from the shortage of nurses in wealthier nations and the business interests of recruiting agencies in India. In 2004, India had more than 1,000 accredited nursing schools, which collectively graduated about 1.4 million registered nurses per year.[76] In response to rising demand from wealthier nations for well-trained, English-speaking Indian nurses, many nurse graduates received additional training to prepare them to work overseas. Of all the nurses trained each year, about 75 percent emigrated to various parts of the world. The majority of emigrant nurses went to Gulf countries, the United States, Australia, New Zealand, Singapore, Ireland, and the United Kingdom, in that order.

In response to the rising demand for Indian nurses in the global market, many Indian hospitals have morphed into business process outsourcing (BPO) agencies.[77] These hospitals recruit and train Indian nurses and prepare them to take a foreign nursing credentialing examination. Licensing and visa processes governing migration to different countries vary markedly and require deep knowledge of the systems on the part of BPO hospitals. For example, the waiting period for migrating to the United Kingdom is as short as six months, whereas for the United States it is up to two to three years. The recruitment and training of nurses for the international health care industry occurs across all the big cities in India. Despite the nationwide nursing training facilities, 85 percent of these nurses are from one state in India (Kerala), and the majority of them are Christian.

Since 2003, New Delhi has been the hub of Indian recruiting agencies that partner with US recruiters. The largest ones are Max HealthStaff, Western International University (Mody Private Group), Escorts Heart Institute, the Apollo Hospitals, and Jaipur Golden Hospital. Khadria found that these agencies invest $4,700–$7,000 to train each nurse and earn as much as $47,000 when a nurse is placed abroad. In recent years, the Indian government, much like the government of the Philippines, has started taking an interest in facilitating the international migration of nurses. Recruiting agencies, with the help of governments, have exponentially increased Commission on Graduates of Foreign Nursing

Schools (CGFNS) examination centers in India since 2004. New government policy has increased nursing migration to the United States many times over. Since 2010, India has become the second largest supplier of foreign nurses to the United States, after the Philippines. Indian nurses, like Filipinx nurses, must undergo a long, cumbersome, and expensive credentialing process to work in US health care.[78] Between 2005 and 2009, Indian recruitment agencies have exported about 100,000 nurses to the United States.[79]

Most of the nurse participants in this study arrived in the United States between 2000 and 2010 on H-1B visas or EB-3 visas through a recruiting agency. The nurses who came here on a H-1B visas had their bachelor of science (nursing) degrees, because to qualify for an H-1B visa the applicant requires at least a bachelor's degree in the relevant field. Upon graduation, they were recruited by agencies and trained for potential employment with a foreign hospital. The recruiting agencies organized interviews with several US health care firms on behalf of the nurses. Once selected, the nurses prepared for the CGFNS exam. It often took multiple attempts and up to two years for some of my participants to pass the CGFNS exam.

After the nurses passed the CGFNS exam, they were eligible to apply for an H-1B visa. The H-1B application process for nurses is similar to that for tech workers. The agency sets up an interview appointment with the US consulate in the city nearest where the nurses live. The visa interview requires nurses to carry their passports, visa forms, their appointment letter from the US hospital, CGFNS certification documents, educational documents, and visa fees (which, in the case of nurses, are not paid by the recruiting agency). The nurses reported that, if their paperwork was in order, they could expect fewer questions at the visa interview, but at a minimum they were asked the name and location of the hospital at which they would be working in the United States. Once the visa was granted, the nurses prepared to leave. Most of the nurse participants in my study on H-1B visas would arrive in Chicago to start their jobs in various parts of the city's metropolitan area. Participants in this study told me that most had to pay for their own travel. Some were reimbursed by their employer in the United States, but others were not; this depended on contract details that the Indian recruiting agency had drawn up with the US employer.

The hospital that decided to hire the nurse would send a contract, typically for a term of 18 months to three years, to the recruiting agencies. The nurses were bound by the contract to work with that hospital for the duration of the contract or up to three years. If the nurse broke the contract, the Indian recruitment agency would have to pay a penalty of $10,000–$30,000 to the hospital. To insulate themselves against that risk, the recruiting agencies drew up contracts of their own, which required nurses to pay up to a $50,000 penalty if they decided to terminate the contract with the hospital before its completion. My participants were of the opinion that the agencies made profit "even from the contract fees." According to Missy, one of my nurse participants: "If the hospital in the United States wanted $20,000 to break the contract, the recruitment agency would charge us $50,000." When recruiting H-1B nurses, most hospitals offered to apply for permanent residency on behalf of their nurse employees after three years of employment under the National Interest Waiver (NIW), a program in the Department of Homeland Security that allows for expediting the process of permanent residency for foreign workers in the defense, biotechnology, and health care industries, which need trained personnel to fill worker shortages. Employees were required to remain with an organization for a minimum of three years by law before they could file for permanent residency under the NIW. The nurse participants saw this both as a benefit and as a problem. Lily told me:

> The only thing we bargain on during the hiring is so that we get a permanent residency fast, but that also makes us stay with the hospital we go to for three years. I wanted to leave my job even if I had to pay money, I hated my first job so much, but I stayed on the three years for the green card. . . . Before coming, you are not thinking of how it would be to work there, you are thinking of your family and your future, so we make sure we have the green-card thing in the contract. But sometimes it becomes [a] catch-22.

In this candid assessment of her situation, Lily unfurls a common dilemma faced by most participants in my sample in which the promise of permanent residency becomes both an incentive and a tool for exploitation, as detailed in chapter 4. However, the nurses, unlike the tech workers, had the possibility of negotiating for an employment-based immigrant visa as opposed to only having the option of the non-immigrant H1-B visa like the tech workers did. I found during my field recruitment that most nurses came to the United States not on non-immigrant H-1B or H-1C visas but on employment-based immigrant EB-3 visas. When US employers of migrant workers apply for permanent residency for their foreign employees, they do so under different categories of employment-based (EB) visas. EB-3 is one such category, and it can apply to Indian migrant workers. Nurses and other foreign workers whose services are deemed necessary for the national interest and in high demand in the US labor markets by the US government may be issued EB-3 visas for immigration before they have even arrived in the United States.[80] Although the qualifications, requirements, and application processes for EB-3 visas are almost the same as for H-1B visas, nurses must meet additional requirements to be eligible for an EB-3 from India. First, they need to demonstrate that they have three to five years of experience working in a world-class health facility as a full-time registered nurse in India. Second, they must produce a "Visascreen" certification.[81] A Visascreen certification is required by section 343 of the Illegal Immigration Reform and Immigrant Responsibility Act of 1996. It entails: an assessment of the applicant's education to ensure it is comparable to that of a US graduate in the same profession; verification that all professional health care licenses that the applicant has ever held are unconditionally valid; verification that the applicant has passed the US English proficiency examination; and verification that the nurse has passed either the CGFNS Qualifying Exam, the NCLEX-RN,[82] or the State Board Test Pool Examination.[83] The International Commission on Healthcare Professionals (ICHP) issues the VisaScreen certificate to indicate that nursing credentials meet US standards. Applicants who successfully complete the VisaScreen receive an ICHP VisaScreen certificate, satisfying federal requirements.

When I asked nurse participants why they chose to come on EB-3 visas instead of H-1B visas, they said it was because the EB-3 ensured a straight path to permanent residency not only for them but also for their husbands. They also indicated that their husbands more readily accompanied them if they did not have to come as dependent visa holders. Spouses and children of EB-3 holders apply for E34 and E35 visas respectively, which allow them to enter the United States as dependents immigrating for reasons of family reunification. Moreover, E34/35 visas do not have the same restrictions on work as H-4 visas.

Given the many difficulties my nurse participants had to overcome, I asked why they decided to migrate instead of working as a nurse in India. I received three overlapping responses, which were consistent with past research on the migration of Indian nurses.[84] First, nursing is a low-paid profession in India with low occupational prestige and slim chances of upward mobility. Most participants cited the "much higher pay" as a foreign nurse as one of the primary reasons to emigrate. Second, within the Indian culture, nurses are looked down on as women who engage in the dirty work of touching unclean bodies. The codification of nursing as dirty work is attributed to Brahminical (caste-supremacist) Hinduism and Islam, two major religions in India, which consider working with the body to be impure, making nursing a niche profession for Christian women.[85] As such, Christian women unsurprisingly have dominated the nursing profession in India owing to the role of Christian missionaries there historically.[86] Medical missionaries or qualified women missionaries were charged with nursing education in colonial India in the hospital-based training schools, which also served as proselytization sites.[87] This religious and colonial history made Christian women more likely to go into nursing as an upwardly mobile profession available to a minoritized group in India. And finally, the main reason reported by the nurse participants in this study, who were all from the state of Kerala, was the severe lack of opportunities in the state.

According to them, because Kerala has been governed most consistently by the Communist Party of India for more than 30 years, it has seen very little foreign investment or industrialization. While Kerala has a robust economy with one of the highest per-capita incomes in India, the economy in Kerala is predominantly agricultural; aside from farm work, very few jobs are available, causing high unemployment rates among young people.[88] Most of the nurses and their husbands came from poorer, rural farming families. Since 1980 or so, Christian women in Kerala have taken up nursing to lift their immediate and extended families above the poverty level and to upward social mobility.[89] This, coupled with the demand for Indian nurses by wealthier nations, has made migration one of the most viable economic options for nurses from

Kerala. As one of my nurse participants put it: "I only became a nurse so that I could get a job abroad and give my family, my children, a chance to live better. It was very hard to leave, but now my parents, my brothers and sisters, my husband's families, all are doing better, and my children will have a better future than me or my husband." This statement posits economic incentive as the draw for emigration for the nurses; however, for these women, the move is rarely for individual gains in career or money but almost always for the betterment of their families.

The Visa Process for Dependent Spouses

The spouses of H-1B holders, as mentioned earlier, apply for H-4 dependent visas to come to the United States as dependent spouses. Recruiting agencies and firms advise that the dependent should apply for the visa when the lead migrant applies for an H-1B visa, but most participants applied for an H-4 visa after their husbands or wives were already in the United States. Most of the women participants who applied for H-4 visas after their husbands had emigrated coordinated with their husband's original labor staffing company in India to prepare documents for the visa application. For the wives of tech workers, the visa fees and travel costs for dependents were usually borne by the firm. As for the nurses' husbands, the nurses (in all cases except two) paid the visa fees and travel costs for their spouses.

The documentation required for an H-4 visa applicant includes a visa form; the applicant's passport, which must clearly state that the H-4 applicant is married to the H-1B-holding lead migrant; the original approved H-1B form (Form I-97) of the lead migrant; copies of the lead migrant's passport; a letter from the lead migrant's company certifying that the lead migrant works in the company and is married to the applicant; a copy of the lead applicant's appointment letter; the lead applicant's pay stubs and bank statements; marriage certificates and photographs showing the couple getting married in the presence of family and friends; and a cover letter stating that the H-4 applicant does not intend to seek employment in the United States. The documentation required for the H-4 visa interview—marriage certificates and photographs of the wedding ceremony—underlines the primacy of the institution of marriage in the immigration process, thereby providing what is perhaps the most tangible evidence that the US immigration regime is inherently heteropatriarchal and heteronormative. [90] This heteropatriarchal norm is all the stronger here because these immigrants come from India: even in 2021, the only form of marriage legally recognized in India is between cismen and ciswomen. Moreover, during the first phase of my research for this book, the United States had not yet recognized marriage equality, which meant that the visa application process for the H-4 visa holders in this study on marriage was predicated on heteronormativity. The legalese surrounding the dependent visa application process then signifies a journey for dependent spouses from one heteronormative state to another, marking dependence in this context as necessarily a heteronormative formation. [91]

The women participants holding H-4 visas shared with me their experiences at the consulate during the visa interview. Most women said they were advised by husbands and people with similar experience that they should wear Indian clothes (sari or salwar kameez) for the visa interview, as well as all the visible markers of marriage based on their religion, such as a wedding ring (for most) and/or vermillion and bangles (for Hindu women).

At the visa interview, women participants had varied experiences. The three women in my study who applied for visas with their husbands told me that the visa officers did not ask them any questions beyond their names and whether the person accompanying them was their husband. The women who applied for visas after their husbands had emigrated had a range of experiences during visa interviews. Some said they were barely asked anything beyond where they were going and where their husbands worked. Others said they were asked several questions. They were asked about marriage. They were asked to identify people in the wedding photographs. They were asked if they intended to look for work in the United States. Participants who faced a barrage of questions were more likely to have previously traveled to the United States for work or other business. Participants who faced many questions thought that, as soon as the visa officers were satisfied that the H-4 applicant did not have any intention to work, they would grant the visa. One of these women, Alka, told me that, when she was asked if she intended to work in the United States, she replied: "Not at all. I want to go, take care of my family, and have a baby as soon as possible." Alka continued: "And as soon as I said that I was like, 'Shit, now they'll think I want an anchor baby,' but thankfully they did not." Alka told me she was being sarcastic; however, the visa officer's unquestioning belief in Alka's statement shows the normalization of the deep-seated hetero-normativity of the migration regime and the construction of the Third World woman/wife as the model dependent.

H-4 visas are denied only in rare cases. None of my participants knew anyone who had been denied an H-4 visa. One participant was asked to return to the passport office after correcting a problem with her paper-work: Her passport did not indicate that she was married to her hus-band, and she needed to have that endorsed by the passport office before her visa could be granted—another instance of heteronormativity in the migration regime's reliance on the conservative institution of marriage for granting family migration (H-4) visa permits.

The H-4 visa applicants had to demonstrate that they were married within the tenets of their religious mandates by wearing gendered sym-bols of marriage on their bodies. The same was not expected of the men, casting the women dependents as a monolith in a heteronormative mi-gration regime. This process also indirectly racialized H-4 applicants at the time of the interview, as they had to appear in what is consid-ered traditional Indian attire and wearing symbols of marriage on their bodies—a requirement the men were exempt from.

The few men who applied for the H-4 visa, however, had to provide the same kinds of documents for the visa interview. In addition, they were required to carry a notarized copy of their wife's CGFNS certificate. The interview experiences of men applying for the H-4 visa was different from those of the women H-4 applicants in blatantly gendered ways. The men were almost never asked about marriage or asked to show photo-graphs of their wedding. Most of the questions centered on whether he intended to work in the United States and how he would spend his time after migrating. One of my participants, George, told me: "The insult starts right there. How am I going to spend my time? You tell me! I know that they see very few men applying for H-4, so they get anx-ious, but it is quite insulting still." While the line of questioning for the women relegates them to subordinated positions to breadwinning hus-bands, questions put to the men dependents are reminders of their lost breadwinning status—instituting the heteronormative as the imaginary for this migration process.

The men applying for dependent E34 visas did not have to go through a visa interview. For all my nurse participants, the EB-3 and E34/35 visas for husbands and children were processed together. The recruiting agency hired a law firm in the United States to apply for the EB-3 and EB34/35 visas for dependents of the nurses. The paperwork for E34 applicants was similar to that of H-4 applicants. After the E34 was granted and the men had traveled to the United States, they would be interviewed at the port of entry by immigration officials about the reasons for their migration before being granted entry. E34 visa processing was assigned more privilege than that of H-4 visas. It is perhaps no accident that most E34 visas go to the men spouses of nurses.

The process of obtaining dependent visas for both men and women is gendered and heteronormative, and becomes racialized in its performance of cultural tropes around marriage and the interrogations at the port of entry. The entire visa-based migration process—from the legal discourse around it to the granting of visas—translates into gendered, heteronormative, and racialized meanings for the migrant subject. These processes make the visa-based migration regime one that is designed to control migrant subjectivities and that exacerbates the gendered and racialized cost of migration for each individual subject of migration.

Conclusion

The purpose of this chapter is to present the unfolding of the racialized and gendered and heteronormative mechanisms hidden in the legal and other details of the migration process. As unveiled here, immigrants have to jump through several hoops to receive visas; however, compared to tech workers, the nurses seem to have to go through even more steps to be hired and to receive their visas. They have to pass the CGFNS examination and obtain VisaScreen certification to obtain a visa. Additionally, the recruiting agencies, through channeled nursing emigration, are even more exploitative than the body-shopping agencies exploiting tech workers. However, nurses have the opportunity to become permanent

US residents much faster compared to tech workers. Unlike nurses, whose EB-3 visas gave them a path to citizenship from the start, tech workers on H-1B visas could not apply for permanent residency until well after arriving in the United States. The experiences of the H-4 applicants seemed to differ by gender during the visa interview process—a difference that persisted even after they had migrated. Understanding the recruitment and visa processes for tech workers, nurses, and their spouses provides insight into the experiences of migrant workers before they even arrive in the United States. While the experiences were trying for some, these difficulties would be just the beginning of the struggles they would come to face.

The research on immigrant families and the gendered division of labor has focused on the gender ideology of the sending country and how it shapes gender within households, as demonstrated by several scholars[92] of gender and migration. An important change that occurs with migration is that women often are required to act as coproviders and, as in the case of the nurses, providers for the household for its survival, which is not often the case in their country of origin.[93] Thus, migration may lead to improvement in women's social positions because of opportunities for employment. Whether in low-wage jobs or professional jobs, employment provided women more control over earnings and greater participation in making family decisions.[94] But does this change or challenge the materiality of gender expectations?

The work of scholars of immigration and gender suggests that, even when immigrant women work for pay, they still do the majority of household work. While the gender ideologies of men postmigration remain unchanged, husbands still do more household work as a result of the nuclearization of the family structure after migration, indicating a change in gendered practices from the home country. The social construction of skill in the context of immigration also creates a gendered framing of households. Purkayastha[95] contends that, when placed in the category of dependent, the wives of highly skilled workers in Indian immigrant families—often highly educated themselves—were "rarely classified as highly skilled and [were] relegated to the undifferentiated category of 'wife,'" a category that devalued their professional skills.[96]

To add to the research on how migrant families of skilled workers experience gender and racialization in the United States, in the chapters that follow, I explore how these visas affect different aspects of everyday life: work, home, parenting, public interactions, and the lives and selves of the participants as immigrants bound by the visa regime in its gendered and racialized dispensations.

2

Model Migrants and Ideal Workers

How Visa Laws Penalize and Control

A broken immigration system means broken families and broken lives.
—Jose Antonio Vargas

Chicago, October 2010. It was a nippy evening. An unusually large number of people—all adorned in an assortment of Indian traditional attire—gathered on a Sunday evening at an urban college campus. For the Indian community in Chicago, it was not an ordinary Sunday. It was the last evening of a two-day celebration, organized by the city-based association of the Indian community, for one of the most celebrated and carnivalesque religious festivals of the Hindu faith. Dussehra, or Durga Puja, is mostly celebrated in the northern and eastern parts of India. I was then an Indian student and an immigrant woman in the United States, and I had attended this event the previous three years, more to connect nostalgically with a familiar cultural repertoire than for religious reasons. On this particular Durga Puja, however, I was conducting an ethnography for my research, to gain more insight into how visa policies affected the Indian families of tech workers living in the United States.

The bustle of the day attracted many Indians and other South Asians—students and families of professionals (many of whom were on work visas)—of all ages and genders from the Chicago area, who participated in the celebrations with aplomb and cheer. Association members and volunteers arranged for three meals that resembled traditional vegetarian Indian fare for the occasion, as well as rounds of chai and coffee throughout the day. The afternoons and evenings were peppered with cultural shows organized and performed by community members. Amid the chatter, the laughter, the small conversation groups, informal singing, formal performances, and multiple rounds of ritual communal worship of the idol of the goddess Durga, which involved chanting mantras and burning incense and lighting little oil lamps, the day passed quickly for me. As evening turned to night, the crowd began to thin. Some 30 men and women spread out in the two large performance halls for a postdinner cleanup party. I sat on the floor in a circle with five Indian women, all in their thirties, who wore elegant silk saris as they counted the cash they made from selling food coupons at the event. This year's Durga Puja had been a success. Engaged in happy conversation with each other., the women shared fond memories of the festivities back home and reflected humorously on the past two days of celebrations.

These five women had organized the event, which had attracted more than 800 people over three days, down to its most meticulous detail. With support from a few others in the community, they raised funds, managed the event's finances, and overseen publicity, catering, decoration, parking, and even the event's website design. On top of all that, they organized two evenings of cultural shows and collectively choreographed the elaborate rituals of worship of the goddess Durga.

Suddenly, one of the women burst into tears. "So, the last month and a half of sweat and fun is over!" She cried: "Now it is back to the boredom of leading the forced housewife life! I had almost forgotten over the last month what it is like to be on H-4!" The others nodded in agreement with somber expressions. One woman turned to me and said with a sigh: "I am glad you are doing this research. I hope it changes something." I understood her remark to be indicative of a general feeling of dissatisfaction with the conditions of life lived while on dependent visa status.

The women with whom I spent that weekend in October were in the United States on H-4 dependent visas. As described earlier, H-4 visas are given to the dependent spouses and children of "high-skilled temporary migrant workers" who hold a H1-B visa. The H-4 visa exists so that family members can join the temporary migrant worker in the United States. All five women—like many others on H-4 visa status—were highly qualified, and almost all of them had held well-paying white-collar jobs in India before coming to the United States. One of the women had an MBA and had worked in middle management for five years in India before coming overseas. Another had a PhD in psychology from a top-ranked university in India. The third had been a journalist of a leading

Indian daily reporting the crime beat. The fourth was a practicing lawyer in India, and the fifth, who held an MS in physics, had taught at a four-year college before joining her husband in the United States. Despite their degrees, experience, and qualifications, the women were legally prevented from working—and thus bound to perform within a family structure akin to the 1950s model of white American middle-class family life, in which the husband is the sole breadwinner in the family and the wife is forced into housewifery. The irony of this situation, of course, is that the family structure in America during the 1950s was embedded in the social mores of the times, whereas for these women the situation was a consequence of the visa regime. Yet, American women at that time still had the choice to pursue a life outside the home, albeit in defiance of social norms.[1] For the highly educated and formerly employed Indian women gathered that evening, such an option remained legally off-limits. The reason they had put their hearts and souls into producing a perfect community event, they said, was from the need to do something that would make them feel like useful human beings again: they wanted to feel alive again and experience a hint of their old selves.

What has been abundantly clear to me throughout the research process is that being juridically labeled "dependent" because of visa laws transforms the selves of the visa holders. The women I interviewed constantly spoke of how the dependent visa reshaped the "self" of the visa holder—a self that was reconstructed through the experience and the lived realities of being a legal dependent.

When trying to understand the self, many social theorists (including, Fanon,[2] Foucault,[3] Stuart Hall,[4] Goffman,[5] and Mead,[6] for example) placed the *self* and its subjectivities within social discourse whether it be within institutions, in cultural constructs and practices, or historical context. In my analysis, the self and the subjectivity of these women was constructed by the legal discourse of the visa regime and the status of being a financial dependent. While the subjectivity of the dependent men was also shaped by their legal status, the dependent men were hesitant to express themselves in those terms. Instead, the men always placed the dependent self within the social and cultural discourse of masculinities.

This was exemplified even in my initial search to find men with dependent status. Finding women on the H-4 visa was relatively easy.

However, men on dependent visas were neither as visible nor as accessible as were the women with the same visa status.

In my search for men on dependent visas, I attended Sunday masses in two Indian ethnic churches for six months. In both churches, the majority of the congregation consisted of nurses and their families. But when I inquired about families with men on the H-4 dependent visa, I was consistently met with silence and found no success at all for a very long time. At a Sunday mass in the December 2010, a week before Christmas, I requested that the pastor announce my research at the end of the sermon, just as he had for many weeks previously. After the sermon, I stood outside the chapel to talk to people. A petite woman in her early thirties came up to me and introduced herself as a nurse, then said in a hushed whisper: "My husband is here on dependent visa." Calmly and discreetly, I asked if it would be possible for me to talk to her and her husband about their visa situations. She said she needed to convince her husband first but agreed to raise the subject with him. "It is Christmas week after all, he might be feeling more generous," she said with a chuckle. Two weeks later, I conducted my first formal interview with this kind and forthcoming nurse and her somewhat reluctant husband. During most of the interview, the husband skirted the issue of dependence, then at one point he had to ask his wife for her credit card to pay for the food they had ordered for dinner. And as he took the card from his wife, he looked at me and said: "This is when I am no one; I don't even have a dollar to my name in this country, but when I married my wife 10 years back, I promised to take care of her. This country has taken that away from me." This first utterance by the first dependent husband interviewee, expressing the burden and the pain of dependence, is emblematic of the emasculation and effacement of the self that men felt upon losing their provider status in the family. While this emotional experience told by the men was not unexpected given previous research on stay-at-home husbands and fathers, I nevertheless had to navigate this emotionality in almost all my interactions with the dependent men as a barrier to them opening up about their own dependent status.

In this chapter, I examine how the legally dependent social actors in this study negotiate the category of "dependent visas" in terms of identity formation and reconstruction of the self in relation to the way they interact with others in public and to gendered discourses of dependence.

Political theorists[7] have engaged with thoughts concerning state power by using Foucault's[8] concept of "governmentality" to explain state domination as dependent on the compliance of individual subjects through ideological self-disciplining. One of the technological mechanisms by which states have seamlessly controlled bodies and subjectivities has been the construction and enforcement of visa laws that, following Mark Salter,[9] I refer to as "visa regimes."

The Visa Regime as the Structural Framing of Discourse

The idea of the visa regime is derived from Giorgio Agamben's[10] theory of the state of exception. In the book *Homo Sacer*, Agamben contends that the power of the sovereign lies in its ability not only to create, institute, and enforce the rule of law but also to suspend it upon the declaration of a state of emergency. It is within this state of emergency that exceptions to the rule are made, and these exceptions lead to the distinction between the political citizen who possesses rights under the law and the "bare life" whose rights have been suspended and stripped away. "Bare life" then resides at the border—in a liminal space, excluded of the citizenry, with no guarantee of protection under the law but nevertheless subject to the law and to coercion. Salter[11] repurposes Agamben's[12] state of exception to show how the visa regime comes to be. He begins with the status of the migrant.

According to Salter, if a migrant whose status within the sovereign state (the United States in the case of the participants in this study) is contingent on a system of visa laws that allows for temporary or permanent membership in the new land, then the migrant "is subject to the law, but not a subject in the law."[13] The visa regime, therefore, is the "internationalization of the body: through biometric capture, the assignation of risk profiles according to race, gender, ethnic, national and religious scripts, and the visa system within the institutions of customs and immigration controls. The visa system as an essential component in the attempt of the state to claim a monopoly over legitimate movement classifies mobile bodies as legitimate through the schema of production and subjection."[14]

Under the rule of law, visa laws are the tools that the state uses to control both the flow of people across borders and the lives of migrants once they cross the border. Visa laws can be suspended upon the declaration of a state of emergency, as President Trump did when he suspended all temporary work visas, citing the COVID-19 pandemic. Visa laws also define the statist identities of visa holders. Guest workers, temporary workers, skilled workers, and dependent visa holders are some of the categories that undergird the identities of those whose movements are managed through visa laws.

An additional aspect of the regimentation of visa laws is that they are at all times implicitly gendered, racialized, and protectionist, as I contend throughout this book. These hidden presumptions are embedded within the political justification of protecting borders, the economy, and the security apparatus. The central questions here are the following: What is the impact of dependent H-4 visas on the intimate selves of women and men who hold them? If we understand the visa as a tool to control and/or foster the mobility of international bodies, what is the nature of such an understanding in the public discourse on this visa regime? If we view the visa as a structure of power, in what way does that power translate into the everyday lived identities of the visa holders? What does this visa-constructed self tell us about larger socioeconomic and political structures in which this self is embedded?

I contend in this chapter that visa regulations govern every aspect of the transnational subject's life as a globally mobile entity. Dependent visas reconfigure identities and notions of the self. They construct particular notions of citizenship, belonging, and migration. Visa policy alters family structures and familial relationships, reinforcing a traditional, heteropatriarchal family form: man as breadwinner, woman as housewife. When, in the interest of economic prosperity, visa policy requires there be a reversal in this traditional family structure—that is to say, the highly skilled woman replaces the man as the breadwinner and the man takes up the role of the dependent homemaker—that also leads to disorienting consequences that undermine identity and self-worth. Dependent visas are closely tied to the employment status of the primary migrant. In this way, the visa system controls the economic resources and legal standing of the individual worker and her family. The dependent visa and work visa statuses are deeply entwined, creating a dependence structure that extends beyond the family and spills into the conception of an identity that is based in the visa regime.

The influences of visa policy are multiple and multidirectional while at the same time destabilizing and disorienting. The problematic state of dependency to which migrant persons are subjected under visa regimes contributes to a high degree of complicated, contradictory feelings, affecting even individual identity. For example, while migrant persons articulate exasperation at the unfairness of the visa regime, they simultaneously embrace the neoliberal discourse of individual choice as well as gendered scripts on family roles when describing their decisions to migrate. Illuminating such contradictions will help illuminate the analysis going forward, as I demonstrate empirically how the abstract mechanism of state power manufactures a concrete web of dependence for the migrant subject. To further this aim, I also report on how the participants acted to disrupt this state of dependency, as well as how such acts of disruption show the interplay between the subjectivities of the self and public, raising serious questions about the effectiveness of dependent visa policy.

Dependent Visas as Governmental Control of Transnational Families

The idea that skilled legal migration is a free, unrestricted process and a personal choice for self-actualization is dubious at best. In the interest of securing a critical transnational feminist analysis of the experiences of the individuals vitally engaged in the flow of people from one place to another, I will subject this idea to an exacting level of scrutiny. Certainly, such notions of individual liberty persist in the subject's register of neoliberal ideological narratives; but it is more appropriate, as I will show, not to imagine such identities as freestanding. Rather, I suggest that the migrating subject holds conflicting, even paradoxical, ideological positions because of the multiple, at times divergent, forces that affect a migrating subject's life. What is often characterized as ambition and a self-realization effort on the part of migrant workers and their families (based on the idea of unfettered possibilities of global mobility) is actually enmeshed in a matrix of dependence on visa policies meant to control and construct the subjectivities of the families and their members.

Visa laws—along with the rights and restrictions by which migrants must abide—can be conceptualized as technologies of domination and control through which various state agencies influence every aspect of the transnational subject's life. This control includes employment, marital relationships, even subjectivity, as well as formal signs of personhood (i.e., the documentation of citizenship status, among other things). For example, one way that the state acts to harness immigrants' subjectivities is to enact controls regulating the real time in which the subject is physically situated within the boundaries of the state's power. That is to say, most migrants possessing visas have a finite duration that they are permitted to remain in the country. This immediately places the migrants, their desires, and their aspirations into a time/space that is temporary and transnational, creating conditions of dependency and contingency. State power in this context is exercised *via* the category of the dependent (H-4) visas, thereby establishing coercive structures of governmentality designed to undo the migrant's previous selves to fit within the dependency structure. In such structures—through the simultaneous techniques of the self and dominations unleashed in the form of the visa regime—subjects discipline themselves and others into conformity. In this book and in the remainder of this chapter, I demonstrate how state power manifests through *technologies of visa regimes*[15] such that visa policies created by the state apparatus to regulate migration have a false façade of gender and racial neutrality.

Technologies of the visa regime coalesce with the construction of women of color from the Global South, especially postcolonial nations considered to be Third World as universal dependents[16] or as the global caregivers within the family and outside.[17] This framework is particularly useful in understanding the constellation of visa systems and their consequences for migrant subjects. Dependent visa laws are especially problematic, as they assume heteronormativity and are available exclusively to legally married heterosexual couples. Visa policy is constructed under the assumption that internationally mobile workers from the Global South have domestic/dependent spouses, which creates a gendered visa structure that assumes a traditional, male-led family status for mobile workers. My analysis details how dependent visas impact the construction of the self for visa holders in terms of how familial gender dynamics operate and how the holders of dependent visas are perceived in public. This demonstrates internalized battles that the self experiences with the dependent other in trying to forge an identity that is simultaneously dependent and resistant of that dependence. This conflict of the dependent self is a testimony that the dependent visa regime assumes the stability and permanence of heteronormativity in families from the Global South, which in fact is the colonizing, orientalist vision that the US visa regime for dependents stands on. I identify moments where, through visa regimes, an implicit subjective contradiction between individual agency and state power becomes manifest. I also conceptualize governmentality as a gendered and racialized phenomenon that forms invisible webs of dependence and material struggles for global migrants that enmeshes their intimate and public selves and subjectivities.

Interfacing with the Public as Legal Dependents: Governmental Discourse and the Public Penalties of Dependent Visas

In the following paragraphs, I reconstruct a few scenes that illuminate the genesis of the public penalties of being a legal dependent and a woman, as well as the dependent woman's experience of interacting with the US government in terms of obtaining visas and dealing with border security. As an immigrant woman myself, I am familiar with these scenarios, which makes it easy to recount these experiences and provide what I hope are vivid accounts of the experience of legal dependents.

Dependent Spouses

The queue to enter the US consulate in Delhi was long, and the midday sun was scorching. The area outside the consulate looked like a war zone, with heavily armed and militarized security guards behind sandbags, at sniper vantage points, and making their rounds. At least 100 people waited in line for their scheduled visa interviews, in 120 degrees Fahrenheit without any shade. After heavy screening, the security guards let in up to 10 people at a time. Afiya stood in line with the others that day, waiting for her visa interview. She had been married to her new husband, a software engineer and a tech worker in the United States, for about three months, and while he was back in the United States she had applied for an H-4 visa. She was herself armed with a heavy folder containing all her documents, including her PhD degree, her husband's employment credentials, her marriage certificate, and her wedding pictures. Afiya let out a sigh of relief after entering the air-conditioned consulate office—but then her experience shifted. She described her interactions with the visa officer and the interview process as intimidating and humiliating.

Speaking candidly about her first experience, Afiya said:

> The entire setup is designed to intimidate you and unnerve you. But once you are at the bulletproof glass window [talking] through the microphone with the all-powerful visa officer, giving your much-rehearsed speech, you forget you are your own person, that you have a PhD. You transform to being just a wife. You cease to exist right on the day of the visa interview, even before you have left India. After asking your name, they begin asking you about marriage, asking for marriage photographs, and then it is all about the husband, where he works, where he lives, blah, blah, blah! And I am no longer a person anymore, and that continues in every interaction after that moment!

In describing her emotions during the visa interview, Afiya is conveying the genesis of her dependency. The interaction with the visa officer—in which Afiya's entire identity is reduced to her status as a wife—is the manifestation of universal dependency assigned to Third World women in the West.[18] For dependents, the public effacement described by Afiya, which begins at the time of the visa interview in India, becomes a material reality in every subsequent interaction with a US public official. This effacement points to invisibilization of the self that another participant, Jaya, poignantly articulated in her description of arriving in the United States as a dependent spouse:

> The immigration officer did not even look at me until he asked me to face the camera for the picture. All he said was, "You know you can only stay in the country as long as your husband has a job," and then, looking at my husband, told him that he should know that he is legally liable for me. I have never felt smaller and more invisible in my life, but little did I know that was just the start of a very fucked-up journey.

Here Jaya elaborates on what it means to be reduced to the singular identity of a dependent wife: it means invisibility of her personhood in the eyes of the state. The discourse on what constitutes a dependent makes Jaya, and other dependent women, charges of their husbands for all legal purposes, thereby erasing their existences beyond those of their husbands. This solidifies the heteronormative and heterosexist orientation of the dependent visa laws originating in the coverture laws[19] and points to the systemic world that the visa officers and other public officials also inhabit when they interact with the interviewees.

The experience of having one's individuality stripped away that Afiya and Jaya describe was visceral and immediate, as their status changed from being employed, independent women to spousal legal dependents in the United States. Every participant with dependent status consistently described these experiences of interfacing with public institutions as an omnipresent reality. Participants felt dehumanized, disenfranchised, and alienated in almost every encounter they had within the public sphere, including when trying to obtain a driver's license, buying things that required valid IDs such as cigarettes or alcohol, and attempting to find a job commensurate to their qualifications so that they might change their visa status.

One of the women participants in my study provided me a copy of her H-4 visa (figure 2.1). It was striking that the visa had the name of the husband and his employer in India as the guarantor of the H-4 visa, and while the start date of her visa was different than the start date of the husband's visa (the wife came to the United States after her husband), the expiration date was identical to the expiration date of the husband's H-1B visa. The layout and appearance of the visa stamp rendered the holders of these visas publicly and institutionally dependent and invisible. The dependent visa holder did not exist legally but for the lead migrant, the H-1B visa holder. Many of the women described the visa not as *their* visa but as a "derived" visa, which, interestingly, is what the dependent visa was called before the Immigration Act of 1990. In describing her visa, one of the women told me that, every time she opened her visa page, she felt she was looking at someone else—"a nobody"—because her past selfhood had been erased to no existence in her new life.

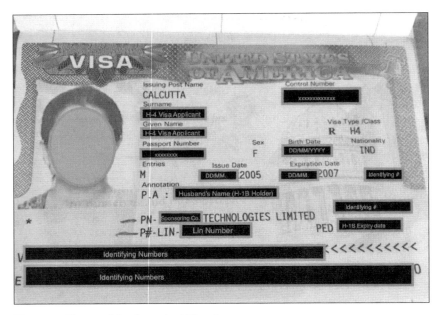

Figure 2.1. Picture of the dependent/H-4 visa.

I interviewed Shivali Shah, a JD and PhD in immigration law from Duke University, who has been an advocate for the rights of H-4 visa holders, to better understand the hindrances these women face and how and why these barriers exist. She said:

In India, the perception is that if you are highly qualified, you should be able to get a job, just like the H1-B [visa holder] that their daughter, their sister, or their friend is about to marry. That is true to the extent that, if that person had a work permit already, it would be very easy for them in the sense that there would not be extra hindrances to obtain a job. There would be a level playing field for them.

Citing her extensive legal work and expertise with women H-4 visa holders, many of whom she had helped to modify their visa statuses, Shah explained that the two most common and challenging reasons the women face in changing their current visas into work visas are:

1. In order for an H1-B visa to be processed, one's qualifications must match the job one is looking for. However, many of the women who come on H-4 visas look for jobs that do not match their degrees/qualifications. For instance, someone with a journalism degree might be applying for a position of a business manager. In such cases, an application for an H1-B visa cannot be processed.

2. Most employers, other than the tech firms and large financial firms, do not know how the visa processes necessary to sponsor the employment of foreign workers work. "Simply, the visa process is too complicated for many employers to handle." This disadvantages women H-4 holders because even when they are better qualified than many other legally eligible job seekers, employers shy away from treading uncharted paths with visa applications and paperwork for foreign employees.

Additionally, H-4 visa holders are restricted by their spouse's geographical location. As has been documented in research on human capital, for immigrants of color from the Global South, even exemplary qualifications and skills become difficult to transfer to the US job market. Shah claimed that many women found these two barriers to be more expected and reconcilable, as opposed to the first two listed.

The greatest demand for migrant workers in the United States who can qualify as "highly skilled" is in the field of tech work. It is usually easier for workers trained in the tech field to find a job and change visa status because most tech firms are well-versed in hiring foreign nationals; however, very few of the women H-4 holders had a tech background. According to Shah, if the H-4 visa rules were less restrictive, and the women holding H-4s could thus obtain a work permit more easily, this would significantly level the playing field for highly qualified women. But until recently the US government was resolute in its unwillingness to amend dependent visa laws to be less restrictive.

In a PBS panel discussion aired in 2012 on the status of H-4 visa holders, a congresswoman remarked:

You know, I greatly sympathize with these women. The feminism in me sympathizes with these women. The congresswoman in me said, "Wait one moment!" Look who these women are. They're almost all upper caste, if I may say so, women. These are not your average women coming here. They have had the ability to come here and live. They made a family decision. Meanwhile, we're accommodating many legal and illegal residents from all over the United States. We give a special visa to her husband. I don't know. Then the feminism in me shouts, "Hey, wait a minute! Why should it be two for one?" We're giving a visa to him because he's applied for it and because he has a skill other[s] here do not have. Who knows that she has such a skill? What is to say that she isn't competing with the 9.4 million American workers who can't find jobs? And why should we? Why should we say—you who get every privilege in India, privileges that are denied to almost all in India—you get special treatment when you come to this country? Love you, but not that treatment. Wait your turn.

The congresswoman's statement reflected a common strand of thinking among the public and government officials, which is: Why should we make it two for one? or Why should we favor a privileged group of women with more privileges? While it is true that many of the participants in this research enjoyed class and caste privilege in India, what constitutes class privilege in the United States, and how much of the class privilege in India transfers to the United States, is debatable. Research by Engzell and Ichou[20] and Kofman and Raghuram[21] has shown that almost all immigrants experience downward mobility and dismantling of class status when they migrate to the Global North from the Global South. The dismantling of privilege is further exacerbated given the racial landscape of the United States, where immigrants of color are automatically relegated to lower social status in relation to whiteness.[22]

Further, the argument that H-4 visa holders take American jobs is fatuous, given that the entire pool of H-4 visa holders from all countries, including children below the legal age of employment (who are therefore technically not legally employable), forms only 0.1 percent of the total employable US population. We also see an example of the *narrative of choice* in the congresswoman's statement. In this instance, the idea of one's "choice" to migrate transnationally is deployed as a means to disencumber the state of responsibility for exploitative power regimes at work within its boundaries.

As I stated earlier, the research participants who had H-4 status often felt disenfranchised and disadvantaged, even when they were trying to accomplish simple tasks within public institutions such as procuring a driver's license. Jaya, who had been driving since she was 18 years old, related her experiences trying to get a driver's license in the United States:

> To start with, there is only one DMV in the entire Chicagoland where you can get your license as a dependent spouse. You go there and you have to stand in separate queues meant for people with no SSN. And when you go up to the counter and talk to the people, they constantly make you feel like a second class. . . . They will ask why I don't have an SSN and why I need a license, why I don't have a utility bill [with] my name. The reason is because your freakin' government will not let me . . . have any sort of power in this country! It has been the most harrowing experience of my life. I had to go back five times to get my license, and all my friends on H-4 [status] had the same experience. I came back from the DMV crying three times! Please, please make sure you have this in your research!

Jaya's narration of her harrowing and demeaning experience at the DMV is intrinsically tied to how public interactions served to efface the existence of H-4 visa holders by denying them personhood that is conferred through state-issued identification (SSNs and driver's licenses). At the same time, interrogating them about their legality for not having those items delegitimizes at the moment their very legal existence. One of the participants, Mili, found out, during the course of our interview, that my driver's license was not tied to my visa status and not based on the visa's duration. I had a five-year expiration period on my license, much like a regular American citizen's license. Immediately, she called her husband at work and found that his driver's license was the same as mine. Then, Mili, pursing her lips and skewing her eyebrows, visibly angry, brought out her driver's license (see figure 2.1), showed it to me, and said:

> I don't understand this! if my status is based on my husband's status, why in hell do I have a license that is aligned to my visa expiration and his is not? Even in this they would have to privilege H1-Bs over us! This is completely unfair! You know I have to go and get my fucking license

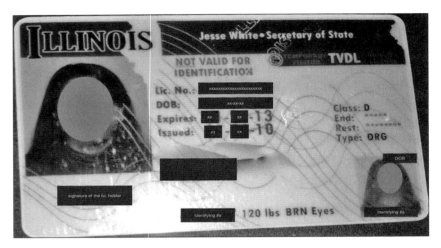

Figure 2.2. Driver's license for an H-4 spouse.

extended every year because my visa extensions are for one year at a time? And last time, I had to go twice in two months because . . . my visa was expiring in December and the new visa was to begin in January and they gave me a one-month extension on the license. I had to go halfway across town again in a month's time in this cold weather to renew my license. Gosh, and then this stupid license is not even valid for identification. Is this a joke?

Mili's righteous indignation over the ordeals she endured to procure the most basic official document—a driver's license—is emblematic of the raw and uneven emotional landscape and the public penalties to which dependent visa holders are routinely subjected. The picture below, which was given to me by one of the participants, shows the format of the driver's license for H-4 visa holders. Mili also gave me the copy of the letter she was issued from a Social Security office when she applied for a Social Security number (see figure 2.3).

A driver's license that is not valid for identification and a letter from a Social Security office asserting her work ineligibility in the US until her "alien status changes" have serious implications. She is not eligible to work, even though her husband (who was her coworker in India) is eligible to work; and her identity and very existence in the United States depend on him. Such denials of basic rights carry genuine material consequences for the participants and also lead to the symbolic effacement of their past selves as independent professional women—only to be relegated to a dependent status imposed by the state.

A comment by the lawyer Shivali Shah on the experiences of H-4 visa holders during the PBS panel that I referenced earlier exemplifies what such effacement entails legally. As she put it:

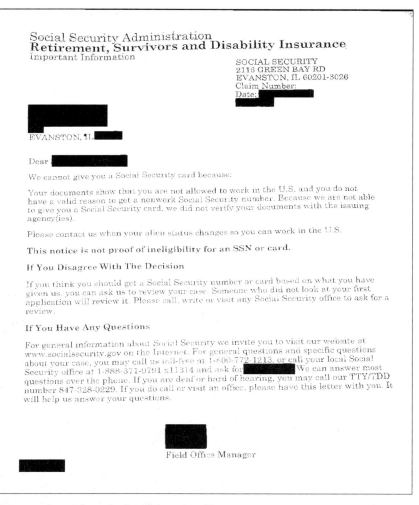

Figure 2.3. Letter from the Social Security office.

These women are not given Social Security cards or Social Security numbers—no Social Security cards. In many states, they're not allowed driver's licenses. In the states they are allowed driver's licenses, the process is
very long and difficult. I mean, when we think about what's in our own
wallets, like the things that I carry in my wallet! Every single thing that's
in there are things that these women need to either get through their husbands or they're not allowed to have. It's like being perpetually without
your wallet while you're in the [United States].

This sense of being dispossessed of one's wallet amounts to stripping
these visa holders of most rights that any long-term resident generally
has. This stripping-down of rights leads to real-world experiences of
marginalization and disenfranchisement, with significant ramifications
for the lives of dependents.

Dependent spouses (both husbands and wives) described how their
everyday lives were disrupted as a result of their legal dependence. These
included not being able to do basic things in everyday life, such as buying alcohol at grocery stores and going to a park without carrying a passport. Matthew, a nurse's dependent husband, said:

I felt most humiliated twice since I came here: once when I was not
served wine in a restaurant because I did not have my passport, and once
when I went to pick up my daughter from preschool and the substitute
teacher wouldn't let her come with me because I had my license and not
my passport. I felt like a criminal. They need to change this rule.

About a month after our initial interview, Mili called me one night crying in anger to tell me about a similar emotionally charged incident. She
was not allowed into a bar because she did not have her passport:

I called you to ask you to put this in your research. I am freakin' 29, and I
was not let into our neighborhood bar because I did not have my passport
and they won't accept my driver's license even when it has my DOB! And,
of course there were 16-year old American citizens with fake IDs in that
bar! This is after all the land of freedom! How bloody hypocritical! I hate
it, I hate it! I am sick of this humiliation!

Titash, also a dependent visa holder, described an incident in which she was almost arrested because she, her husband, and some friends were visiting a Cook County forest preserve and had stayed in the park after closing time. The park ranger who was making the rounds asked them to leave but wanted to see everyone's IDs. When Titash could not produce one because she was not carrying her passport, he expressed his intention to arrest her. After much pleading from her husband and the other friend, the ranger gave her a warning. Titash exclaimed:

> Who would think of carrying a passport to a state park? It is not safe to carry your passport everywhere! You lose it, you are without a visa then. And I don't drive and can't get a state ID, what am I to do? This is the stupid shit that goes on in our lives!

Titash's experience with the park ranger, in which she could be illegalized for not carrying her passport, is a stark example of the precarious legal status of dependents that Agamben[23] calls "bare life": one's existence under the law might be suspended at any moment because of the law itself. Living with a legal precarity of this nature makes the self lose its sense of security in one's legal as well as social status, upending the confidence one must have when interacting with the state.

Work Visa Holders

The accounts of marginalization provided above demonstrate how immigration policies can directly affect the day-to-day experiences of people whose lives are subjected to those policies. What's more, the *spouses* of these dependents—including the nurses and the high-tech workers—were also affected by those policies, albeit in different ways. Akash, a manager in an IT firm and Jaya's husband, relayed his frustration with the invisibility of the dependent status of his spouse in his workplace in the United States:

> The worst and the ridiculous part is that no one in your workplace, your coworkers and your bosses, know nothing about dependent visas or how they work; so, when my wife goes to my office parties she is bombarded

with questions about why she does not work even when she is so qualified. Explaining that she is on a dependent visa is humiliating, but even
more frustrating is [that,] . . . after you explain, people [still] don't get it.
They merely assume that she does not work because we are Indians and
[that] I don't let her. One of my white coworkers even joked about it. This
is wrong on so many levels.

On one level, Akash alludes to the ignorance among native-born
Americans about the immigration systems and laws of the country.
At a second, deeper level, this means that dependent visa holders are
left unseen. On a third level, the ignorance about visa laws among the
general public—which includes the coworkers of H-1B visa holders—
reifies the stereotype that Indian families are crudely patriarchal and
lack awareness of gender equity. Ironically, it is the heteronormativity
of US immigration policy that requires these workers to tolerate conditions that situate them in what they often see as archaic gendered family
arrangements.

Raj, a financial consultant and the husband of a dependent spouse,
cites a graver experience of how being on a dependent visa affects the
families' institutional status. Raj pointed out to me that, whereas H-1B
holders receive a two-week extension (a so-called grace period) after
their visas expire to search for jobs, dependent spouses are required to
leave the country by the day of the visa's expiration, which is usually the
same as the husband's. Raj said: "Imagine the ridiculous[ness] of this
law! Does it make sense to you? It does not to me!" An immigration
lawyer from one of the leading law firms in the country, who specializes
in H-1B and H-4 visa issues, confirmed this, stating that the majority of
the cases they accept involve (1) H-4 spouses who lose their visa status
and risk deportation because of this mandate or (2) visa holders who are
not aware about the renewal policies for H-4 visas.

Women breadwinners (the nurses in my study) had similar concerns
when their husbands held dependent visas. One of the nurses, Nancy,
whose husband possessed a dependent visa, said:

I get it when men don't want to come here on a dependent visa. Everyone
here, the neighbors and my kid's teachers, keep asking him why he does
not work. *I* find it insulting more than he does. The immigration officer

at the airport looked at him funny. I understand if he wants to go back, but our daughter: Why should she have to live without her father or her mother?

In this anecdote, Nancy evokes the dehumanizing marginalization that many of the participants experienced in their interactions in the public sphere that placed them in the status of second-class or partial citizens because of their dependent visas. They were deprived of agency in their interactions with most institutions in this country because of the visas they held. My conversations with public officials, as well as my archival research, demonstrate how little discussion there was of the social and political impacts involved at the time the H-4 visa category was created. Among the 14 public officials I talked to (except for three, one of whom was an expert on H-4 visas), not one knew very much about the characteristics of the H-4 dependent visas or the situation such visas create for visa holders. The reactions I received when I tried to inform some of the public officials about the situation was often one of apathy and disregard and sometimes even mild hostility. I am calling the dehumanization, alienation, and disenfranchisement the dependent visa holders experienced in their day-to-day interactions in the public sphere "dependency penalties of public interactions." It was, however, disconcerting to observe the degree to which these penalties were invisible to the same government officials and legislators who were responsible for upholding these laws. The ignorance and unconcern surrounding the angst of H-4 visa holders represented the public muting and obliterating of any discursive space for any meaningful engagement at the policy level about the public face of state-imposed dependency.

The Rhetoric of Personal Choice

This denial of recognition[24] in and by public institutions of the very existence of H-4 visa holders and their experiences caused the women on H-4 visas to imply a rhetoric of "choice" in explaining their decision to migrate to the Unites States with their husbands. They often claimed that they "chose" to come to America on the H-4 visa for the sake of "keeping the family together." This sense of "having a choice" is complicated by the knowledge that their immigration status is deeply tied to the labor status of their husbands, creating a gendered labor regime not only for the migrant worker but also for the entire family.

Dependent Wives

Mili, with her voice choking up as she described her inability to work, said: "I feel so helpless and unhappy, I would work anywhere, even if it is illegally, like . . . in a Jewel-Osco [a supermarket chain] or whatever, but Ravish [Mili's husband] is chicken. He won't let me. He says I will someday get us deported or jailed."

During this interview, Mili seemed so exasperated with her situation that she was almost ready to risk her and her husband's legal statuses just to be able to work. Like many of the other husbands, Ravi was uncomfortable with his wife working because it potentially jeopardized the legal status of the family. Jaya, much like Mili and many other highly qualified women on dependent visas whom I spoke to, articulated their frustration with the state-imposed prohibition on their right to work. She alluded to the fact that the oppressiveness of the dependent visa is multiplied because it is so intrinsically tied to the work visa and the legal status of the family as a whole. I asked her if she had tried finding a job in the United States, given that she had an MBA and was a certified accountant. Jaya said:

> I did [attempt to find a job] for three years; but, with the economy tanking it was hard. Also, no company was ready to sponsor my visa. I was so frustrated I often thought of working illegally in one of those accountants' offices in the South Asian enclave, but I don't want to jeopardize my husband's job status and get us all thrown out of country. My poor little boy [pointing to her son] has done no wrong. That would be selfish of me. No?

The various dilemmas Jaya faced are palpable in her words. She struggled with reconciling her past identity as a professional with her current identity as a dependent spouse, a dutiful wife, and a mother. Her desire to work was strong, but her worry for her family was stronger. Given all this, she characterized her inability to work as a choice she made voluntarily for the sake of her family.

Neoliberal discourses of global capitalism construct the Global North, particularly the United States, as the coveted fruit for transnational labor migration.[25] Before coming to the United States, most of the women did not think it would be difficult for them to change their dependent visas into work visas, especially given their educational accomplishments and that America was the land of opportunity. Suchitra, a PhD in mathematics from India who was a faculty member in math and statistics at a four-year college before she came to the United States, had been in this country for five years on a dependent visa at the time of our interview. She said: "I *chose* to come to the United States despite knowing about the restrictions on H-4 status because I had known America to be the land of milk and honey." She quickly realized that such was definitely not the case.

Suchitra's disappointment—wrought from facing constant barriers to opportunity, her inability to change her visa status, and the realization that the "milk and honey" of America is only "available to people . . . wanted by the American markets"—was shared by the majority of highly qualified women dependents depicted in this book. Suchitra, as with many other women, could not change her visa because "none of the employers were ready to sponsor a highly skilled worker's visa for [her] as stated by Jaya." Most often, the women appeared to be baffled and disheartened by such a response.

Dependent Husbands

The women on dependent visas were vocal about their marginalization within the public sphere and the frustrations emanating from that; however, men, aside from those quoted here, maintained that they did not experience marginalization related to their visa statuses within the public sphere. They often deployed the *choice* rhetoric to defray the weight of the dependency status. For instance, Jejo, when asked what he thought of the H-4 visa policy, with a dismissive hand gesture said, "I have no opinions on this. I decided to come here because of my family, otherwise why would I? I made a *choice*, no point grousing." Many of the dependent men underscored the (masculine) virtue of standing by their choice without voicing complaints. Adopting a personal choice narrative also meant not having to grapple with the ambits of their lives that loomed over them but that they could not control, like the visa regime. This could as well be a mechanism employed by the men in this study to cope with the multitude of conflicting hardships in their transnational experience that collectively deprived them of the power and privilege that the Indian hegemonic social and cultural system had given them as a birthright (i.e., the right as men to be the patriarch and head of the household). During their lifetimes, the global capitalist system had presented many challenges to the male privilege we speak of here.[26] Men's loss of social power has been intensified as a result of intense poverty and a lack of economic opportunity in the state of Kerala, particularly for Christian minorities. This has led Christian women from Kerala to take the lead in the economic arena by fulfilling a need in the feminized nursing market in the Global North.[27] The irrelevance of these men in the local economy and global economy, along with their further disenfranchisement because of the restrictive US visa system, is commonly perceived by them as disempowering and emasculating. These strong economic and social forces have left the men I spoke with feeling the strain of internal contradictions that they are not often willing to fully face or come to terms with. At the very least, this internal struggle made them unwilling to verbalize their personal suffering during our conversations.

The interviews I conducted with men on dependent visas were often difficult and tenuous, because confessing emasculation was difficult for many; yet, my analysis—synthesizing the narratives of women and men on dependent visas and incorporating the testimony of their spouses—illustrates how the state visa structure reconfigures the lives of the visa holders, organizes their daily lives, and has lasting and consequential impacts on how individuals understand and experience their migrant subjectivities and their selves.

The H-4 Visa Identity and the Construction of the Gendered Self

The phrase "Not Valid for Identification" (see figure 2.2) on the driver's license showed to me by Mili, an instance previously referred to in this chapter, deserves analytic revisiting in the context of the *self*. Particularly, in the light of the questions Mili raised as she handed me her license: "What does that even mean," she asked with a hint of sarcasm, "an ID not meant for identification? Who am I, then? Who is this person? Whose picture is on there?"

Women and the Dependent Identity

These rhetorical, poignant questions, raised by Mili, went unanswered, but the lawyer and H-4 legal activist Shivali Shah offered some explanations. In a statement describing what it means legally to be on a dependent visa, she told me:

> I recognize it is a *dependent* visa, but it is so, so dependent that it makes the women not a person. Essentially, legally, it makes the woman the child of her husband, and she has as many rights in the United States as an average person's child would in relation to the legal system and [. . .] the world outside the home.

In a practical sense, concerning the driver's license in question, this relegation of an adult to a child by legal definition creates a legal bind such that she is allowed to drive (being of legal age in some states), yet she is not allowed to use the driver's license for run-of-the-mill identification (as all other adult citizens and noncitizens on every other kind of visa do). This legal absurdity illuminates the loss of self that accompanies living under H-4 visa status, as well as the resulting—and often traumatic—search for a new identity. I observed a recurrent theme in the narratives of the participants. In describing their relationships with the H-4 dependent visa structure, they would often testify to the ways in which their relationship with that structure had affected, altered, and reconstructed what many of the women called an "H-4 self": an identity solely defined by the visa.

H-4 IDENTITY: AN INCURSION ON THE OLD SELF

On April 4, 2009, PBS broadcasted an episode of the talk-show series *On the Contrary* exploring the unfairness or fairness of H-4 visas, featuring multiple stakeholders including visa holders, activists, lawyers and lawmakers. This broadcast was organized as a reaction to a documentary film titled *Hearts Suspended*, produced by an H-4 wife on her life as a dependent wife. During an interview, as part of this panel discussion, that filmmaker (and a former H-4 visa holder), Meghna Damani, spoke about how she felt being on the visa status:

A lot of sense of self-worth, our meaning in life, comes from what we do; and, we have so many associations around that we don't even realize until we don't have it anymore. So, I think a lot of just who the person I was—I felt like I just left that person. Not even I left, but, like, that person was just cut off from me the moment I landed in this country.

The sentiment Damani expressed in the phrase "that person was cut off from me" is a sentiment that almost all the women participants on H-4 visa status in my study articulated in myriad ways. Most of the women used similar phrases—"I did not know who I was anymore" and "my entire identity as person, a woman was taken away"—to describe how they thought and felt about their own H-4 status. When Mili attempted to answer this question, her voice quivered with emotion. She was not only poignant but also expressed the shock she felt after finding herself ripped from what once was her personhood:

I landed in this country and what I was, what I became, was just an H-4. I was just Ravish's wife, a housewife, with no identity of my own. Yes, when I chose to come here on H-4, I gave up what was me. My work ID back in India that stated my name, what I did, who I was, was gone. I became invisible just like what my driver's license says: *not valid for identification*. It took me a while to come to terms with it, but I did.

For most of the women I interviewed, this loss of self emerged primarily in response to being stripped of certain basic rights—and they were shocked by this new reality. Educated, independent, mostly upper-caste, middle-class women in India, they had become accustomed to these basic rights and understood them as being fundamental to their personhood itself. The shock grew as they found their premigration imagination of the United States incompatible with the postmigration reality. Before migrating, they perceived America as it had been described to them: the "land of opportunities," "the land of women's rights," "the land of liberty"—the tropes of neoliberal modernity touted as American exceptionalism to the rest of the world, especially to the Global South.[28]

However, after migrating, the America these women experienced was very different: an oppressive regime for dependent migrant women that relegated them to positions of subservience in the home and in the broader society. Tona, mocking her status in the United States, said: "I was quite shocked to learn that the only liberty in this country for me is the statue [of Liberty]." The shock Tona evokes here was often traumatic for H-4 visa holders. In a follow-up interview, Mili (who would change her status after five years on an H-4 visa to that of an international student after becoming a full-time graduate student in 2012) said of her experience:

> It was very weird for me. I was very excited during the process, but when it finally happened, I felt nothing. I got a social security number, and my husband and my best friend were so happy, but I was like, what is this number? I did not have it for five years, and now I have it, and it makes me a person again. It was very weird, and it was weird to change my driver's license to a real license that was valid for identification. I felt like this one thing was making me visible from being invisible. And I somehow did not want to give away my old license. It was a part of me I hated so much, but it had become my identity, my H-4 identity for five years, and I still feel like I am a H-4 even when I have a real identity now. I can earn my own money now, and I am no longer on that visa. I hate it, but I can't get out of it. It is almost *traumatic for me.*

Here Mili discusses a *real identity*—her premigration self that she ontologically considers to be human versus her dependent identity, which to her and the worlds she inhabits is less than human given the deprived recognition she experiences.[29] Almost all the women I interviewed shared Mili's "traumatic" relationship with H-4 identities. They used the language of bondage and indicated that being on an H-4 visa caused frustration, depression, and even thoughts of suicide. Mia, one of the women I interviewed, called H-4 status "paralyzing," Survi called the H-4 visa a "prison visa," and Afiya called it a "death sentence." When asked what she thought about being on the H-4 visa, Jaya (also quoted in the introduction of the book), who had worked in a high-level management position back in India, said:

> I call this the vegetable visa. . . . It is meant to take away all your identity and make you vegetate. See, I knew my husband before I married him,

but I have friends who had arranged marriages and hardly knew their husbands when they came here. [T]heir entire lives, whether they lived or died, ate or not, all depended on this one man! You are constantly reminded that you are nothing without him! That is scary! Don't you think?

What Jaya is conveying here is the realization that being legally dependent robbed her—and the other women holding a dependent visa—of any possibility of independence and made them beholden to one person: the husband. This situation creates a familial structure of intense compulsory heterosexuality[30] in which, even when the commitment between husband and wife is one of equity, the structure of dependence imposed on them by the state creates the default position of subjection of women to men that Jaya alludes to as "scary." (Notably, many of the couples in my study in which men were the breadwinners at least superficially described gender equity as a key pillar of the relationship.)

Mia, who called the H-4 visa "paralyzing" and "shameful," shared concerns similar to Jaya's: "The funny part is my husband also feels very uncomfortable, guilty, and ashamed that I have to be so dependent on him." Mia's expression of shame, also shared by her husband, plagued most of the women and men on dependent visas. While the women had a community of other women on H-4 visa status, they still felt an overarching sense of isolation and personal struggle, especially at community events and gatherings.

PAID WORK AS VALIDATION OF THE SELF

I was struck by how most women reconstructed their dependent selves as a totalizing feeling of worthlessness. While the injustice of a state-imposed dependence is undeniable and must be questioned, there is a deeper concern here that needs to be addressed (even if in passing) within the context of this book. I say this because most of the women dependents wanted me to engage with their dependence from a place of unfairness. I would be remiss in my analysis, however, if I did not interrogate whether it is possible for people—especially women of privilege due to their being highly educated, middle-class, cis, and (in the case of most of the women dependents in my study) upper caste—to not associate self-worth with work given the global neoliberal capitalist logics of the current times. Many of the women dependents brought up the fact that they were not their mothers—who pinned their dreams of the future squarely on their children but were mostly happy raising them. "I can't be my mother" was a common refrain among the women dependents. "She was happy in her domesticity, and I wish I could be like her, but I need more from life—I can't, can't be just a dependent," said Tona about her mother. Why is it so difficult for Tona and those like her to find meaning in the care and nurturing work that they were undertaking as dependents? I contend that a potent combination—the neoliberal capitalist ideology that underscores work for pay as the only path to self-worth, plus the second-wave feminist position that educated women often imbibe as paid work being the path to liberation—stripped the participants of any possibility of finding happiness or fulfilment in the intense nurturing work they did as mothers, wives, and community members. Some of the men dependents, by contrast, found fulfillment in caring for their children, which is not surprising because men are often praised when they take on nurturing work, whereas women's nurturance is both devalued and dismissed.[31] Another instance of the dependency-induced effacement of the self is to be found in the absence of concerted and organized collective action on the part of most participants in the study.

Besides the occasional short-lived outbursts of frustration, which I observed at events where only the women met to socialize during the first phase of my fieldwork, there was hardly any collective engagement with the topic of H-4 visa status. However, during the interviews, all the women I spoke with told me that the H-4 experience was central to their lives. A sudden outburst usually ended in awkward silences at these events until someone moved the discussion to other topics—children or food. Women often actively denied their circumstances. When the conversations turned to careers and jobs, women talked animatedly about the "glories" of their work lives in India; they avoided talking about current disappointments or concerns about how their careers had stalled. This changed somewhat after 2012, with the rise of social-media platforms such as Facebook and the blogosphere. Women across the United States began to share their stories of dependence on these sites, but the conversations remained largely online and cordoned off from analog social gatherings, at least among my participants.

Consistently, there was a sense of shame in talking about dependent status. Naureen, who possessed an MBA and a law degree, confided that she was so ashamed of her H-4 status that she would absolutely not talk about it with other people—even to other women on H-4 visas. She felt that verbalizing her visa status made the issue real, made her husband look bad, and made her family appear as if it were troubled. She did not want to make herself any more vulnerable than she already felt. The sense of shame and isolation I observed in the participants closely resembles "collective trauma."[32] All the women were exposed to similar experiences resulting from state-imposed sanctions based on their visa status, and they collectively felt a deep sense of isolation and alienation. Most even shied away from accessing treatments for mental health issues related to their situations. Those who did seek out and receive help felt intensely guilty for "wasting their husband's money." This guilt about money, for many of the women, emerged from having been financially independent, professional women before coming to the United States as dependents. However, this is also how compulsory heterosexuality frames the relationships between men and women: women are to remain grateful for men's material provisions for the heterosexist structure of dependence to be maintained.

The complexity of shame and alienation is interesting on two levels. First, it prevents women from forming a social support system or even a bond of solidarity with each other because the shame and alienation catalyzes a coping strategy based on silence. The struggle to cope with or change one's situation immediately becomes an individual struggle, subject to one's own individual responsibility. This logic of individual choice and responsibility leaves the women feeling alone and unsupported in their struggles, presenting them without an exit strategy other than breaking up the family.

Second, the collective experience of shame and alienation disrupts the hegemonic narrative of the United States being a leader in women's rights, because it challenges the Western discourse of "Third World women as universal dependents."[33] The accounts of angst and even anger clearly show that the Indian (Third World) women did not consider themselves to be natural dependents. In fact, they actively resisted that label, even as they experienced what can be described as collective trauma and a crisis of self and identity. The US visa regime shoehorns independent, educated women from India into roles that the second wave of the women's rights movement in the United States had fought hard to leave behind, reinforcing a sense of intense shame and dejection.

Men and the Dependent Identity

The power of gender in self-construction comes to the forefront when the accounts of the men who held H-4 statutes are examined. Men on dependent visas also shared a sense of alienation and shame, but they expressed it in qualitatively different ways compared to the women. Some of the men expressed anxiety and embarrassment, shying away from discussing their personal experiences on dependent visas. Instead, the men were clear about their motivations for coming to the United States on an H-4 visa, saying that they accepted dependent visa status on moral grounds: "It is what a man should do for the sake of his family" was a common theme. Others indicated that their visa status compelled them to withdraw from the transnational Keralite (ethno-regional identity) community so as to avoid questions and "sneers." Others dealt with shame and alienation by developing destructive habits: excessive smoking and/or alcohol consumption. Some men became physically and/or emotionally abusive toward their wives because they perceived them as the immediate reason for their emasculation.

During my observations, an encounter with a man named Johnny at an ethnic church illustrated this pattern. I was attending an after-sermon social lunch following a Sunday morning mass. Approximately 90 percent of the 400-person congregation consisted of either nurses or members of nurses' families. Most people came to the Sunday mass with families. Earlier, during the sermon, I noticed a man sitting by himself. He held his head down, sometimes swayed from side to side, and sometimes fell off the pew. I could not tell if he was praying, sleeping, or inebriated. While one of the church members, a nurse, introduced me to some other nurses, the man came up to me and nudged me. He could barely stand straight, and his breath smelled heavily of alcohol.

He said: "You want to hear about families of nurses, about men being on dependent visas? You need to talk to me."

I was startled by his forthrightness, because men on dependent visas generally avoided talking with me about their visa statuses. We arranged to conduct the interview immediately, in a quiet and empty corner of the church but in public view. We sat in an empty corner of the large prayer hall while the rest of the members socialized at the other end of the hall. Johnny was in his early forties, although he looked much older.

> I am sure you are pitying me. I am sure you are thinking what a loser I am. Well, you are right. I *am* a loser for coming to this country as a dependent, for letting myself do what a man should never do: be dependent on a woman [garbled speech]. She took my son and my daughter, turned them against me and threw me on the streets. She brought charges on me that I am alcoholic, I abuse her, beat her up. I am an alcoholic . . . because of her—she kept being in my face with her money. I worked in the gas station but did not have papers, so they treated me bad. She told the police I would kill her, and these *good* friends of hers, these other nurses, told her to put me in jail. . . . I spent four days in the jail. I come from a respectable family. Now I have nothing. I sleep here in the church. I can't go back to my village. Please write this in your report.

Johnny was explicit about living in an abusive situation where he was the abuser, which was confirmed by his wife in a later interview. He even justified the abuse he unleashed on his wife because, to him, this was the only hegemonically masculine power (violent, misogynistic, and unhinged) that he could exercise given his situation. This is reminiscent of the mobile masculinity that Bangladeshi men in Amrita Pande's[34] study in South Africa deployed to recoup masculine power in circumstances that dependent men saw as extreme powerlessness.

Other men interviewed expressed exasperation at their inability to adjust to the new life. Daniel, an H-4 visa holder, described the hard transition: "[B]ack in Kerala, I was poor but was respected. Here I have money but no respect and no friends." The nurse wives of men on H-4 visas often talked about the mental toll it took on themselves as they dealt with a "husband" who was either "depressed" or "angry at everything."

Unlike their women counterparts, dependent men on H-4 status usually avoided answering questions about their visas. Those who engaged the topic indicated they struggled with feelings of humiliation and loss of face, particularly when associating with other men in the community who were not on dependent visas. Joseph, 38, bypassed the H-4 question and talked about how his transnational experience left him intensely lonely. He said that his new life "is a very alone life, like, you have no real friends, can't talk to no one. I don't like religion, and I don't like church. Indian people laugh at each other, but even they all had [the] same experience." Some of the men on H-4 status spoke about alcohol as an escape from their situation. Alcohol was touted as a masculine way of dealing with the issue. Jejo, a husband on H-4 visa, said: "If I were a woman, I could cry; but I am a man, so I drink." George, an emigrant who initially chose to stay in India while his wife worked as a nurse in the United States, said: "I refuse to lead a life of a houseboy. I would rather live in my village than live in grand America with no honor." Men talked about dependent visas in terms of being humiliated and associated such humiliation with the loss of their male privilege, which in turn deprived them of male camaraderie, or what Patricia Yancey Martin[35] described as the privilege of mobilizing their masculinities. Drinking as a performance of masculinity has been well documented in studies of masculinity. Michael Messner and Jeffery Montez De Oca[36] and Helana Darwin[37] in their studies, decades apart, have illustrated how one way to perform masculinity is through drinking, though the type of drinking varies depending on the institutional and social contexts. In this case, dependent visa holders used inebriation to gain what Tristan Bridges[38] calls "gender capital"; social practices that are least associated with femininity—drinking, as opposed to crying, in the case of the dependent men—warrants the highest gender capital.

Despite the gendered difference, all dependent visa holders consistently reported the same three themes: (1) an intense sense of shame, alienation, and loss of identity causing "collective trauma" that thwarted the formation of solidarity groups; (2) an assumption of personal and individual responsibility for coping, blaming oneself, and/or possibly changing one's situation; and (3) gendered frames of masculinities and femininities that simultaneously questioned and made sense of one's situation. Most of the women, unlike the men, had the consciousness and the language to articulate the structural oppression of the visa order. But in the final analysis, women tended to readjust their actions to conform to this structure while at the same time training themselves to live with the trauma and the alienation. The men mostly suffered from the humiliation or acted out in response to it.

The concept of neoliberal governmentality[39] posits that the success of global capitalism lies in the successful transfer of responsibility for discipline from the state to individuals. Individuals discipline themselves and each other to adjust to the governmental disciplinary state order, thereby rendering the structures of such oppression invisible.[40] I would contend that the challenges faced by these women and men, while different, resulted in their disciplining themselves to adjust to their new lives while also resisting becoming the "vegetables" that the visas require them to be. Resistance to structural oppression in the form of visa regimes comes at a price: constant negotiations with the contradictions that belie the lives of these women and men. While women agonize over and resist becoming helpless dependents in their minds, men reject the idea of dependence and claim patriarchy through other assertions of masculinity. Women and men resist state power through gendered resistance. They actively resist total state control of their selfhood but, in practice, capitulate often by way of manifesting performances of conventional masculinities and femininities in the familial context. The effort and performance required to negotiate such contradictions shrouds the unanticipated costs of transnational labor migration to migrants and their families. As individuals go through this process, the mechanisms of how dependence is created and sustained eventually become invisible.

Interplay of the Self and the Public: Acts of Disruption

In this section, I present evidence of participants' individual struggles as they resist the structures of dependence imposed on them. These acts of disruption show how individuals push against the power of government and governmentality. I illustrate how dependent subjects actively resist dependence and also challenge the intent and purpose of laws designed to ensure "stable families" for migrant workers by way of levying restrictions on the agency of the dependent visa holder. I contend that this active resistance suggests that the current dependent visa policy is a failing policy.

The structural constraints of the visa regime seem to engulf the entirety of the identities, actions, and behaviors of visa holders. Individual acts of disruption, therefore, challenge the power of dependent visa structures as well as the validity of the policy itself. Most of my participants could not perceive the entirety of their contribution to disrupting the oppressive power of the visa regime. Many of the women on dependent visas said that they saw their participation in research, such as this project, as a way of making their voices heard against the oppressive structure. They engaged with research intimately and often indicated the importance of emphasizing specific episodes of their experience. One of the women I interviewed said: "This is the only way anyone will hear what we have to say, so you need to make sure this gets out. When your book comes out, make sure to send one copy to Michelle Obama so that the issue that no one cares about and is trivialized may get some attention." However, I will show that the disruptive and constructive accomplishments of the women and the men that I interacted with throughout the course of this project go far beyond the research I present here.

Most of the women on H-4 visa status that I interviewed engaged in some form of voluntary work, either for social service agencies or business organizations. About a third of the women donated time to multiple volunteer agencies because most work organizations allow an individual to perform only eight hours of volunteer work per week without a work permit. Ria volunteered at four social service agencies per week and spent more than 50 hours per week volunteering, which often was more time than her husband spent at his job. This left her very little time for housework. Ria's husband, Sumit, told me that he shared the housework equally and could very rarely work weekends, unlike some of his other colleagues on H1-Bs, since his wife was often volunteering over the weekends. The heteropatriarchal family structure that the state imposes by way of its visa regimes only intends to secure the optimum efficiency of an imported skilled labor force. Ria and Sumit, as with many other couples, upended this structure by maximizing the family unit's community impact via volunteerism without sacrificing the family's participation in the commercial economy. Further, they disrupted dependence and gender inequality by enacting empowering cooperation within the family group.

While most women decided to have children so they could use their "unproductive break in career to reproduce," some of the women I interacted with consciously decided not to have children until they were able to restart their careers. One woman said: "The social and the family [here meaning extended family] expectation is that, since I am not working, I will use this time to have and raise a child, but that to me is crazy. That just takes my dream to restart my career farther away. I am NOT getting into that trap!" Her resolve in relation to this issue should be interpreted as a form of dissent against the gendered reconfiguration of the family structure that the visa regime endorses.

A follow-up interview with some participants two years after the initial interview revealed that a few of the women who were trying to change their visa status had succeeded in doing so. Mili had joined a full-time PhD program; Poonam had enrolled in a computer-engineering graduate program; and Mia had made a resourceful move, securing a job at the Indian consulate—the only organization she could work for on US soil without changing her visa. Karuna, who had a two-year-old child, joined an intensive professional graduate program in the hope that it would help her move to a work visa upon the completion of her studies. A few women had tried working despite H-4 visa regulations; they often quickly stopped, however, for fear of being reported and/or being taken advantage of.

Such life changes required full-time commitments and years of planning. As for Karuna and Mia's, they had to convince their husbands, since they had young children. The women who worked without permits engaged in serious arguments with their husbands, given that such actions could compromise the work and immigration statuses of their husbands. Yet some women leaped at opportunities, even if they would jeopardize their husband's work status and the family's continued presence in the United States. In follow-up interviews, the women who pursued higher education shared their fears that, if they did not find a job to facilitate the conversion of their visa status after graduating, they would have to slip into their previous H-4 lifestyles. Karuna, who had a master's degree in hospital management from India, told me:

It would be much harder to reconcile myself the next time around. I did a MSW after I came to the United States while my son was a year old. It was hard as hell. I hardly slept, but I did it just so that I did not have to be on [an] H-4 visa. And then I did not get a job and had to go back on H-4. That was hard enough. I could not do it for much long[er], and now

I am spending $50,000 to get this professional degree. I am killing myself
to do this. I have a child. I travel two hours every day to go to the university and I still do . . . most of the caretaking of my son, though Aniket
[her husband] helps a ton with the housework. It took a lot [to] convince
Aniket. I hope something good comes out of this. After all this, I'd better
get a job after this, or I will be suicidal if I have to lead an H-4 life again.

When I interviewed Karuna's husband, Aniket, about the new situation, he said it was hard to reconcile the work/life conflict, given that
now both he and Karuna had full-time commitments; however, he did
stress the fact that he could not have been happier. It was "physically
exhausting but mentally peaceful to not to have an unhappy wife," he
said. The other three husbands of women who had either begun working or studying echoed Aniket's sentiments. Mia's husband, Rex, said: "I
was worried in the beginning, given we had a young kid and I travel so
much, but, believe me, Mia starting to work has changed our quality of
life. We are so much happier now! I never want us as a family to go back
to the old life." Titash's husband, Gopal, a research scientist, set up a lab
with sophisticated computer systems in their one-bedroom apartment
so Titash could continue the research she had begun in India as a PhD
student, research that she had terminated to join her husband in the
United States. Gopal was kind enough to show me the computer lab and,
in other ways, demonstrated personal commitment to his wife's professional development. Gopal emphasized that he did not want "hot meals
every day." Rather, he wanted his wife to be professionally independent.
When families were unable to change the conditions of their lives under
this restrictive visa regime, the husbands actively tried to relocate to
other global markets, in which the constraints on dependent visas were
not as draconian as they are in the United States.

In drastic acts of disruption, three highly qualified women, all in
their thirties, decided to return to India and start their lives over after
being on dependent visas for five years. They made this decision despite
extreme parental and communal pressures against their decision. The
women left the stability of their married lives in the United States to find
jobs and restart from scratch as single women in new cities in India. The
long gap in their careers disadvantaged them even in the Indian professional labor market and required them to settle for jobs that were below

their qualifications. Still, when I called them for a follow-up interview, they said they were happier than they had been in the last five years.

These radical decisions by women led some of the men on H1-B visas to reconsider their circumstances in the United States. Some husbands considered returning to India to join their wives, while others considered divorce. Most of the women were still married when they went back to India, but they did not intend to return unless they could do so without needing an H-4 visa. Such decisions forced the husbands to rethink their jobs in the United States, and many were actively trying to find jobs in the United Kingdom or Singapore, which don't have dependent visa laws. Others were planning to move back to India to join their wives. One woman in this study got a divorce after she went back to India because her husband was unwilling to move back for various work-related reasons and his green card was still about five years or more away. The wife did not want to come back on dependent status, and so they filed for divorce. In a follow-up interview, the husband, who was still in the United States, told me they remained on very good terms, and even their respective two families were close. He told me that "her visa fucked it up for us," as he explained:

> We had no issues as a couple, but with the visa situation and the mounting frustration, I think this is the best solution. It is sad, and I am back to being single, which is hard, but I can't quit my job for a few years since my green card is in the works, and it is unfair for her to stay on being unhappy. It is unfortunate!

The struggles of these women and their families, their resistance to H-4 identities, and their desperate attempts to change the situation can be construed as merely personal. But they may also be perceived as acts of political dissent that disrupted the carefully crafted labor strategy of the United States from achieving the consequences its policies intend.

The disruptions that men with H-4 visa statuses caused in the state-imposed family structure tended to be less about upending systemic oppression and more about preserving their status in relation to their masculinity. Men dependents tended to jeopardize the stability of their wives' jobs by working in the informal economy and disrupted any semblance of work-family balance that their nurse wives could have had by maintaining a transnational conjugal/parental family situation and forcing the nurses to live within a transnational commuter relationship. When husbands refused to come to the United States on dependent visas, the nurses would often go back to India to see their husbands and children, even at the risk of losing their jobs. This put additional pressure on the nurses in the workplace and also brought the crisis these families faced to the attention of hospital administrators. According to some of the nurses who participated in my research, one of the reasons that the hospitals in the United States are less keen on hiring Indian migrant nurses is that many return to India for long periods to be with their husbands and children, interrupting their work duties. However, the serious shortage of nurses in the United States has contributed to the possibility of expedited permanent residency for migrant nurses, which substantially reduces the duration of the dependent visa status for the spouses of nurses as compared to the spouses of tech workers. Nurses can receive permanent residency in three years or less, thereby ending the dependent visa status of their husbands fairly quickly, whereas for the high-tech workers and their wives, permanent residency can take six to 20 years or more.

The short-term duration of visas makes the issues and consequences appear manageable to affected individuals, at least initially. This in turn makes the issue of visa policy reform appear insignificant to public officials who construct and implement visas. In a television interview, a representative from the US Department of State dismisses the problems affecting dependent visa holders by indicating that she has too much to do to be concerned with a short-term issue. She explains: "Their husbands—predominantly husbands—get visas for six years, and they can then apply for a green card. They might have to wait it out 10 years [. . .] and they can work." The participants who decided to come on H-4 visas saw the green card as their ticket out of state-imposed dependence and considered waiting it out. Yet, when faced with the reality of the circumstances, most of the women participants reacted by expressing views through the language of oppression. They viewed the time frame governing the transition of the visa status into lawful permanent residency as an enticement binding them to their status. Tona said: "By dangling the green-card carrot, they keep us quite quiet, but how long can we be silent? The carrot gets farther and farther, and my life gets messier and messier. Someone needs to say something." The carrot-and-stick metaphor reemerged often in my interviews, given that the trope of permanent status in the United States was one way the visa regime controls the subjectivities of migrants.

Conclusion

In this chapter, I present an analysis of the dependent visa category and its lasting costs on the lives and subjectivities of individuals and families involved. I show how dependent visas are used by the state as a technique to regulate and control labor and family migration. I demonstrate the ways in which H-4 visas affect the self, and public interactions of dependent visa holders. This, I contend, reveals the mechanism of techniques of state domination[41] producing what I call "technologies of visa regimes" whereby visas are used as tools to exercise and maintain control over the self and subjectivities of transnationally mobile individuals. I further argue that technologies of visa regimes represent a gendered project. This chapter illustrates the mechanistic aspects of the construction of gendered identities in relation to the dependent visas. It also shows the inherent contradiction that this notion of technologies of visa regimes contains. It altered the behaviors and the sense of self among the participants—but not their consciousness. Each of them tried to find individual ways to negotiate and survive the rules, including illegal work, schooling, and motherhood as well as alcoholism, leaving husbands, or never joining wives in the first place.

My analysis of dependent visas presents a critique of the US state's implied discourse of women of the Global South as traditional, heteronormative wives and dependents, which appears to be a strong assumption underlying the regime of dependent visas. The so-called immigration experts, particularly lawmakers, seem to justify and defend the dependent visa policies constructed on the idealized 1950s model of traditional and stable families in the United States, complete with a provider who goes out to work and a dependent spouse responsible for household labor—which is actually rare in the contemporary landscape of the United States.[42] The accounts of lawmakers seem to reflect a conservative ideology of stable, traditional transnational families and the Western assumption that women from the Global South are "universal dependents."[43] At the same time, an analysis of the public discourse on skilled worker visas reflects a commitment to making it possible for corporations to import the required skilled labor from the Global South on their own terms.

Visas become tools of exploitation as they impose multiple forms of regulation on migrant subjects, including an arduous annual process of reapplication and reapproval. These impact family structures in very real ways. Participants who held dependent visas indicated how any small violation of their visa rules—such as not carrying a passport or volunteering beyond stipulated hours or performing any work without a permit—could jeopardize the renewal of their visas and the work visas of their partners. These otherwise invisible structures of dependence seem to operate as mechanisms of a gendered and racialized governmental technology of power that shapes and reshapes individual lives and experiences.

However, their acts of personal disruption help form communities of dissent[44] and challenge the unquestioned assumptions and invisible gendered and racialized structures behind visas regimes, particularly for dependent visas, and help to unravel the profound and lasting impacts such regimes have had on the lives of individuals and families.

3

Beholden to Employers

Gendered and Racialized Dependence

> In recent years, one in four high-tech startups in America
> were founded by immigrants.
> —Barack Obama, January 29, 2013

About 50 miles outside Chicago. Around 3 p.m. on a spring day in 2011. I was sitting with Sambit, having coffee in the cafeteria of his office building, which unostentatiously hosts many of the back-end technology offices of major global corporations. "You want to know how H-4 visa affects my wife and my family, but maybe I should first tell you about how my H1B [visa] affects my work life and my life in general and my journey. That will give you a fuller picture." The cafeteria, with counters for Starbucks Coffee, Intelligentsia Coffee, Argo Tea, and a few other cafés, was teeming with people, mostly men, wearing pastel-shaded or light-colored striped shirts and dark khaki pants with employee ID tags hanging from lanyards around their necks. Glancing over the cafeteria floor, I estimated that about 60 percent of people in the cafeteria were Indian men. Sambit told me this was "techie coffee-break time—in India it used to be the techie smoking-break time; in America everything is politically correct, but half of the *boys* are outside smoking."

I was struck by the predominant presence of men in this space. There were at least 60 people in the cafeteria during the hour, with only about seven women including myself: two women who were tech workers, and the rest working in the coffee stand. Sambit confirmed that the project he was currently working on had about 35 people, 27 of whom were men—Indian programmers on H-1B visas with a woman manager who was white and a native-born American.

Sambit went on to talk about his career trajectory. He acquired a bachelor's degree in computer engineering from a midranked professional engineering college in India, which led to his first entry-level IT job, at a large IT body-shopping company, two quick promotions, and a final promotion for which he was sent to the United States to work for a major global bank in its back-end IT division. He had arrived on a temporary H-1B work visa and at the time of the interview had been in the job for four years. A year into his job, he returned to India to marry a woman he met online, who then joined him on a dependent (H-4) visa his company had sponsored. His wife's H-4 visa, as all dependent visas are, was linked to the terms of the visa that he himself held. His company had sponsored him for permanent residency under the employment-based third preference skilled workers visa category (EB-3). The approval of permanent residency in the third preference category usually takes more than 20 years for workers because of the huge backlog in processing requests from countries (including India) that send the most number of workers to the United States. However, once the permanent residency application has been filed, the employer can renew the work visa on a yearly basis until permanent residency is approved. After permanent residency is approved, the dependent spouse is able to obtain a work permit. If an immigrant employee wishes to change jobs in the United States, the application for the permanent residency is annulled and needs to be started anew by the new employer. If the work visa expires or if the employee gets fired, the employee and employee's spouse are required to leave this country within one week and return to the home country.

The permanent residency process, coupled with the long processing period for a work visa, creates a condition that I conceptualize as "legal liminality" for professional workers and their families. I develop this concept based on Cecelia Menjívar's[1] theorization. She coined the idea of liminal legality (slightly different from legal liminality) in her 2006 article as the "gray area" of legality or the in-between status—not fully documented and not fully undocumented. In the context of immigration, it means different things for individuals and families with various immigration statuses. Menjívar[2] constructed "liminal legality" as a status that undocumented immigrants experience as they navigated their various personal and institutional relationships. She contends that the statuses of "documented" and "undocumented" create two different and deeply hierarchical social classes among immigrants. I am not arguing against this claim, for there certainly exists an almost unbridgeable schism between undocumented and documented workers, especially in terms of their experiences as prospective immigrants in the United States. And yet, when analyzing the experiences of immigrant and transnational workers, in particular on US visas, I feel compelled to think of their legal statuses as liminal. The legal status of highly skilled workers on work visas is tied to their employment and employer, and therefore their dependents' legal visa and immigrant statuses are tied to the same employment-based visa statuses. The sponsorship of permanent residency for high-tech workers is an additional leash that the employers can tug at will. In conjunction with legal status, the nature of tech work itself and the hierarchical structure—both formal and informal organizational structure—had a clear racial and gendered pattern to it, creating conditions of constant uncertainty for workers and their families.

How long immigrant workers hold legal visa status in the United States depends entirely on how their performance as a worker is being perceived by their employer. The perception of employers and their expectations of the immigrant worker are informed by two distinct and intersecting sociological constructions. The perception and expectation of being an ideal worker and a model minority largely frame the experiences of mostly Asian workers and their families in the United States. These concepts will be unpacked further in this chapter in relation to the way the lead migrants and their families experience paid work.

The legal visa status then becomes the cue for who the high-tech workers are in the United States; how they must conduct themselves at work; how they must craft their identity as workers; what they and their families are able to do or not; how they relate to their home countries; and, most important, how they perceive their place in the US immigration regime. Sambit describes his condition as being stuck between a "rock and the hard place," which is a poignant metaphor for legal liminality. Many of the other lead migrants in my study, especially the men tech workers, expressed similar sentiments. They were never certain whether they were merely temporary workers or had a future as immigrants in the United States. This uncertainty, closely tied to their legal status, created a condition of legal liminality—a legal status that is always at the risk of slipping into illegality through denial or revocation of the workers' and their families' visa status and/or through dismissal from their jobs.

Sambit's statement that afternoon—about how I should try to understand the politics and consequences of the work visas for the highly skilled workers (H-1B) in relation to the dependent visas for their spouses (H-4)—reoriented the course of my research. When I began this research project, I was singularly focused on how both spouses in Indian professional families negotiated the issue of the dependent visa being so restrictive for the dependent spouse. After my interview with Sambit, who was one of the early interviewees, I realized that it was impossible to gauge the extent of the dependence structure created by the visa regime without interrogating the effects of the temporary foreign workers' H-1B visas as well as the dependent spouses' H-4 visas. Going forward, when talking to the lead migrants, (the men professional workers and the nurses and their spouses), I pointedly expressed interest in their professional lives in relation to the visas they and their spouses held.

This chapter analyzes how the participants—the high-tech workers and nurses—experience intersectional dependence at work as immigrant visa-holding workers in gendered workplaces. I examine patterns of commonality and divergence in the experiences of the nurses and the high-tech workers in the ways that they are constructed as *ideal workers* with presumably unlimited labor time and no family responsibilities. I base this analysis in part on Joan Acker's[3] conception of the ideal worker in her work on a white heterosexual man who had no physical limitations and no responsibilities outside of work. However, the immigrant workers in my study were not white, and neither were they all men. So how can these immigrant workers be cast in the image of Acker's ideal worker? Evelyn Nankano Glenn[4] contends in *Unequal Freedom* that, along with race and gender, having full citizenship greatly shapes work opportunities for minorities and immigrants in the Unites States. Both the kind of work available and the rights associated with being a worker in that occupation are largely dependent on whether or not the United States considers a given worker to be a full citizen. Historically, according to Glenn, the race, gender, nationality, ability, and sexuality of a given subject dictated whether they would be considered a citizen or capable of full citizenship in the United States. In this chapter, in line with this idea and in developing the construct of legal liminality, I also explore how the participants—whose legal status in the United States is predicated on their status of being skilled workers—wrestle with the burden of the gendered and racialized model-minority status imposed on them as they lead their lives within the legal liminality of the visa regime.

The Carrot and the Stick: The Visa Regime and the Nonimmigrant-Immigrant Worker

In the United States, what distinguishes migrants or foreign workers categorized as "low-skilled" by the state from those categorized as "highly skilled"? Supposedly, the answer is simple: whether they have a clear pathway to becoming lawful permanent residents. And yet, according to the stories told by Ravish, Lily, and Sambit, this pathway to lawful permanent residency is anything but simple.

Most temporary skilled workers who migrate to the United States on work visas are eligible to be sponsored for lawful permanent residency (a green card). The Immigration Reform Act of 1990 made it possible for immigrant workers on H-1B visas to possess temporary worker status and apply for permanent residency through their employers.[5] However, the process of attaining permanent residency depends on complex immigration rules and numerical caps; the transition is far from being smooth, efficient, or guaranteed, making the "H-1B program neither fully a temporary program" nor a "permanent visa program."[6] This neither/nor condition creates a situation of legal liminality for highly skilled workers in negotiating and understanding their place and position in the new country. The uncertainty of being simultaneously nonimmigrant *and* immigrant creates great challenges for the families I studied and shows the many facets of dependence that structured the lives of the participants. The aspiration of settling, belonging, liberation—especially for the dependent spouse—and becoming American that is entangled with the possibility of permanent residency was completely at odds with the visa and work situations of the families. The visa regime thus creates an inescapable dependence on the employer for an anticipated future of rights and liberties, making families vulnerable on multiple levels.

In this structure, the legal precarity of temporary visa status intersects with the gender and race of the lead migrants to create a conundrum of dependence that is predicated on keeping the workers on a seesaw, balancing the hope of future stability through lawful permanent residency with remaining indefinitely in a workplace whose profitability hinges on the exploitation of racialized migrant workers. And yet the intersection of gender and legal status creates different experiences for the nurses and the tech workers.

"Here's the Stick": Tech Workers as the Lead Migrant Worker

This neither/nor situation was described by many of my participants aptly as "the carrot and the stick." Ravish, in describing what his visa situation means to him, said:

> I am on H-1B visa now for seven years, and the only reason I am still in the United States for a seventh year[7] is that my company has applied for my green card [permanent residency]. So, you'd think I am happy because not many companies do this and they don't do it for all their employers, but I am not. This is a carrot and a stick situation for me. So, if I were really a temporary worker, I would think, *After six years I can start over, but now I am basically bonded to my employer.* So, the "carrot" is that, once I am a permanent resident, I practically have all citizenship rights: I can move jobs, I can look for a better-paying job, maybe in a different field. I can drive cabs if that makes me happy, and most importantly my wife can work, and you have talked to her, you know how important that is for her and me—so that is the carrot. But *here's the stick*: It can take another seven years or more to get the green card, and if I want the green card, I need to stick with this company because (A) I have no option of extending my visa with another company. I have to go to back to India because my six years are over, and (B) even if I do get a job, I will have to restart the green card process again, and that does not help me at all because that sets my wife back again. So, my options are to remain with this company or go back to India, and the additional "stick" is that if I have stuck it out so long, let's see when the green card happens, and what that means is that my company and the US government own my ass.

Ravish was particularly articulate in explaining his situation. He laid out the various layers of dependence that translate into structures of exploitation embedded in the visa and permanent residency policies for temporary workers. The invisible nexus of the contracts of employment with the validity of the visa status makes sure that workers and their families are kept in an uncertain state of instability regarding their futures in the United States. The promise of lawful permanent residency (i.e., obtaining a green card) spells a future of privileges for the worker and his family, but the temporality of the visa trajectory creates an uncertainty and vulnerability in the present that can be and is exploited by employers. Therefore, when Ravish uses the metaphor of the carrot and the stick for the green card application and what it means for him as a worker to be beholden to his employer—and the consequences for his family's future as well as the time already invested in moving toward the goal of becoming an immigrant—is what I call "legal liminality." This status of "nonimmigrant immigrant" makes highly skilled workers on these visas vulnerable to exploitation by holding out the hope of permanent residency—as long as they remain obedient workers and model minorities.

"Always on Call": Nurses as the Lead Migrant Worker

The nurses also experience legal liminality, albeit with the added dimension of gendered dependence. Many described how the possibility of the green card and the threat of losing it made them more exploitable at work. When I asked what it was like to be on a work visa, Lily, a floor nurse, provided a vivid description of how the visa and the possibility of the green card dictated work conditions and family dynamics for the nurses:

> I am always on call. I feel like H-1B nurses are always on call. They know we will not say anything because we Indian women never say anything, but it is also because we know if we say anything, they will refuse to process our green cards. And they also know that my husband is home, and I should put my house responsibilities on him. You know how hard that is, right? One of the recruiter agents told me, "This is why we pay for him to go." They never do it to American nurses. They have their fixed shifts, holidays, and promotions. It is always us, and what can we say as foreign nurses? I should never have come on H-1B. I can't wait for the three years to be over and for the green card.

When Lily says that Indian nurses are "always on call" and that "Indian women never say anything," she unknowingly unlatches the intersectional analysis of how being an immigrant of color, of being a care worker/nurse with a precarious legal status in a feminized profession (nursing), builds up the idealized version of the docile feminine worker.[8] Despite these trying conditions at work, Lily hoped that getting the green card would be her ticket out of "being always on call." Little did Lily know that green card processing would take far more than three years of her life. Though the processing time was quicker for the nurses than for the tech workers—because they migrate as health care workers to fulfill acute labor shortages in the health care industry—it was at least six years nonetheless. The gendered and racialized aspects of the demands on the nurses' time, predicated on their visa and green card situations, were unmistakable. While employers of tech workers and nurses were aware of a dependent spouse at home, the nurses felt extra pressure because a dependent man at home is not the same as a dependent woman at home (as will be analyzed in detail in chapter 5). The green card, however, had a similar exploitative hold on the nurses as it did on the tech workers, at least where work was concerned.

"The Stick is Real": Dependent Spouses' Experiences

In their independent interviews, the dependent spouses also evoked the carrot-and-stick imagery in relation to the green card and their lives as nonimmigrant immigrants and their dependent statuses. Jaya's poignant observation revealed much about the situation, as far as planning a future for the family was concerned, because of the wait to obtain lawful permanent residency:

> The "carrot" is that that one day we will be fully part of this society with no visa sword hanging over us, but it is still the carrot, it is a perishable veggie. But the "stick," *the stick is real*, and the "stick" is made of steel, it will kill you but leave no marks. We have been waiting for the green card for seven years now. I almost wish we were not the chosen people picked for the green card. I almost wish our green cards were not in the works. Look at Rishi and Reshma [her friends to whom she had referred me]— the company refused to sponsor their green cards, and they said fuck it,

and they are now back in India starting their lives, and Reshma has already found a job. We pitied them when they had to move back, but now I pity us and myself. God knows how long our lives will be held hostage to this immigration situation.

Jaya uses many metaphors here to describe her situation. She refers to permanent residency/green card as the carrot and her dependence status as the sword hanging over her. And then she uses humor to say that even the green card does not guarantee them a safe life in the United States. However, the metaphor of the steel stick that kills without leaving marks—which Jaya used rather casually while she and I were having coffee one afternoon in a coffee shop—left me rather shaken. Her words expressed strong emotions and a sense of "being stuck" in a legal situation that made families more vulnerable and less secure.

Given the centrality of the green card in the lives of the families I interacted with, unsurprisingly, permanent residency/green card was a common topic of discussion among both the nurses and high-tech workers. However, the men tech workers seemed to be more preoccupied with it compared to the nurses. This can be considered a gendered phenomenon. They did not take on as much responsibility toward their family's everyday caregiving as the nurses did—so the spaces in which tech workers gathered were rife with discussions about green cards rather than households, as in the case of the nurses. At weekend get-togethers when the men hung out after dinner over whisky and cigarettes, anxious conversations were often raised about the status of green card applications. Or when the men met up after a game of cricket at a local bar, where I accompanied them almost every other week during a six-month period, the discussion often steered to green cards, and the men compared notes on where they were in the process. More often than not, they expressed deep frustration with the process, calling it a "trick to make them work without complaints." More than once, I heard men say how important the green card was to the health of their marriages. For instance, after a couple of drinks in the bar on a Saturday evening after the weekly match of cricket, Jeet looked at the five other men on the table and sighed, "If this fucking green card is not processed quickly, my marriage is going to end, man. I keep telling Piyali that her miseries will end soon, with the green card, and I hope it really does, and she is able to work again. We [our marriage] are in crisis." The other men, who were not as open about the health of their marriages, nodded in unison and understanding. One of them turned to me and asked, "Can you take note that this green card is screwing us big-time?"

The issue of permanent residency is analytically interesting because, as my participants suggest. On one hand, the companies use it as an almost forced and coercive retention policy;[9] on the other, they use it as a reward structure for the migrant employees, adding to the burden of being the "ideal migrant employee" and all that that label entails.

Scholars[10] who have studied tech workers on H-1B visas have shown how the recruitment structure and working conditions contribute to racialized and sometimes gendered disadvantages for workers. Banerjee, in her 2006 article, showed how visas were used to control tech workers. She argued that tech workers interpreted their "marginalization as being determined by the visa";[11] my own research takes it a step further and shows how the visa structure and paid work create conditions of dependence and disenfranchisement not only for the high-tech immigrant worker but also for her family. I also show how paid and unpaid work are related to each other and how it structures spousal interactions in a gendered way in the context of labor migration and how that is further reinforced by the visa regime. This regime of granting specific visas to workers and their families along with employer-dictated pathways to permanent residency represents cost-effective immigration policies.[12] Such policies filter out nonproductive immigrants and favor "productive immigrants" by selectively granting them rights when it benefits the institutions of power. This also is an effective tool in the making of the ideal "model minority" immigrant worker so central to the unhindered functioning of the global economy.

A Gendered "Model Minority" Paradox and the Visa Regime

A 2009 *Forbes* article[13] titled "The Indian-Americans: The New Model Minority" touts Asian Americans in the United States as the new model minority in comparison to the original holders of this designation: the American Japanese, the Chinese, and the Koreans. The article used the phrase "model minority," coined by the sociologist William Pettersen in

1966, and indicated, in line with contemporary public and media discourse, that earning that label was an achievement in the context of the American racial demographic landscape. The model-minority discourse is based on the stereotype that portrays some immigrants of color, particularly Asians, as quiet, hard-working high achievers who rise to the top of the socioeconomic hierarchy against all odds.[14]

To support his claim, the author of the *Forbes* article cited statistics from scholarly research and research organizations such as the Pew Research Center, the Migration Policy Institute, and the US Census. In claiming that Indians in America are in fact the new model minority, the author provided numbers indicating that a very high percentage of Indians in America have college degrees, are employed, and are physicians and engineers, as well as that the median income of households headed by Asian Indians is significantly higher than all other native-born and immigrant populations, including whites.

These numbers paint a rosy picture of the social positioning of Asian Indians in America. But they dangerously legitimize narratives of the American dream and the privileges that come with it for minorities who work hard and consequently succeed despite the adversities of racial discrimination. My comment about the American dream is deliberately tongue-in-cheek because critical race scholars[15] and scholars from other fields have proved that the American dream is at best ephemeral, at worst a myth, and that it insidiously gives cover to institutional racial discrimination that has been instrumental in the historical and generational oppression of people of color. As is often the case with dehistoricized, decontextualized, and misappropriated statistical evidence, the numbers highlighted about Asian Indians in the United States hide more than they reveal. Critical scholars who study Asians in America[16] have since at least the 1980s undone the model-minority discourse and established that the model minority is a myth and a detrimental stereotype for various reasons, including that: (a) Not all Asian Americans are doing well, and in fact, Asian Americans make up a disproportionately high percentage of those living in poverty; (b) the narrative delegitimizes the everyday and institutional discrimination faced by Asian Americans; (c) it isolates Asian Americans from other minorities by creating a false dichotomy of ideal and less than ideal people of color; and (d) it undermines the Asian American struggle for citizenship and belonging by assuming that Asian Americans are readily accepted and handed rights and resources because of their model-minority status.

Researchers[17] who study Asian Americans have problematized this assumption of privilege and high status attached to highly skilled immigrants from India. Rudrappa, in her 2009 article on Indian IT workers, labels them "techno-bracero," who—much like the Mexican agricultural workers (*braceros*)—are guest workers in this country, racialized and commoditized for the exploitation of their labor. Rudrappa contends that the tech workers, who do hold more advantages than braceros, were nevertheless similarly beholden to their work and employers for their legal immigrant status under draconian visa laws that allowed for little flexibility over work and day-to-day lives while in the United States.

Yet the model-minority rhetoric in connection with Asian Indians here is pervasive. In my interviews with immigration experts, lawyers, immigration activists, and legislators, Indian temporary workers were consistently referred to as "privileged immigrants" who were diligent workers. One immigration lawyer described Indian immigrants as: "They are well-educated, middle-class people, who are great workers and not surprisingly make good money. They are unlike most immigrants coming into this country. They don't need a whole lot of support to get on their feet." This way of reinforcing model-minority rhetoric was present across the board in my interviews with the "immigration experts," some of whom were immigrants themselves. The roots of this discourse go so deep that any mention of Indian immigrants in the United States is followed up with how efficient they are as highly skilled workers. A heart-wrenching *New York Times* front-page story about an immigrant Indian engineer, Srinivas Kuchibhotla, who was killed in a hate crime in a Kansas City bar on February 2017, describes him as "so well regarded that his boss routinely asked if the human resources division could 'find more Srinivases.'" Dave Wysong, his supervisor, added: "This is not hyperbolic when I tell you he was almost the perfect employee. . . . He was a great engineer—technically, very, very good. He was quiet and very, very friendly."[18]

"Technical efficiency," "quiet," and "friendly" emerge as the key characteristics of the model-minority worker. The presence and pervasiveness of this rhetoric is in no small way the result of the immigration histories and trajectories of Asian Indians to the United States since

1965. Most Indians that migrate here do so for postsecondary and graduate education (see chapter 2). These types of migrations contribute to a disproportionately high number of highly educated and highly skilled Asian Indians in the United States, leading to the model-minority narrative both inside and outside immigrant Indian communities.

My interviews with lead migrant participants demonstrated the extent to which they had internalized the concept of the model minority while also being acutely aware of the discrimination they face as immigrant skilled workers. The tech workers and the nurses enmeshed in the gendered nature of their work and workplace understood the internalization of this concept as well as the discrimination they experienced from their gendered and racialized positionalities. Both sets of workers often viewed the day-to-day work they did as immigrant workers as heroic, calling themselves "soldiers in the trenches." For the nurses, the imaginary trenches meant meeting the demands of what they described as "noble work" or the "higher calling" of healing work and patient care. For the tech workers, the trenches were the demands of the tech industry from immigrant workers. "Sticking it out" at work was how they thought they would build a viable future in a new country. At the same time, the powerlessness of their situation did not evade them. They felt they had very little control over their lives or work. They felt beholden to employers and the government because of the conditions of their visas. They saw themselves as "indentured" to employers, with severe consequences if they faltered. The consequences, which I present in the remainder of the chapter, were different for nurses compared to tech workers. The intersection of a gendered labor regime and the racialization of professional immigrant workers—which deeply influenced their understanding of their positionalities and subjectivities in the United States—is what I call a "gendered model-minority paradox."

Soldiers in the Trenches: The Ideal Model-Minority Immigrant Worker

Immigrant Nurses as Ideal Care Workers

"This is going to take, how long? My friend Carmen is covering for me for one hour while I talk with you. She is Filipina—a nurse on my floor. We look out for each other, you know. We are also considered the best workers. We never take days off, and we are always in the trenches." That was how Gina opened her interview with me, in the busy cafeteria of the city hospital where she worked. She went on to tell me that being the best worker also meant not participating in "union activities," not taking time off, and never saying no to additional shifts or extra hours. She added: "They know we, the Indian and Filipina nurses, the immigrant nurses, are always ready for what the job needs, and we are quiet, not challenging the doctors and admin staff all the time. We just want to heal patients. In that way, we are different from the other nurses." "Who are the other nurses?" I asked. "You know, the Black and Latina nurses," Gina replied.

Gina's choice of words and expressions in describing the qualities of the Indian and Filipina nurses resonates with the ideal worker and model minority.[19] Three distinct elements in Gina's narrative are theoretically important. She said that the best workers were quiet workers who did not challenge authority; she also suggested that immigrant nurses never said no; and finally she made a distinction between immigrant nurses and other nurses of color. In Gina's mind, Latinx and Blacks did not represent immigrant workers, even though some of the Black and Latinx nurses might have been immigrants. They are minorities, but different from her type of immigrant minorities because they are not, in her description, quiet and obedient workers. The distinction made by Gina between Asian and Black and Latinx nurses is indicative of the racist discourse that underlies the making of model minorities and that in turn is internalized by model minorities.[20] Gina was not the only one of our nurse participants to use this type of discourse; it was a common theme among the nurses in my study and was also was present on a more structural plane. Indeed, I attended a national conference of Indian nurses that had embraced the model-minority discourse. The keynote, by a white American professor of nursing, the speech of the president of the organization, the numerous sessions and presentations on caring and healing—all these reiterated the discourse that immigrant nurses were the backbone of the US health care system. The keynote speaker unequivocally said: "We love Indian nurses in our profession because [of] how committed to healing and nurturing they are." She also spoke about how medicine and medical care were secondary to nursing, saying that the expertise of nurses lay in healing at a spiritual level. The president of the organization, an Indian nurse practitioner, building on the keynote, reiterated the reason why Indian nurses were relevant in the United States: "We prioritize our work and patients even before our own families. So many of us even leave our precious children and our husbands in India so we can care for our patients in America. This is the kind of sacrifice we Indian nurses are capable of and willing to make." Florence Nightingale and the "higher calling" of doing healing work was invoked numerous times in the conference. In descriptions of why they chose to do their feminized work as nurses, it was not uncommon for the research participants to invoke religion. Many participants told me that it was their duty as Christian women to take care of others, to heal.

Feminization of nursing work is not uncommon in regular parlance and in the occupation, as noted by several scholars.[21] What struck me was not this feminization of the job, which was quite stark in the rhetoric about nursing work in the conference and among the nurse participants. Rather, it was the thorough and yet masked construction of Indian immigrant nurses as especially caring and nurturing, as women who put patients before their own families and who were on a mission to heal. When asked about the demands of the work, many participants said similar things. They acknowledged that they have to keep very long hours, the job itself is stress inducing, they often sleep very little, and their work is physically taxing. Yet they justified it by saying, "We are at the front line." This phrase has assumed added meaning during the pandemic, but the "we" in this phrase means immigrant nurses—a group that has indeed been the "soldiers in trenches" (to quote one of my participants) in the fight against the pandemic. The nurse participants often said, "We the immigrant nurses are always on call." Rose, a nurse, explained as follows: "As immigrants, we are always on the front line. We do have to work harder than many, but the kind of work we do makes it worthwhile. As women and from the culture we are, it just makes us better at dealing with what our work demands." While the interviews were done much before the pandemic, I am left wondering how the demands of the pandemic appropriated this internalized notion that immigrant nurses are better at dealing with the heavy demands of the frontline work.

For the purposes of this research, the concept of *appropriate labor* coined by Wooten and Branch[22] allows for deconstructing how the professional work performed by the immigrant nurses is crafted as a type of work that can only be performed by this category of workers. Wooten and Branch use the construct to demonstrate that, in the twentieth century, for white women to go to work, Black women had to be cast as ideal domestic workers because of their race and gender, justifying both their exploitation as domestic help and exempting them from the type of heteronormative domesticity available to white women. On "appropriate labor," Sharla Alegria[23] points out that nursing work, along with care work and emotional labor, requires long shifts, physical strength, and endurance to the point of extreme exhaustion, making women the ideal and appropriate worker for nursing work because feminized labor hinges on submission to the demands of the task at hand. Immigration status is an added dimension of the labor performed by nurses. It makes them the ideal model-minority worker for this feminized profession. The professional norms, legal limits of the visa status, and gendered cultural beliefs reinforce this gendered and racialized definition of nursing work. Following this logic, my participants made sense of the demands on their persons through the model-minority framework. The framework gave them a sense of control over, and ownership of, the grueling work asked of them daily. It seemed an aberrant way for them to regain agency over their challenging and exploitative work conditions. As discussed in greater depth below, the nurses claimed agency in other ways as well. The skilled male workers in this study were more deliberate about deploying the model-minority discourse to gain some perceived control over their work lives. The model-minority discourse gave them the tools to create distance from other minorities by casting themselves as more deserving of the American dream through their silent march toward achieving whiteness in the deeply unequal racial landscape of the United States.

Immigrant Men as Model Tech Workers

The tech workers men, much like the women nurses, endorsed a narrative of the superiority of Indian workers and their dedication to work. Not surprisingly, this motif of the superior worker was constructed through a framework of masculinity, in the image of a focused and diligent worker engaged in the steely world of tech work—untouched by the emotionality found in the nurses' narrative. However, both narratives—of the ideal tech worker and the ideal nurse—built up the image of the model minority. A condition of believability for the model-minority discourse is the construction of the deserving minority in contrast to the underserving minority. My nurse participants did so by comparing themselves with other minority nurses. The tech workers worked in spaces that mostly had other Indian immigrant workers. Aside from occasional meetings with their American bosses and counterparts who were mostly white, they had little interaction with other minority workers.

In the absence of such interaction, the participants often referenced the abstract "other" minorities as less deserving than they were. For instance, when Ranveer, a tech worker, was asked about his future plans, including whether he would like to live in the United States or return to India given that he was reaching the end of his H-1B visa term, he responded by saying: "We work hard, we contribute to the economy, we are here legally, and we do not make any trouble. We deserve to live in this country, but no, it's the precious illegal immigrants who are called dreamers and whatnot. They are the ones who will get amnesty, and we have to rot for years and wait in line forever to get our due." Ranveer uses the term "precious" with sarcasm, in his reference to people protected by the DREAM Act,[24] but in actuality he is drawing a moral distinction between his kind of legal immigrants and other kinds of immigrants (undocumented immigrants) by drawing on the legality of his status and casting himself as more deserving of living in the United States. This rhetoric was present among all of the participants, with dependent spouses often drawing this comparison by saying, "Why are we treated like illegals when we are here legally and have the qualifications to contribute?" Whenever the question of permanent residency was raised, the default for most participants was to point out the unfairness of the situation in comparison to "illegal immigrants."

The rhetoric of deserving versus undeserving immigrants/racial minorities among immigrants of color in the United States is as old as the social construction of racial hierarchies. It began with early immigrants such as the Mississippi Chinese,[25] the Italians,[26] the Irish, and other Eastern and Southern Europeans[27] once considered not to be white, claiming whiteness by embracing white supremacy, by distancing themselves from Blacks, and even by committing atrocities against Blacks. The racial middle (those who reside between whites and Blacks in the racial hierarchy) in the United States have continued to vie for whiteness at the expense of racialized groups constructed as less than them, based on the socially, politically, or culturally available bigoted and discriminatory repertoire of the time, which for the Indian professional workers was the trope of "legal" versus "illegal" status.

However, for the tech workers, the story of the deserving and underserving immigrants often went beyond using discriminatory language toward other minorities and hit closer to home. They often justified the dependent visa status of their wives by saying that, since their qualifications were not in demand in the United States, they *deserved* to be on dependent visas. When Shubham, an economist by training who was employed as a tech worker in a stock-trading company, was asked about how he felt about his wife being on dependent visa, he said:

> Oh, it sucks for her. She has a masters in Philosophy. But, come on, what can you do with a Philosophy degree? There are no jobs with Philosophy in the United States that needs to be filled, but there is demand for tech work. We are growing the market. So, I have the visa I have, she has the visa she has. We can complain all we—I mostly mean she—want, but honestly, that is the only visa she could come [to this country] on.

Shubham established two things here. First, he claimed that he and other tech workers deserved to be in the United States, given the posited demand for tech workers in the economy. He viewed himself and others such as him as adding value to the economy, thereby setting the stage for the "model minority" label. Second, he distinguished his skill set from his wife's qualifications and claimed that his qualifications and skills were more desirable. Despite her graduate degree, her qualifications, in his view, were redundant in the US economy, which is why, he indicated, she deserved to be on a dependent visa despite the unfairness of the legal constraints. Perhaps Shubham's training as an economist led him to articulate the visa situation for him and his wife from a market-oriented supply-and-demand-perspective, but this line of thinking was not uncommon among the tech workers. Many of the men indicated that they as tech workers were more deserving of the work visa than their wives, who, despite holding advanced degrees, were not tech workers. Here, the framing of skill and qualification as deserving and undeserving pivoted on a masculinist, technocratic imaginary that is endemic among techno-scientists, especially cis-white male scientists who see scientific/technical knowledge as universal and consequently as a conduit to symbolic power and thus a deserving skill to possess.[28] In the case of many of the male Indian tech workers in this book, the equivalence and transference of the ideation of deserving lies in the privilege of ascribed dominant caste status (*savarnas*) at birth in India and an unfettered access to the universal knowledge economy generationally only available to *savarna* upper-caste men.

While most men agreed that the dependent visa system was unfair, they said they were able to "objectively reason with the policy" from the perspective of the state. For example, a common sentiment I heard reasoned that it is not possible for the United States to provide jobs to everyone. Gopal, a tech professional, said:

> H-4 visas are not bad . . . [in themselves]. They are the easiest visas to get, but, they are bad because they create stupid tensions in the family. I will be sitting at work and worrying if my wife is getting bored and calling 15 times to make sure she is okay. That is stressful—[it] affects my work.

Men tended to express disapproval of the dependent visas because of how their wives' dependent status affected *their* lives and not how the dependent visa negatively affected their wives. Most men reported that they were frustrated that their spouses were unhappy; however, they were much more concerned about how their wives' unhappiness was affecting themselves at work and thereby their image as the ideal dedicated worker.

The image of the ideal dedicated worker was deeply entwined with the nature of the work that the men did on a regular basis. Most Indian immigrant tech workers were doing back-end software development, described by many as "repetitive grunt work." Because of visa restrictions, Indian workers did not have many opportunities for promotion and had very few chances of moving into management. But when asked what their professional aspirations were, most unequivocally said they wanted to become a "tech guru," much like their white senior engineer bosses. Their idea of the tech guru was modeled on Mark Zuckerberg: excessively involved, "wired," and busy to the level of being oblivious of every other aspect of their lives. They also saw themselves as the silent hard workers who, according to them, constitute the backbone of the American IT industry and its future. Underlying this construction of who an ideal tech guru ought to be is what Marianne Cooper[29] sees as the new masculinity of the new economy, which requires that the best tech workers be "men [who] must be technically brilliant and devoted to work. They must be tough guys who get the job done no matter what."[30]

For the Indian tech workers, however, the aspiration of someday becoming a tech guru was also intersectionally cloaked in a masculine articulation of the racial model-minority stereotype. When asked about the situation of Indian workers on visas in the industry, Satya, a tech worker in a large education technology company, had a mild outburst and said, in a somewhat irritable tone:

> Who was Satya Nadella, the present Microsoft CEO, or Sabeer Bhatia of Hotmail fame, or who was Sundar Pichai, Amit Singhal, the Google biggies, before they became who they are now? They all came to America on H-1B [visa] like us, quietly did their work, worked as hard as a man can, did not worry about who was being an asshole to them, who was talking down to them, kept their focus, their eyes on the target, and look where they are today. And, of course, we Indians are smart, and we make the system work for us. We have two choices here: . . . to beat our heads [*gesticulates head-beating*] about our visa situation and why we have to work more than Americans—or keep our heads down, do our work, and show the world we Indians make it despite everything. We even have role models.

Noticeably, Satya named only the Indian men who are tech leaders in the United States; none of the few women leaders captured his imagination. Satya's minor outburst is indicative of what it means to be a male, ideal, model-minority worker among aspirational, middle-class, educated immigrants. The imaginary is one of a disembodied worker (whose body does not fatigue) and emotionlessness, a model minority who overcomes the disadvantages faced by immigrant workers of color so that he can achieve the American dream without being distracted. The only qualities

Satya notes in these role models are their construed hard work and their perceived brilliance, keeping the eyes on the target of reaching the top and silently continuing to work until they have achieved this idealized target— qualities he views as inherently Indian attributes. We know, however, that of the 85,000 H-1B workers, most of who are tech workers, coming into the United States every year since the 1990, only a handful (less than 10) have become the industry leaders whom my participants hold up as role models and ideals. Given the level of education, the targeted skills of the workers, and the number of Asian Indians in the US tech industry, the proportion of Asian Indians in positions of power in the industry is fairly low. Most of the people who run the industry and hold important positions in the tech industry are still white men.[31] And yet, through this framing of the successful Indian immigrant worker, Satya evokes Joan Acker's[32] male ideal worker and Pettersen's[33] model minority who, against all odds, work toward and achieve the elusive American dream.

Indentured Servitude: Racialization of Immigrant Workers

Tech Workers and Presumed Indentureship

The American Dream, used as a lure in the formation of the model minority, is only a pipe dream. The model minority is not a positive stereotype. It hides more than it reveals. When coupled with the legal liminality of H-1B visa status, the model-minority concept produces conditions for worker exploitation and racialization. Payal Banerjee[34] and Biao Xiang[35] have argued that, in the recruitment of H-1B workers, labor migration becomes a racialized process. In addition, H-1B status is used to exploit migrant high-tech workers through wage cuts, exploitative working conditions, lack of benefits, and frequent relocations, as well as social alienation and isolation at work. The high-tech workers in this study described similar exploitative and alienating conditions at work. Rex, a high-profile financial analyst at a large consulting firm, explained his work and his visa status:

> If you ask me, slavery is not over. Before they would get black people on boats. Now they get us brown people on airplanes. The concept is the same: Yes, they pay us for our work, but it is much lower than what they pay American white workers. . . . We know that, but what can we do?

What we can do and cannot do in this country is tied to our work and our visas. Okay, I will say we are more like indentured servants, not slaves. I feel like an indentured servant who lives in an expensive company-arranged downtown apartment but will lose all legal status if I am fired tomorrow. I and my family become illegals if I am fired. You can imagine how much pressure, fear, and bondage that can create.

The language of slavery and indentured servitude was used by many of the men workers to describe their work and visa circumstances. I do not endorse the analogy to slavery given its history in the United States. I acknowledge that the analogy, as used by the participants, is misplaced and exaggerated. But there is no denying that the overwhelming emotion that accompanied this language of servitude emanates from the sense of powerlessness they felt in their work and family lives. Sambit, referenced earlier, a tech contractor in a large American insurance company, said about his work life:

I feel like a glorified servant, I have so little power to change my situation . . . We Indian IT folks usually have 12-hour workdays: 8 a.m. to 8 p.m. Our American bosses go home by 4 p.m., and really we are supposed to only work till 5:00 p.m., but I know of three people in my company whose contracts were terminated on two days' notice, and they and their family had to go back to India within the week. They had not screwed up or anything at work, they just went home at 5:00 p.m. like the Americans and would not show up on weekends when called in like we do, and bam, they were gone.

Sambit, like many of his fellow tech workers, felt an overwhelming lack of control over his work life, especially because of the liminal condition of his legal status. The link between visa status and employment status for H-1B visa holders places them in legal liminality, which in turn makes the position of the workers vulnerable and tenuous. What Sambit described is a coercive model of forcing immigrant workers to work longer hours not only by holding their jobs hostage but also by threatening their ability to remain in the United States. Getting fired from the job also meant a loss of legal status and a forced departure from the host country.

This situation of not being in control of one's life course presented the participants with a difficult paradox. On one hand, being a highly skilled worker, especially in the tech field, is associated with certain elements of masculinity—not being affected by anything outside work while also being emotionless, aggressive, and in control. On the other, the legal liminality of the position emasculates the worker for not being able to control his destiny and his field of work. This is best exemplified in the words of Kaushik, a tech worker who had been in the United States for 10 years at the time of the interview. When asked to describe his position in his company, he said:

> I mean, . . . I have been here for eight years, and I started low, but slowly I have risen through the ranks. I am a VP now, but that really means shit. I still have so little control over anything I do. How I interact with my team, how I process a code, what my team works on, is all decided by my superiors—the whiteys, you know. The thing is if you are in the tech industry, you need to be tough, aggressive, in charge, but when your lifeline hangs on the string of a visa, which can be pulled at any time, you feel like nothing. I feel like my wife, even on a dependent visa, has more control over her time and activities than I do in this glorious job. Apparently, I can hire people, but in the past three years, I have made one hire that I wanted. Every other hire was overturned. It's stressful and frustrating, but then there is hope that someday I will be in control. That's how they get you. But you can't talk about this to anyone. You can come off as a weakling.

The constraints of the visa and the long path to permanent residency, as explored above, induce powerlessness and the feeling of being stuck between a rock and a hard place. This feeling, as identified by Kaushik, was common among participants, even among those who performed bravado in their work to reestablish the model-minority framework. But what Kaushik highlighted here, which was not being explicitly articulated by anyone else, is the paradox that encumbered the lives of the tech workers—the paradox of feeling pressure to inhabit a masculine orientation at work and feeling emasculated at the same time because of the iron clasp of the visa regime. As Kaushik said, he was supposed to at least pretend that he was in charge and not appear to be a "weakling."

And yet he felt less in charge of his time than his wife and thus felt emasculated. For immigrant tech workers, the structure and demands of tech work was at odds with the conditions of the visa regime. One demanded a performance of control and masculine prowess, whereas the other took that ability away from immigrant workers by making them vulnerable to legal disciplining that ensured that they would be model immigrant workers—quiet, obedient, and outwardly friendly.

Nurses and Unspoken Indentureship

The discrimination that the tech workers experienced resulted mostly from their legal status in the United States and what the work demanded of them. The struggle to reconcile the paradox of such an existence was central to shaping their subjectivities as immigrant workers in the United States. The nurses, by contrast, carried the entire burden of their intersectional identities as they navigated personal lives with their families and as immigrant nurses of color.

Nurses on H-1B visas spoke about the exploitation, the isolation, and the overt racism they faced at work, which also affected their family lives. Gina, who arrived on an H-1B visa, said that her recruitment agency told her that she would be paid less than her American counterparts because "that's just the way it is" and because nurses were expected to work their way to more pay. Rosy told me that H-1B nurses were usually paid the minimum that is required for the H-1B visa, or $35,000 plus benefits, "which is much less than what US-born nurses make." American Association of Colleges of Nursing statistics from January 2014 show that, while the median income of American nurses varied across states,[36] the average salary for registered nurses (RNs) in the United States was $66,620, while the average for RNs with a bachelor of science in nursing was $75,484.[37]

Another problem highlighted by the nurses on H-1B visas was also troubling: if they did not perform what was expected, they could be moved to another branch of the hospital in a more rural area or to a different location. The nurses wanted to avoid this because it would mean moving their families and being uprooted from the community they had formed through churches in the Chicago area. At a national conference of Indian nurses, one session, on the migration process of

Indian nurses, focused on the exploitation of immigrant nurses on H-1B and EB-3 visas as well as unethical recruitment practices. One of the speakers, Dr. Patricia Pittman, professor at the medical center of George Washington University, spoke about her work with the labor department to stop such practices. Stopping such practices, both historically and in the present, has led to a temporary moratorium on visas for Indian nurses and the migration of Indian nurses to the United States. The Indian nurses at the conference were quite vocal about the unfairness of this line of action. One of the leaders of the organization said, "Stopping nurses from coming to the [United States] is further punishing the nurses and their families instead of the corrupt agencies and hospitals." For nurses, their visa status was only one part of the discrimination they faced at work. It was the intersection of their social identities that shaped the totality of their experiences. Unlike tech workers, they did not struggle with the paradox of reconciling gender identities at work with visa statuses. Multiple aspects of their identities—being immigrants, being women of color with families, and working in nursing—all shaped their subjectivities as well as their experiences as workers.

Beyond the nurses with H-1B visa, nurses with green cards (or lawful permanent residence) and even nurses who had become naturalized citizens all felt that their social location as immigrant women nurses were instrumental in shaping their experiences at work. When asked about her experiences, Josi, a permanent resident, commented:

> It is okay. I get more respect here as a nurse than in India, and more pay, but we are still immigrant nurses. Even though I have a bachelor of science in nursing, I have been a floor nurse and bedside nurse for years, but I see when it is an American nurse, they become administrators in two years. And then, you know, the patients hate us. They say, "We don't want these brown nurses. They don't know anything. They can't speak," but we cannot be angry with them, we are there to take care of them. And whether we have visa or not, we always get the bad shifts! As immigrant nurses we are always threatened with firing and sending us to other locations, and as the main earner, I can't take those risks. I can't make my family suffer, so we just let everything go.

Like Jenny, most of the nurses understood the expectations of work through a gendered and racialized lens—that is to say, as women nurses from South Asia, they are expected to be more nurturing and caring while taking care of their patients, even when they have a higher glass ceiling than their American counterparts and their patients racialize them in the unkindest and most discriminatory ways.[38] Amy, a nurse who made house calls, told me: "The reason patients like Indian nurses was because they were so caring and went beyond the call of duty, and even when they are bad to us, we are not [bad to them]." The women I interviewed so consistently performed this feminized professional identity—involving silent caring and nurturing—that it seemed almost as though an organizational mandate governed how Indian nurses had to conduct themselves. At the national conference of Indian nurses, one of the keynote speakers noted how words such as "loving," "caring," "nurturing," and "healing" were markers of Indian nursing ethics.

Despite their hard work, nurses felt underappreciated by their superiors. Sheila, a permanent resident who arrived in the United States from Kuwait seven years prior to our communication, had been a nurse in her home country. She told me that, even though she never complained and took care of her patients with all her heart, her boss—a white woman and an important administrator—had repeatedly mistreated her over a three-year span. Her boss had assigned her to night shifts, insulted her, and laughed at her English and the lack of her knowledge of American culture. "It was almost as if she hated me," she said. She was never given a raise, and her applications for leave were never approved. When I asked whether she had reported this to anyone, she said:

> I have not even said this to my husband. I just keep it all in me and pray that this woman leaves soon. My husband does so much for the family. I can't burden him with this, and if I tell him this, he will ask me to leave my job, and I don't want to do that. And then my hospital is so close to my home that I can come home on my breaks. I was working 45 miles away for five years, and I don't want to do that anymore. And it is hard for us immigrant nurses to get the job we like and where we like. And it is always that we immigrant nurses are first to be fired. If I said anything, I would be fired, and that's the end of it, so what's the point?

Sheila's experience was harsher compared to the other nurses, but such issues were common across the board. Many were mistreated by bosses, coworkers, and patients. Even nurses who did not experience overt discrimination identified the constant sense of threat and the fear of being fired. Almost all the nurses complained about how hard it was to be promoted as immigrant nurses. An Indian American nurse administrator told me that it took her five years longer than her less qualified white American colleagues to become a nurse administrator. "I was lucky to be born here, not to have an accent—the only reason I probably became an administrator. If I was a nurse coming from India, even if I had all the qualifications, I would probably be a floor nurse forever."

The issues of accents and cultural integration were sore points for the nurses. Not being able to pick up on American cultural references alienated them from American colleagues and patients. The immigrant nurses felt socially isolated. In Carolyn's words:

> My American colleagues are more interested in their pets and pets of their friends and talking about *Friends* and *Sex and the City* [TV shows] than if I talk about my children. I don't have pets, and I don't have time to watch TV. So, I don't know how to respond to them. So, they think I am dumb. They talk to each other and not me. And they keep asking "what, what" [*simulates a nasal Midwestern accent*]. It's embarrassing for me. So, I keep quiet. It is like I don't exist.

The struggle for inclusion was experienced by the nurses and the tech workers in a similar manner. The nurses worked in more diverse spaces depending on the location of their facility; the tech workers worked mostly with other Indian tech workers.

The immigration statuses of the nurses were not uniform in this study. But every nurse indicated that immigration status was still the primary lens through which they understood their experiences as a migrant care worker in the United States. My analysis shows that nurses faced more cumulative disadvantages compared to the men professional workers in the workplace. For nurses, the outcomes of being an ideal immigrant worker (always being on call) were distinctly different compared to the outcomes for tech workers. Even when visa status was used to force the tech workers to work longer days, if immigrant men lived up to the expectation of being ideal workers, they were often rewarded with pay raises and promotions. By contrast, nurses were expected to always be on call as well as docile, obedient, nurturing, and kind. For advancement at work and pay increments, docility was crucial. If nurses showed resistance, they could be assigned to undesirable shifts, reassigned to undesirable locations, or even fired. They were consistently confined to the same position—that of floor nurse or bedside nurse— for years, whereas their American counterparts were promoted, as Adia Wingfield[39] shows in her book *Flatlining*. The glass ceiling for immigrant nurses was clearly much higher than it was for immigrant high-tech workers. I argue that, although immigration status disadvantaged both tech workers and nurses, the nurses faced gendered racism. Being an Indian worker did not hurt the prospects of the tech workers in the same ways that it hurt the prospects of the nurses. Given the feminized nature of nursing work, the demands of the work from the nurses was intersectionally more gendered and racialized. Additionally, nurses were expected to do more domestic labor in their homes (as shown in chapter 4). The nurses I observed in this study had to negotiate more layers of oppression and dependency.

Work-Family Dynamics and Visa Regimes

Nurses' Perspectives

Much of the discussion about work visas revolved around the relationship to dependent visas, which the spouses held. When I asked participants about their experiences as immigrant nurses, they presented a complex view of the dynamic between work and family lives. They almost always referenced their families and their own role in the family when talking about work and the constraints they faced as women immigrant workers.

A unique dimension of the structure of dependence created by the visa regime became apparent when the nurses talked about their own visa category in relation to the visa category of their spouses. Nurses expressed guilt and angst because they felt they were the reason for their husbands' dependent status. Alma, speaking of how she felt about her husband being on a dependent visa, said: "It eats me up. I hate it that he had to come as a dependent due to me. I feel ashamed to say this to my friends and family. I try my best so that he does not feel it." Unlike the men tech workers—who predominantly did not view their wives' decisions to move to the United States on dependent visas as a sacrifice that the wives made for the husbands' careers—almost all the nurses said that it was because of their husbands' "permission" and "sacrifice" that they were able to work and have a career. For example, Mary said: "It was because he sacrificed, and he gave me permission that I could take this job. He did it for our family, but I don't know many men who would make such a sacrifice. I am very grateful to him." The feelings of gratitude felt by the nurses was part of their internalized gendered emotion because they believed intrinsically that they were undeserving of their breadwinning status within the household.

This sense of guilt and constraint was aggravated by immigration status and conditions at their workplaces. About a third of the nurses I interviewed arrived on H-1B visas, a third on EB-3 visas, and the rest as permanent residents upon marriage with their current spouses. The nurses who arrived in the United States on H-1B and EB-3 visas were placed by commercial recruitment agencies, which was not without cost. It often meant lower pay, hefty fees to the agencies, and binding contracts with employers. Penalties for breaking a contract were severe and could cost the employee anywhere between US$20,000 and US$50,000 at the time I conducted the research. The high cost of breaking such a contract has been widely documented by other scholars studying nursing migration.[40] It is also well documented that foreign nurses are often given salaries and assigned sites, shifts, and workdays that are unattractive to native-born nurses.[41]

Missy's story testifies to how recruitment practices and visa structures control both the paid work and the families of nurses. Missy arrived in the United States in 2007 on an EB-3 visa obtained through a recruitment agency. I met Missy, 27, a registered nurse, in the afternoon of December 23, 2011. Missy worked in a hospital located in a northwestern suburb of Chicago. I waited for her in the hospital's lounge. It was my fourth attempt to meet her.

Missy was working extra shifts and extended hours during the holiday season because the "American nurses" were on leave. Missy was assigned to an emergency patient during the time of the interview, so I had to wait for more than an hour. She arrived in her blue nursing scrubs, seeming rushed. She asked me whether it was okay if she ate her lunch during the interview, as she had not had a chance to take a lunch break that day. Because I felt as though I was encroaching on her free time, I asked if she would like to reschedule again, but Missy told me that she would be working through Christmas and New Year's and then would take a four-day leave to visit family in Florida. There would not be a more convenient time to talk. I asked her whether she chose to work through the holidays and would be paid more for her time. In a hushed voice, looking over her shoulder, she said:

> Oh, no! You know we are immigrant nurses, and since we are on visas, we get the worst shifts no one wants! That was in our contracts with the agency. We work any shifts we are asked to. Right now, in my floor, there are only two nurses—me and another Filipina nurse—and today I was suddenly assigned to the emergency-patient floor. It has been just crazy, you know? I want to leave this job, but I can't for the next three years because otherwise I have to pay the agency $30,000. How will I pay them that money? I already gave them extra money to find me a job near Chicago because my aunty lives here. That was the term of the contract. You know, a friend of mine—you should talk to her—who worked with me in India and came with me through another agency was sent to a small hospital in a village in Texas, and her working hours were even worse. She was forced to stay in an agency-rented place with other nurses, and she could not even bring her husband and children, and she was also pregnant, so she wanted to leave the job, but she had to pay $50,000. They had to sell their house in Kerala to come up with the money. Now she works in a city hospital, but her husband is still not here. I feel so bad for her, just talk to her.

Missy's description of her working conditions reconfirms what others had said about immigrant nurses being assigned the worst shifts. In addition, Missy explained the mechanisms through which such discrimination was made possible. It was part of the contract she and others like her signed during the migration process through their recruitment agencies. Missy had two young children. Her husband emigrated to the United States on the EB-4 visa and so was legally allowed to work. But he decided not to look for a job and to stay home for a few years to take care of the kids. Missy told me that, given her work pressures, his decision to stay home to help raise the children was the optimal choice because her husband would probably find an "average job," and sustaining her income was more important for the survival of the family. She also said:

> Without him at home, there is no way I could keep the hours I am keep-
> ing. It creates a lot of stress, but I am lucky to have an understanding hus-
> band. Everyone is not that lucky, and this is why the agency prefers nurses
> whose husbands are willing to come with them, or unmarried nurses,
> because otherwise this kind of work is just not possible.

What Missy adds here is theoretically key to how the work of skilled migrants is structured in the United States. It is either assumed that workers have a full-time caregiver at home—in Missy's case, her "understanding husband"—or that they have no caregiving responsibilities because they are unmarried women. This logic is emblematic of the purpose that dependent visas serve whether by design or not: it ensures a steady supply of supposedly unencumbered ideal immigrant workers.

In my conversation with Missy's friend and other nurses, all on H-1B visas, I discovered that far fewer preferred arriving on H-1B visas, as they generally experienced more exploitative working conditions and had greater difficulty balancing work life and family life. Rose, who arrived on a H-1B visa to work in a rural Texas hospital via a recruitment agency, told me that according to her contract she had to live with other nurses in housing arranged by the agency, which required her to pay rent back to the agency, which she learned was much higher than rent for compa-rable housing in the area. This stopped her from bringing her family— her husband and three-year-old child. Out of fear that her contract would be terminated, and that she would have to pay exorbitant fees for break-ing the contract, Rose did not tell her recruiters when she found out she was pregnant soon after she arrived in the United States. Ultimately, she decided to terminate the contract and paid the fees to do so. Then she changed jobs so that her husband and child could come to the United States.

I met Rose in her one-bedroom apartment in a Texas city in October 2010. Her apartment was unlike any of the other nurses' houses I had visited. It was small and had barely any furniture other than a tiny dining table and two lounge chairs. The walls of the living room had pictures of her daughter and one large wedding picture of her with her husband. On a little side table, in the space meant for a television, there was a shrine to the Virgin Mary.

Rose told me that her husband refused to come to the United States on the dependent visa, so after she had her second child here, she went back to India to leave the newborn with her husband. Her work schedule would not afford her the time necessary to care for an infant. She said she could not afford child care because she had hired a lawyer to expedite her green card process (permanent residency) with the goal of having her husband and children come to the United States as soon as possible. Pointing to the shrine, she said:

> I pray day and night that my husband and children can come here quickly. My heart bled to leave my tiny baby in India. They have the whole family, the grandparents, uncles, and aunts to take care of them, but, you know, children need their mother, and I need them more. [Rose paused for a long moment, sobbing.] I feel like a terrible and a heartless mother, but I did this for my family. I know once they come, they will have a good life. Kerala is so less developed and poor. The kids would have no chance there. They will be like my husband and me; when I have this chance, I want to give them a better life. I wish my husband would come, but, you know, he is a man: How can he come as a dependent? He had no problem taking care of the children, but he just does not want to be called "dependent," but I think God has listened to my prayers! I think they will be here in March! I hope so! [Rose smiles for a moment in silence.] It is so lonely here, you know?

Rose was one of two nurse participants who had a transnational family because of the visa restrictions combined with the structure of nursing work for immigrants; almost all the nurse participants, at some point, either experienced or considered transnational living. As feminist transnational scholars[42] of migration have shown, many women immigrant workers find themselves negotiating transnational families and transnational mothering, which is emotionally vacuous and physically taxing for the mothers. The burden of transnationality is accentuated by the isolation and racism that immigrant nurses face at work. Rose continued:

> My hospital has only one other Indian nurse, and other nurses don't talk to me. They say they don't understand how I speak English. The patients are bad to me because it is natural that they don't like foreign nurses and I am new, so I am a little scared. And I always get the night shifts and extended hours, and when I am home, I feel so alone and tired. And then my family in India does not understand why I have to work night shifts! They think badly of me! But I bite my lip and do what I have to. I try to be the best I can for the sake of my family. I don't know anyone here, I have no family, I can't talk to anyone! I just come home and cry to God and then go back to work. [Rose begins to cry again.] I am just waiting for my family to come. That is my dream. I want to give them the best life possible.

Unlike tech workers, nurses tended to blame their perceived inability to assimilate for the discrimination that they faced at work. They blamed their accents and their cultural lag for the exclusion and affront they faced. They embraced the suffering as inevitable for what they have to endure as a woman and as a breadwinner for the betterment of their families and, in Rose's case, to be reunited with her family.

The nurses attempted to submerge the onslaught of inequities they faced in their aspirations for a better future. The power of aspiration created by the neoliberal capitalist project of "manufacturing consumerist dreams," as Anna Guevarra[43] contends, douses any resistance that might emerge from the oppression. Instead, it repurposes aspiration to build the model-minority family that the racial structure of the United States expects of them. What is distinct for the nurses is their focus on the betterment of the family, in contrast to the discourse of personal growth and development so present among the tech workers and their spouses.

Tech Workers' Perspectives

Tech workers often treated work as separate from the conditions imposed by their own work visas and their spouses' dependent visas. When talking about work, the men habitually ventured into minute technical details of the actual computer coding they did (which most of the time was beyond my knowledge or understanding). They also talked about their experiences at work in relation to immigration status. So, I pushed them to think about what their visa status meant in the context of the entirety of their experiences in the new country. For instance, I would ask: "How does the H-1B visa inform other parts of your everyday lives?" It was in response to this question that tech workers drew a connection between their own visas and the visas of their wives and talked in more detail about the interplay of paid work versus the unpaid work done by their wives.

The tech workers communicated a perception regarding dependent visas that was different from the nurses' perceptions. Most men indicated that the constraints of their visa status not only affected them personally but also extended to their family because of how inextricably visa status was intertwined with the dependency status of the spouse. The tech workers understood the relationship between the work visa and the dependent visa from a perspective of work dependency and the impact on their work lives, as exemplified in the conversations we had about their understandings of the visas. When asked what his work and his visa status meant to him, Rex, a high-profile financial analyst at a large consulting firm, said:

> Come to think of it, they own me through my visa, but actually, they not only own me and my work, I feel like they also own my wife's work. They paid for her visa and her passage, and so they expect me to have no family obligations. I have a job that has me travel for five days a week, and sometimes I am away for months. We have a four-year-old. There is absolutely no recognition that I have a family that might need me, that I have responsibilities of being a father. One time, my wife was sick while I was in New York. I requested a two-day leave so that I could come back and take care of our son. I was denied the leave. I was not explicitly told that it was because I had a wife at home, but it was like, "We don't care about your family. You need to have that taken care of. We only care about how much work we can get from you."

Most high-tech workers had reflected deeply on their situation at work. They understood the pressure and, as Rex put it, the "fear of bondage" and servitude that their visa situation produced. In addition to the perception of servitude, the tech-worker participants, as Rex previously articulated, felt that the recruiting companies owned not only their labor but also the labor of their dependent spouses. Shobhit, a computer programmer at a large bank, said:

> My company paid for my family to come here. Do you think that was for nothing? They expect us to be in office as long as they need us to be there. They know I have a wife at home on a dependent visa who will take care of the family.

Adding to this sentiment, Sambit said:

> I feel like a glorified servant. I have so little power to change my situation. . . . The fact that my family was allowed here, and my company paid for it—I got a job in Belgium in the same company and they don't allow dependents to come—creates an additional pressure. It is as if now they own the entire family. I am grateful that I could have my wife and my kid here, but nothing is free in this free market, you know? Everything comes [at a] cost.

When I asked Sambit whether this sentiment was conveyed to him by his bosses, often white Americans, he said:

> Not directly, but I know of people who have been fired because they stuck to the 9 a.m. to 5 p.m. routine and did not go beyond. That is a lot of duress to work under. You are the single earner in the family, so you are completely responsible for their well-being. My wife sacrificed her bright career for me, and so I can't fail even if that means being an absentee father and a husband. It's not like I can find another job if I am fired. If I am fired, my entire family loses legal status, and we have to run back to India at the earliest. And if I am fired here, my mother company fires me too, and I don't get passage money back, and I don't have a job here *or* there. This is too stressful. And I also support my parents so I am pretty screwed! This is why you will find IT workers moving around with stressed-out *ullu* [Hindi for owl] faces! [Sambit laughs.] Not our fault though.

On a similar note, another tech worker, Akash, said:

> I can't say I am unhappy here. I don't have to deal with the dirty corporate politics like in India, but yes. . . . If my white boss's dog is sick, he takes off at midday, but I can't take off even when my baby is sick. They know I have a wife at home who will take care of the issue.

By revealing that their employers are aware of the dependent status of their wives, Rex Sambit, Shobhit, and Akash are underscoring how their wives' dependent visas are inextricably linked to their own work lives. Further, the theme of extreme stress as the only breadwinners, and of being absentee fathers and husbands, came up several times. In Marianne Cooper's[44] research, some of the white American tech fathers also articulated a sense of loss at not being present in their children's lives because of work; for the Indian tech workers, being an absentee father was typically seen as a necessary condition of being the ideal migrant worker. Sambit's description of the consequences of getting fired highlights how visa status is used to control work hours and illustrates the multiple dimensions of dependence that migrant families face. Just as many tech workers viewed being an absentee father as a necessary evil that helped ensure a degree of stability in employment, they also viewed their dependent spouses' unpaid labor at home as necessary to construct the image of the ideal migrant worker—an image uniformly perceived to be key to success in the American tech market. Shobhit explains:

> It is a lot of work and stressful, but the payback . . . is good, I would say. I have gotten many quick promotions in the last 10 years that many of my counterparts, even Americans, have not, but that is because I have not taken even a day of leave besides what I have [been] allotted, if that. I could only do this, of course, because my wife is on dependent visa and I don't have to worry on the house side.

Here, Shobhit clearly articulates the relationship between his success at work and his ability to ignore his responsibilities at home because of his wife's visa status. Satya, another IT worker, thought it was very unfortunate that his wife had to quit her job. Satya and his wife had the same jobs in India at the same company, but Satya was offered the opportunity to take an offshore position, but she was not. Still, he reasoned that, given the circumstances he encountered on his arrival in America, it was probably a good thing that while one spouse worked, the other stayed home. His employers' expectations concerning time commitments at work would have made it all but impossible for him to chip in at home and help with housework, cooking, or raising a toddler, which he recognized as a full-time job. He further explained:

> I just see it as a sacrifice we as a family make so that we can do well here, and doing well means proving myself as a good and wanted employee. Why do you think American companies like Indians so much? Because we do the least hanky-panky about family time and all that. I go in and do my work, give the best I have, and my bosses absolutely love me as an employee. You don't want to bring a bad name to Indian workers, and, yes, that means sacrificing family life to a certain extent, but you do what you got to do.

Satya's and Shobhit's understandings of what it means to be an ideal migrant worker were deeply entwined with the expectations that mainstream America holds for model minorities, viewing them as obedient minorities with high human capital who refrain from claiming personal or family time at work.[45]

The accounts presented by the tech workers about how their own visa status is intertwined with their wives' visa status demonstrate that the perception of the "ideal worker," or what it means to a be successful migrant worker, hinges squarely on performing a narrative of the self that is both wholly free from family responsibilities and able to invest an unlimited amount of labor time. This creates traditionally gendered organizational expectations, assumes a gendered family structure, and marks men's labor as paid and women's labor as unpaid.[46] Additionally, these visa regimes, which govern the lives of high-tech workers and their spouses, racialize the labor the workers and their spouses perform.

Visa regimes create multiple dimensions of dependence for both immigrant nurses and immigrant tech workers. These dimensions of dependence are embedded in the structures of power governing the lives of migrant workers. The presence of these dimensions of dependence indicates that there are unintended yet insidious consequences stemming from state policies that aid the corporate and state exploitation of migrant workers and their families.

Despite the internalization of the model-minority discourse by the lead migrants and their families, the narratives of struggle, readjustment, and conflict common to the experience of all my participants undermine the discourse of the model minority. Their lives and struggles dispel the model-minority myth framed by the rhetoric of opportunity, choice, and stable and happy Asian Indian immigrant workers and families common in master narratives of the US social structure. These struggles illuminate the multiple layers of dependence to which both the lead migrants and their dependent spouses—particularly women immigrants—are subjected in the course of the migration process.

Conclusion

Visas become tools of exploitation as they regulate migrant subjects in multiple ways, creating anxiety around reapplication and reapproval and outright fear over rejection. This affects the lives and subjectivities of immigrants in real ways. This analysis of the effects of employment-based visas illustrates the creation of what I call multiple invisible "structures of dependence." My analysis shows how government-sanctioned visas, issued to large corporations to import skilled labor, create conditions of exploitation and oppression for migrant workers at work. Visas put legal migrants in a position of legal liminality by functioning as a mechanism for controlling both their labor and their lives. At the same time, highly skilled Indian immigrants come with the added burden of living up to racialized expectations of being a model minority and gendered expectations of being an ideal worker. These expectations and their performances play out differently for the nurses and the tech workers. The way the tech workers frame their gendered subjectivity at work has parallels with Gerstel and Clawson's[47] research, in which they found that male doctors recognized the need to be more involved at home while using the gendered frame of being the family provider to justify spending long hours at work away from their families. The nurses in their study, much as in this book, recognized they were doing double shifts but still fell back on gendered cultural scripts to justify their high level of involvement at home. However, in my study, the nurses felt guilty about being the main breadwinners and bringing their husbands to the United States as dependents—and therefore they blamed themselves for their circumstances. The tech workers, meanwhile, because of their masculine ideas around deservingness, more readily identified structural inequities—the visa regime and the racialized workplace—to be the source of the challenges they faced at work rather than blaming themselves.

Despite these gendered differences in perceptions of inequity, both groups experienced the lasting negative impacts of a visa regime founded on a gendered and racialized understanding of immigration status of migrant workers and their families. The visa regime creates and supports intersectionally oppressive conditions of work for immigrant workers.[48] Indian tech workers face racialized exploitation as foreign workers. They are often held hostage to the liminality of their legal status in the United States. Further, the H-4 visas given to the wives of high-tech workers heighten the sense of constraint for tech workers, who perceive their wives' unpaid labor as instrumental in constructing the image of an ideal immigrant worker. The nurses, as representatives of migrant professional labor, experience racism at work while dealing with gendered expectations of caregiving both at home and at work, creating a more complex condition of inequality for them compared to tech workers. They faced more severe demands as so-called ideal workers and experienced stronger glass ceilings as immigrant women. The experiences of the nurses in my study reflects Glenn's[49] argument that immigrants and women of color have historically been coerced into paid and unpaid care labor, a form of labor that is feminized and that demands docility, obedience, and servitude. This form of labor historically has severely constrained the rights of immigrant women and women of color because it affords little or no protection from the state. Also, as chapter 4 will show, the paid labor that makes workers "ideal" hinges on the unpaid labor performed at home by women and is therefore usually unavailable to women breadwinners.

4

At Home

Dependent Spouses and Divisions of Labor

[Immigration reform is] an economic issue, too, but it is at
its heart a family issue.
—Hillary Clinton, May 5, 2015

It was dinnertime on a cold March evening in the spring of 2012. I sat
at Naureen's kitchen table while she reheated leftover pizza for her children. She had migrated to the United States on a dependent visa with
her husband, who was a head software engineer at a major financial
institution. As we talked, she said she was frustrated with her life and
explained: "You see, I am the cook, the chauffeur, the housekeeper, the
teacher. . . . what I was supposed to be was a lawyer, but as an immigrant in this country, my job is defined by my visa." Naureen juggled
her duties during the interview, keeping an eye on her two elementary-
school children while preparing their dinner. When dinner was ready,
she asked to stop the interview to feed her children and get them ready
for bed before running to pick up her husband from the commuter train
(Metra) station. He had worked a long day outside the home, while she
did the same inside the home. As she drove away to pick up her husband, I sat at their kitchen table making small talk with the children.
However, I couldn't help but silently observe and ponder the stressors
that the dependent visa brought to this family.

When Naureen returned with her husband, Aasmaan, she quickly
prepared him tea, as he grabbed some snacks and play-chased after his
children to the basement. During this time, I finished interviewing Naureen. Over the soft sound of her rollicking children floating in from the
basement, Naureen lowered her voice and whispered to me at one point
as we were wrapping up the interview: "I never thought when I was getting all those degrees that this is what my life was going to be, and it's

nobody's fault. Aasmaan is so tired after a grueling day, I don't have the heart to ask him to help me. . . . You are seeing firsthand how immigration [status] dictates how we live."

After Naureen's interview, she directed me to the basement so that I could interview her husband. She hustled the kids upstairs to help them with homework, while I sat down to interview Aasmaan—me on the sofa, him on the floor in a conversation that would run 2.5 hours, until about 10 p.m. When the interview ended, Naureen had already put the kids to bed, and it was now time for Naureen and Aasmaan to eat dinner together. Naureen kindly invited me to join them, and I gratefully accepted. They also volunteered to be jointly interviewed as we ate together.

Aasmaan apologized over dinner for not helping prepare the meal, then looked at Naureen and laughed as he said: "I say sorry for not cooking almost every day. But then, I guess we both do exactly what we are supposed to do. I work my ass off at the office; she works like crazy at home. Given my job, I don't think we could have [it any other way]—this is probably [the] reason for these visas we have." Like many other couples among the tech families, Naureen and Aasmaan provided a detailed account about the paid and unpaid labor they performed as part of their transnational lives as immigrants in the United States. Upon my request, they graciously maintained time diaries of their daily chores, which they later shared with me. Before I loop back to Naureen and Aasmaan later in the chapter, I want to present another context of dependent domestic life in another family.

A few months after meeting with Naureen and Aasmaan, I visited George and Gina's rather large home in another Chicago suburb on an unusually chilly October afternoon. Gina was a nurse, and George, her husband, had joined her on a dependent visa. It was Gina's day off. I reached there right after the family of six—Gina, George, their three children (four, eight, and 10) and George's mother, who was visiting from India—had finished eating lunch. George opened the door to let me in. He was a tall man, with thick glasses, a moustache, a full head of thick, curly short hair oiled and brushed out neatly, and wearing a loose, striped light beige shirt and black pants. He told me Gina was in the kitchen cleaning and suggested I visit her in the kitchen. Gina was wearing a sequined pink *salwar kameez*, the traditional northern Indian women's attire, with her long hair plaited down her back, adorned with orange flowers. "I wear Indian clothes on my day off. Sick of wearing the same green scrubs every day," she said as she welcomed me to the kitchen and asked me to sit while she finished up. "You missed a grand Malaylee meal—kappa (spicy tapioca mash) and red fish curry and everything else I and Amma [her mother-in-law] cooked. You can stay for dinner; we have enough for everyone even for dinner."

I asked if she cooks such big meals every week. She nodded. "I am sick of wearing scrubs and eating dry sandwiches every day of the week. And I want my kids to know what our food is. So, I go all traditional on my days off." George took his leave of us at that point, saying he would be back after putting their youngest, the four-year-old, down for a nap. Meanwhile Amma, a woman in her early seventies, wearing an off-white, gold- and green-bordered saree with the same orange flowers in her hair, offered to make us some tea. I heard the kids chattering in the basement.

In my observations and interviews with nurses' families, I noted the importance the family, and particularly the nurses, placed on what I call a "gendered performance of culture," which the nurses did not view as oppressive or forced. The nurses often emphasized how much better their lives were from their mothers'. And the husbands took genuine pride in caring for children, which will be discussed at length later in this chapter.

After three intense hours of interviewing, Gina and George invited me to stay for coffee and appetizers. Gina and I sat at the kitchen table, drinking rich South Indian "filter coffee" and munching on an array of homemade Malayalee snacks, while George played basketball with their 10-year-old son in the front yard. Gina had talked about her mother at length during the interview. She showed me an old, sepia-tinted, black-and-white picture of her mother that she pulled out from her purse. Her mother was sitting by a banana tree in the courtyard of what Gina told me was the house she grew up in. While the woman in the picture had a full head of long black hair, she looked 60 and had noticeably blank and tired eyes. Gina told me her mother was 35 when the picture was taken. I was shocked but said nothing. She told me: "I always keep this picture with me, to remind myself of how much of a better life I have than what she had and how much sacrifice she made for us—that really eases much of my pain and puts what I and George have had to give up in perspective."

The stories of these two couples animate the household relationships of the two forms of family in this book. Naureen and Aasmaan represent households with breadwinner husbands and dependent wives, and Gina and George represent the inverse. The familial dynamics in each household were choreographed by the gendered nature of the visa laws, which influence interactions and exchanges that are shaped by internalized gendered scripts that are sometimes cultural, sometimes universal. However, perceptible differences between the two households existed as well. These differences were a function of the transnational histories emerging from variegated regional, religious, caste, and class statuses that co-constituted how gendered unpaid work happened in each of the two types of households. For instance, while Naureen and Gina both did much of the caregiving work despite their different visas and employment statuses, each discussed such work differently. Naureen, a Muslim woman, was more direct about how she felt forced to do unpaid domestic labor, perhaps because of her upbringing in Mumbai (an urban metropolis) in an upper-class family; Gina, a Christian woman, saw her double shift of paid and unpaid work as the cost of her breadwinner status, while also accepting the labor that permitted her to feel deserving of a life more emancipated than that of her mother, who still lived in a rural part of southern India.

I was able to observe and record these nuances because most participants opened their hearts, homes, and histories to me in the most generous ways. What was palpable in these historiographies of families was a seething discomfort, a sense of struggle that each member of the family experienced in their relationship with the work levied on them, whether as nurses or tech workers, by the visa regime they lived under. Some individuals and families were more troubled than others. But the strife was unmistakable. Naureen and Aasmaan, and similar couples, in both sets of families struggled to accommodate a structure of work that was imposed on them, even if the nature of the work was no different than in any other American nuclear family. What was also clear, from a closer look at the family lives of the participants, was how the household work that women spouses, irrespective of their visa statuses, performed in these families belabored the intersecting and yet hidden dependence structure imposed on them. This chapter sets out to unravel this hidden dependence structure by putting the households—and the unpaid work that goes on in these households—under a microscope in the context of the visa regime.

This dependence structure was made invisible through the varied, nuanced interplay of social and legal constructs. The racial regime that labels Indians a "model minority," along with the label "highly skilled workers" conferred on the main migrants (nurses and high-tech workers), projected a class location that was privileged and comfortable for the family—and disavowed any form of oppression these families might face. In the popular discourse, the reified role of the visa regime as an institution, which heightens gender-based inequalities within families, is buried. In reality, as participants in this study show, the visa regime further reinforces the gendered division of household labor that pervades the traditionalist construction of South Asian families and greatly imposes even more pressure toward gendered expectations and performance. The legal premise of the division of labor in the family as defined by the US immigration regime is based on a gendered and classed construction of family—including South Asian families and societies— and represents a heteropatriarchal social norm that espouses the universal dependence of women, particularly wives. Heteropatriarchy as espoused by Indigenous scholars[1] refers to the social systems in which the norms of heterosexuality and patriarchy are perceived as normal and natural and is enforced by a heteropaternal state that presumes a heterosexual nuclear domestic arrangement as the standard. The visa regime, I contend, lies at the junction of these regimes of power— gender, race, legal status, and heteropatriarchy—that directly affect intimate interactions and expectations in the families.

Feminist scholars[2] who have questioned the heterosexist construction of the family and unpaid labor contend that studying the typically gendered division of household labor provides insights into larger structural inequalities. For instance, the act of feeding the family ties women to a structure of nurturance that leads them to shoulder much of the care work at home,[3] and the unpaid labor that women perform at home in addition to their paid work shows that this second shift is predicated on women's work as deliverers of nurture, as demonstrated in Hochschild's[4] famous study. Acker[5] uses the work-family feminist analysis to show

how men shirk family responsibilities to become ideal workers, and Collins,[6] in centering Black families, contends that the labor of Black women in families is not only a function of their gender but also the product of the intersections of gender, race, class, and the nation. Since the end of the twentieth century, research taking on heteronormativity[7] extended the conceptualization of gendered unpaid labor to queer families. Carrington[8] shows how in lesbigay families the partner who takes on the nurturance work of feeding the family also does more of the caregiving work. Moore[9] contends that, in Black lesbian stepfamilies, the biological mother voluntarily takes on a larger caregiving role to maintain control within the household. And Pfeffer[10] demonstrates that ciswomen partners of transmen often take on more of the women's work at home, citing their partner's masculinity as oppositional to competence in feminine work. In the context of migration, gendered divisions of labor often take the form of compulsory heterosexuality[11] given that the immigration regimes are heteronormative and heteropaternalistic.[12]

Following the lead of these scholars, I walk into the everyday lives of the couples in this chapter. I, however, place this *everyday* into a multidimensional integrated framework of gender structure at the institutional, interactional, and individual levels[13] while establishing the implications of the gender regime for the visa regime.[14] In addition, I situate gender and race regimes in a globalized, postcolonial world[15] to interrogate the unpaid work done by the couples in the families—all in the service of unmasking the contours of dependence that are based in strictly heteronormative family configurations created by the visa regime.

I begin by reviewing the institutional constraints that a visa regime imposes on migrating individuals and families and then analyze how those constraints influence gendered selves and societal expectations of marriage and family. I seek to understand the co-constitutive nature of gender at various structural levels, given that the visa laws are allegedly gender-neutral or gender-blind. I specifically focus on the organization of household labor after migration and what it says about gendered selves and societal expectations. I conceptualize household labor as reproductive labor, including child care, plus any other form of unpaid care work performed by either spouse.[16] The analysis focuses on three overlapping questions: Does the visa regime affect or alter how gender is done in the families? How does visa-based dependence of men compare to dependence of women within the families? What does an analysis of unpaid work done in the household tell us about the intersections of the gender structure of families with the visa regime?

Institutional-Level Analysis: Immigrant Families and Gendered Policies:

As readers may recall from the discussion in chapter 2, the formal definitions of the skilled workers' temporary nonimmigrant (or H-1B) visa, according to United States Immigration and Citizenship Services, state that the H-1B "applies to people who wish to perform services in a specialty occupation, services of exceptional merit." The EB-3 (or employment-based) immigrant visa is defined as the "immigrant visa preference category if you are a skilled worker, professional, or other worker whose job requires a minimum of two years training or work experience, not of a temporary or seasonal nature." Finally, the H-4 (dependent) visa states that the "spouse and unmarried children under 21 years of age of H-1B workers may seek admission in the H-4 non-immigrant classification. Family members in the H-4 nonimmigrant classification may not engage in employment in the United States."[17]

Noticeably, the definitions in the visa laws are not explicitly gendered and thus may be interpreted as gender-neutral or gender-blind. However, my interviews and archival research show that immigration experts as well as lawmakers, lawyers, activists, and the general public understand these laws as gendered and heteropatriarchal. In my discussion about the H-1B visas with immigration experts, it was often implied that that the recipients of these visas are mostly men. In talking about highly skilled workers, one immigration activist said: "We offer these men the opportunity to come develop their skills." In confirmation of this statement, the transcripts of public hearings and debates on the committee reports (House Report 112–292) on "H.R. 3012—Fairness For High-Skilled Immigrants Act Of 2011" showed that the public discourse on highly skilled migrants assumes that migrant skilled workers are all men. To quote one of the public-opinion statements: "It makes little sense for American employers who seek immigrant or non-immigrant visas for foreign skilled workers from India or China to have to wait longer. These [men] can easily take jobs elsewhere in the world." Another public opinion read: "[G]iven the economy here, we need to reconsider if we need more imported high-skilled men in U.S. companies." This last statement goes a step beyond gendering the skilled migration: it turns people into capital in the global marketplace. The general assumption, therefore, is that migrant high-skilled workers are men and their spouses on dependent visas are women, normalizing the heteronormative nature of visa laws. While it is statistically true that most recipients of the H-1B visas are men,[18] research, including my own,[19] demonstrates nurses also arrive in the United States as highly skilled migrants. The immigration experts I interviewed had to be reminded that nursing migration is led by women who brought dependent husbands and children.

In the discourse on dependent visas, the default assumption among immigration experts, the public, and legal opinion forums was that the dependent visa holders were women. The rhetoric of "ensuring stable families" was a common thread throughout arguments in support of the H-4 visa category in the public discourse. When a proposal[20] for making changes to H-1B skilled-worker visa laws was floated in Congress in 1996, one of the proposed amendments referred to easing the process of procuring H-4 dependent visas, particularly for tech workers. The most common argument in the five congressional hearings and the solicited public opinion on the proposed changes was that "ensuring stability in the families of transnational skilled labor" and "allowing the *wife*" to migrate was important for the well-being and productiveness of the transnational highly skilled employee. One of the statements of public opinion cited in a congressional hearing was: "Having a stable family, a warm home cooked meal, ensures that we get the best work out of the foreign employee." The formation of stable families through state mandates encouraging a traditional family structure—in which one spouse was a "traditional wife"—to garner the highest level of productivity from the migrant employee includes a neoliberal gendered assumption about highly skilled workers and dependent visa laws. The dependent visa holders themselves viewed the visa as oppressive and constraining and gave it various derogatory nicknames, such as the "vegetable visa" or the "prison visa" or the "handicap visa." Given the contradiction between the actual law and its interpretation, as well as the fact that women-led migration is part of highly skilled migration, I questions how institutional policies translate to the everyday lives of the transnational families bound by these visas. Does the creation and enforcement of such policies create stable families, as conceived in the public discourse? The analysis of gender at the individual and interactional levels of the gender structure in the context of the family provides a convincing and problematized response to my inquiry.

Internalized Scripts of Gendered Marriages and the Visa Regime

Internalized Gendered Scripts: Breadwinner Husbands and Dependent Wives

Chicago's icy wind mercilessly swept across our faces as Tona and I walked back to her apartment after an hour-long Bengali lunch. Tona was on a dependent visa, and her husband was a tech worker. One of Tona's preconditions for doing an interview with me was that I have a Bengali fish lunch with her in a new restaurant. Her husband, she told me, did not eat fish, and Bengali-style fish was her favorite cuisine. She explained, laughing: "I have not had fish in ages because my husband hates fish. I am conflicted between being a devoted wife and being my own woman." Over lunch on that cold day, she described the different hobbies she had enjoyed growing up in India, including long-distance biking, archery, playing soccer, and building toy cars. Her only hobby now was cooking, which she said "was the last thing I ever wanted to do." As we walked toward her apartment, boots pounding the snowy pavement, I asked her why she did not pick up one of her many hobbies besides cooking. "I don't know," Tona replied. She added:

> When I first came here, it was cold and crazy, and I was not used to the Chicago winters. All I did all day was watch TV. I guess I watched a lot of Food Network. Like most girls, growing up, my idea of marriage was to have a "doll's house"—everything pretty and perfect—and then somewhere while doing the PhD in India, I forgot all about it. But then when I came here as a dependent, I became this complete housewife. And I fell back into the pink world of the doll's house. I invested all my energy in building this perfect home.

Indeed, Tona's "doll's house" was perfect on the surface. On the twenty-fifth floor of an apartment building that overlooked downtown Chicago on one side and the frozen lake on the other, Tona's living room was a three-dimensional portrait of an educated, upper-middle-class lifestyle. Dark wood bookshelves held books about art, photography, travel, feminism, and some fiction. The living room was decorated with paintings, vintage posters, and artsy masks, strategically placed indoor plants, comfortable vintage brown couches, and a ceramic bowl on the coffee table with bitter dark chocolate bark to munch on. When I complimented her home, she proudly responded: "It's mostly me, though I have to say Kaushik has wonderful taste and interest in home decor, unlike most men." Like Tona's, most homes of the tech-worker families were tastefully decorated, and the wife usually took the credit. Also, like Tona, many of the dependent wives talked about "learning to be housewives" upon migration while at the same time expressing deep unhappiness about their lives as dependents.

Why would well-educated women give up high-paying jobs in India to move to the United States on a visa with such restrictions? This was my question for the women such as Tona participating in my study. Most of their answers involved gendered scripts around meanings of marriage and family. This allowed them to justify their decisions. Mili, who had worked as a human resource manager in a multinational company in India, said:

> I did not know my life would stall after I came to this land of opportunities. I suddenly became this obedient, good housewife and just dedicated my life to keeping my husband happy. I have worked since I was 16 and lived by myself, supported my own education back in India. I never thought I would have to be so dependent economically and mentally. I call it the "H-4 syndrome."
>
> [At this point I asked: "You knew you were coming on dependent visa? Why did you choose to come?"] Well, once you are married, you are supposed to be with your husband and take care of him and his household. My dad and Ravish's family wanted me to join him ASAP after we got married. Not that I did not want to come, but had I known, I probably would rethink . . . and now those nuts want grandchildren. . . . I am not falling in that trap.

What Mili calls the "H-4 syndrome" refers to adapting to the role of a wife in a traditional marriage, which, for almost all of my participants, was a deeply embedded gendered and heteronormative trope that they were expected to adopt. The trope stipulates that the women must live with their husbands once married, no matter what the circumstances, as Mili and many other women in this study affirm. It is easy to interpret this form of apriorism as a gendered cultural script.[21] However, I contend that what we understand as internalized scripts would not have co-opted the lives of my participants but for the visa regime. Mili's label of "H-4 syndrome" refers to this dormant, internalized, gendered cultural script that crept into the lives of these women as a way of negotiating their legally defined dependent status while being shocked and stifled at the same time at the realization that they are reconciling to their lives being locked in this state for many years.

Mili provides a detailed account, while expressing genuine surprise at how quickly she transitioned from her strong identity as an independent career woman to being "just a wife":

It was quite amazing how quickly I learned to be *just a wife*. Learning to be a dependent is a wonderful thing [said in a sarcastic tone]. I wake up in the morning, make tea for my husband and myself, and fix his morning cereals. On the weekends, he makes the morning tea if he wakes up before me, which is rare, and then if I have not made lunch for him to take with the night before, I make that. And then he leaves. And then I think of multiple ways of filling up my day. So, then I go out for a run. Some days I would go do grocery. I come back, clean the house, talk to my folks in India, or look up stuff on the internet—things I can do. Then I cook lunch because Ravish often comes home for lunch, which is nice because I don't have to eat alone and then I cook dinner—yeah pretty much that. I tried to explore hobbies, but I don't really have hobbies, so I get bored with whatever I start pretty soon. You see my apartment with all these beautiful things—I spent hours decorating my house at one point, looking for nice stuff at reasonable prices, I learned to cook elaborate meals and try to make Ravish happy—that was sort of my reward. Can you imagine, I would dress up as did the other H-4 wives in our apartment building for our husbands to come home from work. Our lives had become all about pleasing our husbands. It took me a while to realize how crazy it was—when I did, I now think, *I was probably moving toward insanity.*

Mili's "thick description"[22] of what her day as a dependent wife looked like paints a picture of a lifestyle drawn from a deep-set archive of gender performance. She also explicitly expressed surprise and discomfort at how quickly she made this transition and how insistent her gender-normative side was, so much so that she called it "insanity." Her interpretation of her transformation points to the insidious sway of the visa regime in pushing this gendered identity onto the dependent visa holders. Mili's portrayal clearly followed gendered notions of what it means to be an ideal wife, and this role was contingent on being on a dependent visa and then primarily on her identity as a legal dependent, as defined by the visa. Even though these depictions are uncannily similar to description of white middle-class suburban "housewives" in 1950s America,[23] the difference is that most women on H-4 visas had experienced a life beyond that of a housewife and led independent lives before coming to the United states and becoming legal dependent. While much of what Mili described was part of normal chores for most of the dependent women, it was endorsed by the belief that if one is a married woman and not working, then one must follow traditional gender norms in household labor.

As the women justified their decision to choose family over career as a direct response to the visa regime, another narrative emerged. They often said that they decided to move to the United States with their husbands because that is expected in a traditional marriage. Uma, who holds an MBA degree and worked in upper management at a large financial firm in India, discussed her decision to move:

> It makes me crazy to be home all day. I feel I am wasting . . . my degree and my career, but I am also really happy taking care of husband and enjoy having a home and family. Simply put, I had to choose one—being with my husband or having a job. I picked the first, and I am not unhappy picking it, but I wish I did not have to choose.

When I asked Antara, who also has an MBA and worked at an investment bank before coming to the United States on a dependent visa, what made her leave her high-powered job to come on a dependent visa, she said:

I *chose* family over my career. Well, you marry so that you can build a family, and I never thought I would have to choose between working and creating a family, but that is what it has boiled down to. The weird part is, this is not my husband or his family asking me to quit the job—it is the United States of America. Our parents did want me to stay with my husband, and that was part of the pressure, but it was after all my choice. I wanted this life, but who knew after the first blush, I would be so intensely unhappy. And what is more tragic is that I only get to spend weekends with my husband since he is always traveling through the week on his consultancy job. We both are finance people, and we think about optimization, so I decided to have a baby while I was not working, but I know with the baby, my life will change as I ever knew it—not sure if for the better or worse. I hope better [*smiling*].

Mili, Uma, and Antara, like most of the women I interviewed, emphasized a "choice." However, they understood the choice to be a difficult one because they had to choose between "stable families" (as many lawmakers I interviewed for this project described Indian H-1B families) and successful careers.

The women on dependent visas clearly were forced into the perception that they were choosing to create stable, intact families at the expense of their own careers, when in fact they had little choice in the matter. The interaction of gendered cultural scripts around marriage with the visa regime created the illusion of a familiar and almost universal gendered discourse of supposed *choice* among the participants. It was a seemingly straightforward *choice* between having a career or being with their husbands after getting married, yet the reality was that, if they wanted to legally work for pay, they could not be in the same country with their husbands. The language of "choice" that the women deployed to explain their situation and decision to migrate was notable. They could easily have asserted that they did not have a choice in joining their husbands, given the difficulties associated with maintaining transnational families. This rhetoric of choosing family over career, I would contend, is a byproduct of the neoliberal discourse imposed on these women by institutions as well as people within their social circles. For instance, many women told me that they were often asked by their working friends why they *chose* to move despite knowing that they would be on dependent visas. As highly educated women with careers prior to migrating, they probably wanted to reject the notion that they did not have agency in their decision to move with or follow their husbands, and the language of choice was a convenient fallback to defend their decision.

Within this illusory mind-set of choice, many decided it would be a good opportunity to have children (if they didn't already have them) because of the dependent visa restrictions that prohibited paid employment. The logic was that they could use the forced sabbatical from work as an opportunity to start a family.

Of the 16 tech-worker families with children, 13 of the women participants told me that it was their decision to have a child because they wanted to make the best use of the time when they could not legally work. Antara, who had an MBA and had worked as a midlevel manager at a large multinational company in Mumbai, India, felt conflicted about the decision to have a family:

> I was like, *gosh, I can't live a life of doing nothing*. I wanted to do something productive, so I decided to have a kid. Reproduce, that is [laughing]. Anik was so apprehensive. He did not think we made enough to have a kid right now, but I was like, "No, no I will raise the kid in these years I am not allowed to work so that as soon as we get our green card and I can go back to working, my kid is all grown up, and I don't get behind because I might need maternity leave." Well, has it been easy? No. I had to go back to India to have the child because Anik has no time. He does not get off even when he is sick—how would he help with the pregnancy? I traveled 4,000 miles by myself in my second trimester, and it was hell. I came back after Suhani was three months, after the first set of vaccinations. Anik saw his daughter when she was three months. He convinced his bosses [to allow him] to go fetch me and the baby, because I was very clear, I *cannot* travel alone with the baby. Even now, Anik hardly gets to spend time with Su, and I often feel like a single mom. I know it was not fair on him, Su, or me, frankly, but I am ready to endure all that. We eventually wanted a kid, and I could not think of a better time to have one. This way I won't be regretting these years of being at home because I have no choice.

As with most of the other women, Antara felt that she was able to exercise a choice in having a child when she had little choice in anything else in her life. Some women deployed traditional gendered logic to justify having a child, and they would say something such as "motherhood is part of being a woman" or "my parents wanted a grandkid." However, like Antara, many of the women mourned the absence of their husbands (the fathers of their children) from their children's lives because of the kind of work they had. Still, they then reaffirmed that "after all it's a woman's job to look after her child, more than a man's," as Nisha said, indicating her internalization of gendered ideologies of nurturing work. Some women went back to India to give birth or had their mothers come over from India to help through the pregnancy because the husbands were too busy at work to be involved in pre- and postnatal care. Yet the women emphasized that it was important for them to have the child right away. Women who made it clear they did not have a child because it was the "normal thing to do" or they were "being pressured by the family" said that they sought motherhood to feel they did something productive with their lives. This is also indicative of an internalized ideology of motherhood being associated with worth for women, generating an interesting form of binary—a middle-class, upper-caste woman can feel worthy either as a mother or as a professional and ideally would manage both with perfection. Anushree said the only thing she liked about being in the United States was that her parents and in-laws had less control over her and her spouse and that they could not pressure her into having a kid when she did not want to. She was happy that it was her decision and not theirs. However, she asserted, "I wish to be a great mother on my own terms not because my parents-in-law expect that of me. I also wish I could work as a great software developer as an MCA [masters in computer application] while being a perfect mother—but I don't have that option so I focus my energy on being a perfect mother." The impossible ideals placed on women in a neoliberal heteropatriarchy with an internalized rhetoric of choice and engrained gendered scripts of motherhood, to be perfect mothers and perfect paid worker, I contend, make the lives of H-4 women even more oppressive. If they were able to escape the internalization of these binarized scripts, they may have been able to find more agency in this situation.

However, when the dependent women do decide on motherhood as a self-proclaimed choice, they are vying to claim at least some agency over their lives. They assert they have control over the decision to have children, even though most of their responses when asked "Would you have a child now if you were working?" were "probably not." In most cases, the reproductive decision was the woman's, where she established control over her "wasted time" through reproduction almost as a protest against the restrictive visa regime.

Some women, though fewer in number, expressed more traditional views about household and reproductive labor. These women insisted that it was their job to take care of their husband and children and to do the household chores. In Jasleen's words: "It is wrong to expect husbands to do household work and take care of the child. It is my job, and I feel happy doing it. That is what my parents taught me. 'Just because we are educating you does not mean you forget your duties as woman,' they told me." Jasleen, who grew up in rural Punjab, a region in India infamous for discrimination against girls and women and female feticide and infanticide,[24] insisted that her parents were progressive in educating her. She said she was one of the few women in her region who had an undergraduate degree and a diploma in computer programming. Piyali, who grew up in semiurban West Bengal and had a masters in computer science, said:

> Even if I was working, I would make sure that I can still take care of my husband and kid the way I do now. It is my duty as a wife and a mother. I have been lucky to have a wonderful husband. You know I grew up in a conservative family, I was not allowed to even wear Western clothes, and my husband never stops me from doing anything. He has no demands, which is why I really want to do things for him. It does not mean I don't want to work. My parents sacrificed a lot in educating me, and I would not waste it. I will work as soon as I can, but it would go to my discredit if I can't take care of family well.

I do not have enough geographical diversity (in the context of India) in my sample to make an empirical claim about how regional differences (rural/urban, location, and demography of states of origin) affected the families' understandings of unpaid household work. However, my interviews do indicate that regional differences, particularly urban-versus-semiurban differences, led to the internalization of different gendered expectations, such that women raised in more rural areas verbalized a gendered cultural script passed to them from parents and families, whereas urban women deployed a rhetoric of choice when speaking about why they perform gender in the household—indicating a possible prevalence of a neoliberal hertropatriachal logic among urban women.

Saba Mahmood[25] contends that women in traditionally gendered societies derive what she calls "docile agency" by using traditional scripts to define happiness and give meaning to their gendered lives. However, most of the women in my sample were not raised to follow the traditional gender expectation of being homemakers. They were given the same education as their male counterparts—an education that would typically make them competitive in a technocratic labor market. The change in social expectations upon migration left the women negotiating many contradictory realities—current family situations, internalized gendered meanings of marriage, their educational and professional credentials, past successes, and the desire to be productive in the labor force.

The tech worker husbands also held strong internalized gendered notions about women's role in the family. Still, none of them expressed a desire for their wives to stay home if they had the opportunity to work. They expressed intense unhappiness about their wives' dependent statuses and at their being forced to "waste their education and careers." But at the same time, they also believed that women should prioritize family over work. When asked if they would have traded places with their wives if the roles were reversed, some men, particularly men from rural parts of India, explicitly said that they would not have chosen to come as a dependent man and suggested that "it's a woman's job to keep the family intact and the men's job to provide and protect the family." I am not suggesting that these men were more sexist than the others, however, because very few urban tech workers did anything to change the situation of their wives regardless of how they answered my hypothetical questions about role reversal. The men from rural parts were just less guarded and more upfront in expressing their gendered expectations. Most of the men rarely contributed to household work or child care or attempted to move to another country with better spouse dependency laws or return to India so that their wives could get back to work.

Men, particularly from upper-middle-class and caste urban India, used the rhetoric of choice liberally to justify their family situation. They liked to say—and likely believed—that it was their wives' choice to come to the United States on dependent visas. For instance, Rex, a high-level financial consultant, when asked about what he thought of his wife being on a dependent visa, said: "It was a *choice* for my wife whether to stay in India and keep her job or come here on a dependent visa. She *chose* the latter—she *chose* to build a family as every woman does and probably should. And I respected her *choice*." He uses the word "choice" three times: it was his wife who decided to migrate with him, and he had little to do with that decision (without, however, acknowledging the pressures his wife may have felt to make that choice).

Some men drew on traditional ideas about marriage, just as the women did, to justify the circumstances. When asked how he dealt with the fact that his wife used to have a higher position at work than him in India and was now not allowed to work, Ravi, a high-tech worker, ruefully and apologetically told me:

> I know the situation with our visas is completely unfair. My wife used to be my HR manager back in India, but when we married, we made a commitment of being together no matter what. We are Indians; to us marriage is sacred, not like the *goras* ["whites," meaning Americans] who marry for only the fun of it. We live through the fun and the pain and savor both but hold on. We as a family *learn* to deal with the hand we have been dealt. . . . We learn how to work with the dependent visa thing. What can I say?

A phrase Ravi used—"learning to be a dependent"—came up several times in my interviews with the legal dependents (men and women) in the two types of families. The notion of "learning to be dependents" was deeply tied to internalized ideas of gender and what it meant to be a dependent spouse in the context of a traditional heterosexual family. However, the ways in which the men and women understood gender was heavily shaped by their transnational social locations. Most families were dual-earner families back in India. However, the institutional policies that forced a state-imposed spousal dependence reorganized how the couples acknowledged their positions within the family. I found they relied on different gendered cultural tropes to make sense of their new status within the family. This differed significantly in the families of the high-tech workers versus the families of the nurses.

Similar patterns of internalized gender beliefs existed in the families of nurses among the dependent husbands and the nurse wives, albeit in different ways, depending on how the nurses and their husbands negotiated the hidden effects of a gendered visa regime.

Internalized Gendered Scripts: Breadwinner Wife and Dependent Husbands

It was a hot summer Saturday afternoon in a Chicago suburb. I was in the house of Shija, a floor nurse at a suburban hospital. I sat on a bar stool across the kitchen counter, sipping on chilled coconut water, interviewing Shija while she cooked for her family for the week. Saturday was Shija's only day off, and she asked me to come at that particular time because her husband had taken the children on a play date at a local park. Shija had four stovetops and an oven turned on. The air-conditioning was off. In the sweltering heat, the aroma from the Keralite food filled the house. As she cooked, she offered me a taste, and I happily accepted. During the interview, she told me that, even though it was hard to spend her only free day cooking, she felt good doing it. She explained:

> This is the only, most real way I can show my kids and my husband that I care for them. Also, I want my kids to grow up eating Malayalee food. It is a big part of who we are. I grew up eating my mother's home-cooked meals, and so should they.

This was a regular occurrence in their household. Only when Shija did not have a day off from work to cook for the week, her husband would take care of meals. Shija went on to explain that her husband did not contribute much to the cleaning in their large four-bedroom suburban house with a spacious living room and large kitchen. She explained: "He sometimes does, but because he does everything for the children, I try to do the other things myself."

This was the story in nearly every family among the nurses. Although the household labor was divided between the nurses and their husbands, the wives also worked full-time while their husbands did not or had minor part-time work. As part of my interview, I asked each of the spouses to keep a diary of time spent doing household chores. All the men, both tech workers and nurses' husbands, mostly evaded recording the time they spent doing housework. The time diaries showed that the nurses' husbands were spending about 25–30 hours per week caring for the children. However, the nurses were spending about 30–40 hours doing everything else. Like Shija, all the nurse participants said that, on days off, they did the majority of the cooking and cleaning for the family. Some of the nurses (11 out of the 30) had either their parents or their husbands' parents living with them; they often helped out, but the nurses still emphasized that cooking was primarily their own responsibility. When I asked whether this was something the family expected, most said they "felt good cooking for their families." Rosa, one of the nurses, told me: "This is the least I can do for my children and my family—give them food cooked by mom. I work so much that I am never home. This is the only way I can give them a mother's touch." Many of the nurses even opted for night shifts so that they did not feel like absentee mothers to the children during the day. Some participants felt it was just easier to take on domestic chores themselves rather than have to train their husbands. As Alma, another nurse, told me, it would be hard to teach her husband to cook because "he's never cooked or done anything in the house. It would be more work teaching him to cook, so I prefer cooking myself."

Given the hours that nurses were required to put in at work, they felt they were not fulfilling their mothering duties. In talking about their children and motherhood, many of the nurses broke down in tears, saying that they were "bad mothers" or that they were "losing out on the children's childhood." In a heartrending remark, Jenny said:

> I picked this life so that I have a better life than my mother, but now I am losing my children. I like it that they are close to their father, but my heart bleeds every time they run to their father when they need something and don't come to me even when I am there. It is like I am the person who makes money but is never there for them. That is not what a mother is— [trails off in sobs].

Here, Jenny's disavowal of her provider role because it stands in opposition to what motherhood is to her—an impossible ideal of gendered nurturance—because she sees the gendered reversal being forced on her family by the visa regime as an illustration of how unthought-out policy decisions causes more harm than good. Along the same lines, the nurses also expressed a deep sense of guilt and shame when their husbands had to accompany them to the United States on dependent visas. In their guilt, the nurses often tried to overcompensate. Alma shared that she has been doing night shifts for three years "so that the kids don't think their mom brings money and dad sits at home." Gina, whose husband was on a dependent visa, said:

> I was only able to come here because my husband decided to support me. It was more his decision to move here. It is because of his sacrifice that I am here, and I am being able to work. I have two kids, five and eight. If it were not for my husband, I would not be able to do anything. We all are all in it together—we just want our family to live better. I am very lucky to have Joseph as my husband.

Like Gina, other nurses whose husbands were dependents—either because of their visa status or because they were stay-at-home husbands and dads—tried to assert that the husbands were still the heads of the household despite their economic dependence. As a contrapuntal move to their breadwinning status in all of the families where the men were on dependent visas, the women handed the reins of the family finances to their husbands. Many of the nurses told me that they did not even know how much their salaries were and that the husbands "managed all money issues." Gina explained: "I only bring in the money, the rest is up to him." When I asked Lily what her income was, she said:

> I am not quite sure; you have to ask my husband. He is the one who handles all the money things. My salary goes into our account, and then he manages it—does what he thinks best. We are still a traditional Indian family. He is still the master of the house. Any major decisions about the kids or money, he takes those decisions. It is important for us as family to give him that respect. Just because he cannot work because of the visa, we

don't want him to feel he is not the head of the family. That's the secret of our strong marriage.

The nurses' emphasis on the men being the "head of the family" as the secret to a strong marriage shows the desire to maintain some semblance of the patriarchal familial structure that the dependent visa regime threatened to alter for the nurses' families. The insistence on cooking for the family betrays an internalized form of cultural gendered beliefs. Because they were immigrants, the nurses felt it important to impart, through food, the ethnic/regional culture to their children growing up in the United States. However, the nurses also construed "cooking for their children" as an essential element of motherhood. Opting for the night shift at work, working the second shift[26] at home, and handing over the finances to the husbands were all attempts to maintain the image of what they considered to be the traditional Indian family.[27] This was clearly important to the nurses, revealing a deep-seated heteropatriarchal commitment to what a family should look like.

This notion was reinforced by the dependent husbands. They harbored internalized understandings of masculinity that became pronounced as they relied on them to cope with their dependent status. Many of the men refused to come to the United States on dependent visas and preferred to live in India, visiting their wives in the United States once a year. All of this was in the service of escaping being labeled a "dependent spouse" and compromising their masculinity in the process. The husbands that did come as dependents tried to negate their dependency by emphasizing that it was because of their "support," "insistence," and "permission" that their wives were able to accept the jobs they had and come to the United States. George, Gina's husband on dependent visa, said:

When my wife got this opportunity, she was not sure if she should take it because you know, for a while, I won't be able to work. But I knew it was important for [our] children and family. I gave her permission to take the job, and then we moved here. It is easier because I can keep a watch on the children, and while this is a bad policy, it is the way. What can we do?

Another husband on a dependent visa said:

> As a man, I needed to make sure my family is okay, and my wife was getting this opportunity to help our family, and for that I would have to sacrifice a little, and I was ready for that. I don't think about these things. Government does what it has to—it is no point getting depressed about this. I am doing my duty of keeping my family secure. That is what a man should do.

This attempt to establish masculinity within the family by using the language of "permission" or "as a man" can be interpreted as a deep-seated gendered belief about a man's role in the family and also as a mechanism to cope with the perceived emasculation they experienced as dependent men. When they did claim to be contributing to housework as the dependent spouse, they expressed antipathy for having to do so. Shijo, a husband on an EB-34 visa with a work permit, stated:

> My wife works 40 to 60 hours depending on how much she is on call. She only has time to cook. I have to do the rest. No choice, *nah* [no]? When you marry a nurse, you know you will be servant of the house [laughs]. But see, I can never say this to my friends and family in Kerala because they laugh at me, say "you became a woman or what," but what will you do? If I earned like her, we get [a] maid but my English is not strong, and my diploma is not good here. So, I am staying home. I don't want to work in gas station like others. I want to start a business later. But for now, I am being houseboy.

The resentment expressed by Shijo about his changed role as the housekeeper was a common sentiment among most of the husbands of nurses, even when they held odd part-time jobs or engaged in informal self-employment. However, it was more pronounced among the few husbands who were on H-4 dependent visas. Johnny, an unemployed husband separated from his nurse wife, had been on H-4 status for five years and had become a permanent resident. Drunk at the time of the interview, he said:

> I agreed to marry Maria without dowry because I thought she was my ticket to being rich and escaping from Kerala poverty, but when people

have power, even a lamb acts like a tiger. That is what happened to Maria. It was the biggest mistake of my life; you better write that down— [trailing off].

Previous research[28] on nursing students in India also revealed that being a nurse saved them from paying a dowry because they were seen as potential income generators for the family. Johnny's drunkenness largely discounts his views, but I found similar (though less aggressive) rhetoric in my other interviews with men on H-4 visas. When I asked Joseph what his day looked like, he responded angrily:

Why do you even ask, to shame me? . . . I am like the wife, okay, I wake up in the morning, make tea, feed breakfast to my son, get him ready for school, and then drop him. My wife does night shift so by the time I come back, she is home and I warm breakfast for her; you are thinking, it should be the other way around—not in this house. And then she sleeps. I warm lunch, eat, clean the house, and do laundry, and then it is time to go pick up my son and take him for soccer, and then drop my wife at the hospital and do the evening chores and go to bed. That is my life, not what a man's life should be. But I see it as a sacrifice for my family, my son. You know if you are a woman in Kerala and a nurse, you can do much more for the family, if you are a man, you have nothing. It was my decision that we come here, but I should have not come like some of the people in my village did. They stayed back till they got green cards. But I did not want my son not to have a good life, so I came, so it is all for him. I am learning to be dependent, but it is not easy because you can't talk about it to anyone. Not many of the men are on this visa. Even if you don't work, but if you are not on this visa, you have prestige. And it is not Mary's fault. She tries a lot . . . but what can she do? I did not ever drink or smoke—I have to now. It's bad, but what to do? Please don't tell her anything. Please. I talked a lot with you."

Joseph's unhappy confession that he has taken to drinking and smoking to deal with his dependent status (or as he calls it, his role of "wife") shows the self-admitted harm the internalized gendered norms about masculinity is causing these men. The wives of the tech workers resented the restrictions on their life choices because of dependency. The dependent men deeply lamented their loss of male privilege within the household even when their breadwinning wives' work undermined their own contributions to maintain the patriarchal status quo. The battle that these families have to engage in with their internalized gendered selves, brought to surface through the visa regime, and bolstered by a neoliberal rhetoric of choice and productivity, leaves little room to explore any meaning that either the women or the men may find in nurturing and caring for their families in the absence of the ability to work, thereby making a deeply unfair situation almost tragic.

Household Labor and the Visa Regime: Gender at the Interactional Level

Gendered Division of Household Labor: Breadwinner Husband and Dependent Wives

I sat on the brown leather couch, drinking chai and munching on snacks in the spacious and well-lit living area of Jaya and Akash's apartment while I waited to interview Jaya. The apartment was tastefully decorated with various Indian decorative artifacts and paintings and many hand-embroidered pieces, which Jaya later told me she had made. When I arrived a few minutes early, Jaya told me she was running late as she was still getting her six-year-old son and husband ready for playschool and a work trip, respectively. The apartment had an open kitchen with a dining space by the kitchen, where I could see Jaya packing lunch for her husband and snacks for her son. While packing lunch, she was also feeding her son what I assume was cereal and milk from a bowl. On his way to his daylong work trip, her husband was to drop their son at the playschool. As Jaya combed her son's hair, she called out to me and told me this is how a typical weekday morning looked like for her, but that Monday was "crazier" because her husband was leaving for a trip, and she had to help him pack before making breakfast and lunch. She said she usually made lunch later because her husband came home to eat, but that particular day she had to make lunch earlier to pack it up for him. In a few minutes her husband came out, dressed for work, said hello to me, picked up his lunch, and waited for the son to finish his breakfast. He told Jaya to take a cab to pick up the son, as it was very cold outside. "Please don't walk, I will feel bad since I will have the car, and Aku might catch a cold." He then picked up his son in one arm while pulling his travel bag with the other. He hugged Jaya and left. Jaya went back to the kitchen, got herself some chai, and settled in for the interview.

This description of Jaya's home and the snapshot of her life that morning was typical of my observations of the lives of the women participants on dependent visas. During the interview, Jaya noted with a sigh that, a few years ago back in India, her mornings were "as crazy" except that she was not cooking but getting ready to leave for her high-level executive job along with her husband. In talking about their lives in the United States, the wives of the high-tech workers often alluded to their previous lives in India to draw a contrast for me and to show me how different their lives had been back in India. They emphasized the different social expectations that they encountered as dependent spouses versus when they were working spouses. Drawing a comparison between her present and previous lives, Mili said:

> My life now is boring as hell. When I was living by myself, I was living like a dude, I never cooked, cleaned sometimes, and partied and traveled on free time. Cooking, cleaning, and this domestic life was the last thing I ever wanted to do, and then after I got married to Ravish and the brief time we lived together in India before coming here, even then I was not cooking and cleaning, I was still working. We had help, and we'd mostly get food from outside. I never felt bound to do housework, and neither did Ravish expected mainly because we had help. . . . But now because I am home, it's like what do I do every day—expectations build that I will be the perfect wife.

The expectations to be the "perfect wife" in the absence of a work life was present across all the dependent wives. As explored in chapter 3, this is one way the neoliberal logic intersects with gendered expectations for women. Thus, it was not surprising that, in the families of the tech workers, the conventionally gendered division of labor seemed to be more or less intact, and the women did the majority of the house and reproductive and caregiving work. When counting hours spent doing household labor, I found that all the women in the tech families were doing a disproportionately large share of household chores. Tona, whose husband belonged to an upper-middle-class, educated family, hailed from an urban background, and expressed progressive views about gendered division of labor, commented on her husband's contribution to household chores:

> I do 90 percent of the housework. His contribution is 15 minutes in a given week when he cleans the bathroom, that is when he does that—he does not do that every week. But he wants the house to be spick-and-span. He would never ask me to do it, but won't do it himself, but complain about it not being tidy, and since I am home, I feel like I should do it. Another thing he does is sometimes he cooks when entertaining guests. . . . oh, but wait a minute. I always help him out. I chop the veggies, do the defrosting, prepare masala [spices], and clean after he has cooked. It is usually a big mess after he has cooked. He, however, gets all the credit for cooking, while I have actually done the hard work. To think of it, he never helps me when I am cooking either for us or guests. Nice strategy, [yes?]!

Tona's mild outrage at the inequity in the division of chores shows her astute understanding of the gender disparities in her home due to her dependent status. Even when her husband engages in some household work such as cooking, she still is expected to do most of the grunt work. Tona's husband, Kaushik, corroborated Tona's description of his proportion of housework. He stated, with a hint of guilt in his voice and a sheepish smile:

> Tona does 95 percent, I maybe do 2 percent, and 3 percent remains undone. I just don't have the time. I manage an overseas team at work, and so I am always on call. I have to work most weekends. It's just that I have no juice left to do anything. But I have to say that maybe if I were pushed, I would do more around the house, but since Tona does it all, I choose not to think about it.

Kaushik provides a different insight into how social expectations of gender operate. While he is aware that he falls short of doing his share in the family chores, he alludes to the demands of his work and confesses to deploying avoidance techniques to escape housework. While he feels guilty for not contributing to household chores, he also knows that he is not held accountable. The hint of guilt that Kaushik demonstrated was present in many of the other tech workers in varied forms.

The men might be feeling guilty because their wives sacrificed their careers and entered a situation of forced dependence to avoid family separation, but I assign this guilt mostly to the social class and upper-caste status of the tech workers and their wives. Most of the tech workers and their spouses came from middle- to upper-middle-class and upper-caste families in India. For this class strata in India, being able to hire household help is affordable and common. Therefore, it was nearly inconceivable that the women from upper-middle-class and upper-caste families would have to do any household chores. Both spouses, and particularly the men, felt a loss of status because their wives now had to engage in household work or "dirty chores," as the men often referred to it, chores that normally would be done by maids or household help if they were in India. Many of the tech workers and their spouses stated that moving had resulted in downward mobility for them, because their standard of living had gone down. In India, most of these families could afford help, child care, cooks, and chauffeurs, whereas in the United States none of that was possible. In the words of Mia: "In the United States, you are the cook, the maid, the driver, the nanny—you are working around the clock practically." Rex, Mia's husband, added: "The only reason I would ever think of going back to India would be so that we can afford help and have a better quality of life. That way Mia does not have to do all the crappy work she does here, and we can have a relaxed life. Especially in a big city in India, our life would be much better at least in terms of family life."

When the tech-worker men contributed to family chores and child care, it was explicitly out of guilt. Sambit said that he feels guilty that his wife does the housework and child care because "back in India this would never happen." He said his way of compensating was by cooking for the family: "I love to cook, and so it is not hard." Most of the women on dependent visas said that, when their husbands helped around the house, it was because they felt that they were not good husbands, unable to provide enough to afford household help. Karuna felt her husband did "all the hard stuff around the house." She added: "He makes roti [Indian flatbread], puts Kitu [their 8-year-old son] to bed, mops the floor on weekends because he knows I did not grow up doing this. I did not move a finger except to study. He feels he is not being a good husband if I, as his wife, am doing this type of work." Karuna and her husband are both upper caste, and the idea that menial work is below one's status is a caste construct as well as a class construct in India. Mia said: "My husband is home during the weekends because he has a traveling job, and he does the week's laundry, cleans the house, and you can say he almost does 45 percent of the household work." Her husband estimated his contribution to household chores at only 20 percent. During his interview, he mentioned that he was trying to find help for his wife even in the United States so she did not have to do "all this useless work."

While some of the women overestimated the number of hours their husbands spent performing housework, which is also found in the literature on housework and gender,[29] most of the dependent women in this book actually underestimated the contributions of their husbands and tended to overstate the number of hours they themselves spent on daily chores. The husbands tended to underestimate their own household contributions. I found this to be the case when I matched the time diaries of the women with their initial perception of how much time they were spending on housework. Granted that the husbands were not doing very much housework, this gap between perception and reality by the men and the women has important theoretical implications. It shows how the visa regime altered the perceptions of gendered work in everyday lives. The dependent women belabored their own domestic contribution because they were bound to their homes and needed to feel like productive members of the household and society. The tech husbands underestimated the little contribution they made toward the household chores. However, they also justified their noninvolvement in nurturing work by citing the high demands of their (paid) work life, which in fact relied on the unpaid labor of their legally dependent spouses.

This routine did change in the realm of child care. The men showed more proactive support in helping out with caregiving for children. They expressed unhappiness at the prospect of not being able to contribute toward child care or not being part of their child's life enough. The men, to combat the loss they felt, often volunteered to take care of the children. As one husband, Satish, put it:

> I make it a point to take care of our son for a few hours on the weekends. This gives me quality time with my son and relieves my wife of child care duties, so that she can have some fun with her girlfriends. Childless fun [laughs].

The complexities in Satish's little humorous statement about "childless fun" is staggering. Satish recognizes that constantly being saddled with child care is hard work, which is why he wants to relieve his wife of what he sees as her duties because of the visa-dictated division of labor. He views the time he gets with his child over the weekend as quality time, not as a chore. This is theoretically interesting in terms of the gendered division of labor at the interactional level as framed by the visa regime. For Satish, in the absence of any built-in family time in his work life, caring for his child (which is grunt work for his wife) over the weekend becomes quality time, a time he cherishes, to save himself from the guilt of not being present in his child's life. Child care becomes dichotomized gendered work depending on who takes it on and when. The gendered organization of work, especially when forced, re-creates heteronormative dichotomies that are oppressive to both partners.

In a similar vein, Sambit, when talking about his and his wife's decision to have a child, said: "I knew it would be hard, but I knew this was the best time for Alka to have a kid because she can't work. It has been hard with the money and getting help and support. I am hardly there, but still it was the best decision." He felt guilty for not being able to help out with child care enough. Like many other men, he recognized that his wife was often working more hours than him in the house, and the unfairness of the situation was not lost on him. He still thought it was an important decision to have the child while his wife was being forced to take what he saw as a sabbatical.

While reproductive labor was an important part of familial social expectation for the men and the women, some of the dependent women reframed that expectation by countering it. Of the four women in the tech families who did not have children, three told me that they did not want to have a child because of their visa status (as I alluded to in chapter 3). Mili said this about her plans for a family:

Just because you are on H-4, you have a kid. That is the stupidest thing to do. You are already fucked, and then you further screw up your life. Not me. I don't want a kid, but if I ever have a kid it will be after I am earning.

Like Mili, who did not want to have child unless she had her own income, Tona thought having a child while on a dependent visa would trap her into the dependent situation even more. She explained:

My life is so uncertain, and I am so depressed all the time. I don't want to have a kid and tie myself to this life more. Right now, if it gets too much, I can go back to India and start afresh, but with a kid, I will be stuck.

For these handful of women, having a child while being dependent felt like the intensification of the dependency trap. Here, they were trying to disrupt gendered expectations of motherhood that came with their "forced housewife" (as many women called themselves) status.

However, other types of gendered interactions were visible outside the confines of the home, such as in the community events that I often attended. As I helped Karuna clean up after a weekend get-together of Indian co-ethnic families to which she had invited me, she told me she considered organizing social events to be part of her job as a dependent wife. She said that life in the United States, especially as a dependent spouse, was so isolating that she intentionally took it upon herself to organize weekend events with other Indian families. As I attended the weekend community parties, I noticed that the women were much more involved in organizing the events, sending out invitations, following up, arranging for the food, organizing playtime for the children, and maintaining connections with the community. At these social occasions, the men hung out with other men while the women cooked together, chatted, and planned other events. Most of the women were responsible for other social activities, such as organizing play dates for the children, organizing community religious events, keeping track of and buying gifts for special occasions for friends and families, and maintaining ties with their transnational lives back in India.

I found that when the men took responsibility for socializing, it usually involved their colleagues at work. However, the wives were still responsible for organizing the parties that the men were hosting. I asked the women how they felt about being the main social liaisons of the family. They said that while they liked to be actively engaged in social activities because it gave them visibility, it also took an emotional toll. Tona said: "Sometimes, I just want to hide, but I am the one who is available always, so I am always the point of contact in this family for anything social." This reflects Rosabeth Kanter's[30] observations in her study of the social roles of the wives of executives whose default job was to entertain their husbands' colleagues.

The women on dependent visas pointed out that they liked participating in get-togethers only when it was with friends in the Indian community because their experiences attending social events at their husbands' work felt emotionally draining to them. Poonam had an advanced degree in physics from Mumbai University and was an assistant professor in a four-year college in Mumbai before she moved to the United States on a dependent visa. In her words:

> I hate organizing Shri's office parties. People there are so surprised that I even exist even when I am one organizing the party. I feel completely invisible. When he introduced me to his boss at one of these parties, he was so surprised. He told Shri, "Oh, I did not know you were married," and then turned away without even saying a hello to me. I was like *really*? You wrote that awful letter for my H-4 visa and screwed up my life, and the only reason he can stay at work until midnight is because I am doing the other half of his work at home. Oh, how I hate talking to his office people. And then some come around and ask, "You are so qualified, why don't you work?—Has it to do with being a Indian wife?" and in my head, I go, *No, idiots, it's because of your stupid and regressive policies that I don't work.*

Poonam's poignant and indignant explanation of the deep emotional experience of invisibilization that she undergoes in social events, especially those linked to her husband's workplace, some of which she puts her unpaid labor to organize, is an exposition of how work is organized structurally for legally dependent spouses—all their labor, whether physical or emotional, is immediately subsumed in their dependent status and undermined.

On the spectrum of emotional labor that dependent women had to put in to maintain social ties, they were also largely responsible for maintaining relationships back in India. The women maintained almost a daily connection with their own and their husband's families in India and made sure to stay in touch with friends and extended families. However, this was not without its emotional toll. As Jaya said, it was particularly "emotionally taxing" to keep ties with friends in India. She explains:

> I feel so ashamed talking to my friends and relatives. They ask such hurtful questions like, "Why did you study so much if you had to sit at home?" My friends who started working with me are now in big positions. Even my parents sometimes get on my nerves. But I don't blame them. They did not raise me to be a housewife. God! It is emotionally taxing, and Akash skips all the drama because he is so busy.

The constant reminder of the dependent status in transnational interactions that the wives of tech workers often maintained to get away from the daily drudgery made the emotional labor of maintaining social relationships more arduous. I coded social engagements as emotional labor because it involved time, effort, and energy that the men avoided on the pretext of having busy work schedules. The women took it upon themselves because they wanted to spare their husbands the time and effort.

In this context, the dependent wives often talked about the labor they put toward their families (to protect their husbands' work time) as a way to claim economic resources for their personal expenses. Tona explained:

> Even though it's not my choice that I am not working, I still feel I need to be able to take care of my personal needs financially. I see the work that I put in as my part of the earning, because if I were not putting in this labor, my husband would not be doing so well and getting the promotions he has been getting, so I deserve a part of those gains.

Here, Tona is claiming space in her husband's work life because his success at work (as rightly analyzed by Tona) was because of the invisible labor she performed at home. Mili added another dimension to this conversation, saying:

> I have always been independent, always taking care of myself, so it is hard to snap out of that, which is why I keep feeling guilty for spending money that is not mine and Ravish adds to that by always saying we don't have money. So, I feel like I need to be doing a good job of maintaining the house, saving the money because that then becomes my money.

Mili, like most of the dependent women, did not consider her husband's money as her own. Mili also invoked how the experience of financial independence premigration made her unable to automatically claim her husband's money as her own and thought of her household labor as a way to legitimatize her ownership on her husband's income. This trait was diametrically opposite to the nurses' husbands who took control of their wives' finances without offering any explanations for it in any of our conversations. This aligns with past research[31] finding stay-at-home wives often viewed housework as a form of economic exchange and justified entitlement to their husbands' income. On the question of finances, the couples all agreed that men were spenders, women savers. In all the families of the tech workers, the men kept tight reins on the finances, from paying bills to investments. Only in two families, where the wife had expertise in managing finances, did husbands consult their wives on financial affairs. But in terms of spending on consumer goods, the men usually outspent the women, buying expensive items, whereas the women almost never spent money on expensive items beyond what they absolutely needed, such as winter coats and cell phones. For instance, in a joint interview, Tona said: "When I buy shoes, it costs at the most $25, but when Kaushik buys shoes, it can go up to $250." Kaushik nodded in agreement with a shy smile. Likewise, Mili complained in the joint interview: "When I buy clothes, it is Target brand; when Ravish buys clothes, it is Armani. I have been conditioned not to spend money because I never think of Ravish's money as my money." Ravish responded by saying, "No one stopped you. You are just *kanjoos* [miserly]." While this repartee was in jest, it underlined women's often self-asserted sense of disenfranchisement in laying claim to their husbands' financial resources.

As participants' narratives show, these restrictive visa laws create gendered social and familial expectations for both men and women, leading to contradictions and reinvented heteronormative dichotomies that the men and women grapple with as transnational families. These expectations are further shaped by class and regional backgrounds and the desires and aspirations of the couples. Based on gender socialization, social expectations, and the legal status of a dependent or the breadwinner, the participants' gender performance was heavily regulated and controlled. This had different consequences for the men and women and dependents and nondependents in each family form. However, the most striking result of this analysis is that, despite the strictly designed gendered expectations in the dependent visa regime that the women were forced to meet, they were not passive actors in this play. They actively participated, made their resentments known, and reclaimed the most intimate choices in their lives—their reproductive labor—despite the limitations imposed by the visa laws. They almost became sociological agents who demonstrated reflexive agency, resisting institutional constraints, which made them active, often rebellious actors in this story. The interactional-level gender story, however, markedly inflected in the households of nurses.

Gendered Division of Household Labor: Breadwinner Wives and Dependent Husbands

It was about 9:30 p.m. on a Saturday, a breezy fall night in a northwestern suburb in Chicago. I was leaning on the kitchen counter at Amy's house, chatting with Amy's friend and colleague Rosa. Amy was a petite woman of 38 and was a nurse at an inner-city hospital. That particular night, all the women were clad in colorful silk saris. The men wore shirts and trousers. Amy owned a large, five-bedroom house, which they bought new about six years prior. It had a spacious kitchen with granite countertops, stainless-steel appliances, a large living and dining area, and a fully finished basement, which served as the children's playroom. The house was spotlessly clean and had heavy, ornate, expensive furniture procured, perhaps, at generic suburban furnishing stores.[32] Adjoining the kitchen was a living area with couches and a 50-inch plasma television. Amy's house was typical of most of nurses' houses I visited, including the layout, the furniture, and the family pictures, which hung in the living room.

On this weekend night, 15 families had gathered at Amy's house. All the families had nurses as the lead migrant and the main breadwinner.

Three of the husbands in this group were on dependent visas, while the rest of the husbands had work permits or were lawful permanent residents or citizens. Very few of them had full-time jobs. Six were entirely stay-at-home fathers. I was invited by Amy to this party to conduct observations as well as interviews. Like all other community events in the Malayalee community, this event was distinctly gender-segregated in its arrangement. The men gathered at one area of the house—at this event in the living space adjoining the kitchen, where some drank beer and chatted while watching Malayalee TV. The women gathered in the kitchen or the living room. The children were often sent to the basement to play. The women usually took charge of warming and serving the food. There were usually between seven and ten dishes served, mostly cooked by the host family, with a few dishes brought by the guests. Most of the food was cooked by the women (the nurses), while the husbands often declared that they had cooked the meat dishes. Cooking meat was understood to be a mark of masculinity by the men. As I helped Amy[33] lay out the food, she whispered to me with a chuckle that her husband usually helps around the kitchen, but when he is with other men in the community "it is not the done thing to help in the kitchen." If the men helped in the kitchen at social gatherings, it was seen as a sign of diminished masculinity.

This scenario presents the various forms of gendered interactions that occurred among couples in families of nurses and in the Malayalee communities. The segregation in social gatherings was common at most events in the community. The dependent men and their wives were very protective of preserving the masculinities of the men in the presence of community members. The performance of masculinities to fit the gendered expectations of the community was common in public and at social events, including church, among the nurses' families.[34]

All the couples in families of nurses I interviewed had at least one child, and given that the mothers/nurses had highly demanding jobs, the fathers were required to fulfill child care. As one of the men put it: "Someone has to feed the child and put him to bed. If the mother is not there, I have to do it. The child can't go hungry." The men often took care of feeding the children, putting them to bed, dropping off and picking them up from school and other extracurricular activities such as music and dance lessons, arranging and taking them to play dates, reading to them, drawing with them, and taking them to parks or other recreational activities. The nurses made sure to be informed about what was happening in their children's lives but would be able to join in the activities only on their off days. Nurses who taught Sunday school at the church had more time with their own children and with other children in the community. Unlike with household chores, the men assumed the responsibility of child care without much complaint. Some of the men even took pride in the fact that their children were closer to them than their mothers. In tune with this trend among the men, John said:

> My children really love me. If they need anything or if they have to share anything, the first person they run to is me, not their mother. It makes me feel important. It is a wonderful feeling to be loved by your children.

While not being explicit, it was clear that the dependent men drew agency from their fathering duties and the nurturance work. The nurses also felt that the children were closer to the fathers than them and experienced regret and pain for being absentee mothers, much as the tech-worker fathers did. However, the pain and guilt were more severe for the nurses compared to the tech workers. When it came to household work, nurses were vocal in saying that "it was important that the men contributed equally in, the household chores," especially when their husbands were on E-34 visas or had permanent residency, where they did not have the legal dependency tag. Missy, a floor nurse in a suburban hospital, affirmed during the joint interview with her husband, a mail sorter in the local post office, that she thought it was very important that men share equally in the household labor. She explained:

> We are not living back in days, like in olden times, and not living in the village in Kerala. It is impossible to run a family when both people are working, and in our families, we as nurses work more to say that the women will still take care of the house. I now know how much hardship my mother had to go through because of this attitude, and I am happy that has changed. Arun does a lot in the house, takes care of the children, and that is very good, if you ask me. I don't think Arun is unhappy. [Arun nodding in assent]

Missy makes the distinction between life in India and life in the United States, where she is the breadwinner and has to work longer hours than her husband and takes on an equity perspective on the division of labor. Similarly, Lily shared that she decided to marry Thomas, who was less educated than her and came from a humble background, because she did not want to end up like her mother. She tearfully said:

> I only wanted to become a nurse and leave my village so that I could help my mother and save her from my father. You know she was the one [who] worked like a donkey both for the family and at the farm, and yet my father would yell at her, push her around, sometimes even beat her. I did not want that for me, which is why I married Thomas even if he was lower status than me. I wanted a man who would be understanding and would take care of my home and children and not be like my father. Thomas is a great husband, and I am happy that he does not think it is bad to take care of children and family.

Indeed, Thomas was one of the few men who did not complain about doing household chores. While there was little diversity in class and region among the families of the nurses, as most came from rural parts of Kerala and were from farming families, there was some indication in my research that men who came from poorer backgrounds were less resentful about having to do household work. Previous research[35] with Indian migrant nurses found that most nurses tended to marry down economically, especially if they were working as foreign nurses or had plans to do so. The few husbands of nurses who were employed full-time or had their own business unabashedly admitted to me that they did not contribute at all to household chores aside from some child care because, they claimed, they were not like the other husbands who "were sitting at home and not earning." They absolved themselves from most household chores because they were also employed, leaving their wives, who worked longer hours than them, to pick up the slack.

In terms of social interactions and emotional work, in the families of nurses, the husbands assumed more public responsibilities such as organizing events at the church or organizing community picnics and games. The men's claim that the church played an important role in their lives, was previously found in George's[36] work. They were also unanimous in their complaint that the church or the community did not provide the same sort of social support they had in India. When it came to keeping in touch with family and friends in India, it was still the primary responsibility of the women (nurses). The men mostly avoided talking to family and friends in India. This perhaps protected their already vulnerable masculinities from being challenged.

While the nurses did perform compensatory femininities in the homes to underplay their breadwinner roles in order to uphold their husbands' status, and their husbands evaded everyday chores, they took appropriate pride in being the primary caregivers and the go-to person for their children. Fatherhood was important to these men, much as it was important to the stay-at-home fathers in other previous studies.[37] They felt productive and important as men in their extended parental role. For the men, caring for children became the replacement for the provider role in their families, which made them reclaim their figurehead positionality.

Reification of the Visa Regime through Gender in the Homes

In this chapter, I present an analysis of gender structure in terms of the consequences emerging from the rules and regulations of dependent visas. The institutional possibilities for the participants are defined by their legal visa statuses. Wives and husbands of the lead migrants are allowed into the United States on a provisional basis as dependents. They maintain their legal status as long as they do not work for pay and their spouses have jobs in the United States. The visa policies are gender-neutral in language. However, the implicit assumption within dependent visas is clearly gendered. Dependent visa policies assume that those migrating on dependent visas are women, that is, wives of skilled workers from the Global South in traditional families in which the women are full-time wives and mothers and financially dependent on the husbands. The primary reason for allowing dependents or wives to accompany the skilled migrant worker was to create "stable" migrant families so that the lead migrant was able to meet the "ideal migrant worker" expectation with no other demands on his labor time.

The dependent spouses, however, actively resisted the implicit gendered assumptions about migrant families. The wives of the tech workers, most of whom came from middle- to upper-middle-class and upper-caste families, were socialized and educated to be independent. All the dependent women were highly qualified with college degrees and more, and all had upwardly mobile careers before migrating on dependent visas. Prior to migration, none of these women wanted or conceived of a future where they would be "just housewives." It was therefore not surprising that most of these women responded to the visa structure with angry, vocal disavowals of their dependent status and the invisibility and dehumanization that came with it, exhibiting a deep mental agony. They resisted vegetating under what they called the "vegetable visa."

The husbands of the nurses, like the women on dependent visas, resented being dependents, albeit for different reasons. Most of the men came from rural Kerala, with strict gender rules about a man's and a woman's position within the family. The nurses described the family structure in Kerala as strictly patriarchal, with the father as the iron-fisted overseer. The men often alluded to male honor as defined by being the provider and the head of the household. Visa-imposed dependency therefore meant loss of male privilege and honor for the men, causing them to be resentful and depressed with their current situations.

The effects of economic dependency differed in the families of nurses versus the tech families. The economic realities of the visa regimes were understood primarily through the lens of gender by the dependents and the lead migrants. Class, religious, and regional backgrounds intersected with gendered understandings of familial roles to produce contradictions and complexities in the lives of the migrant subjects.

Wives of Tech Workers

The wives of the tech workers dispel the monolithic image of the American mainstream of women from the Global South as domestic and dependent. All of the women participants on dependent visas were not docile dependents. And yet their actions completely conformed to the gendered and heteronormative expectations of their dependent positions. They invested themselves in intensive performance of traditional femininities—cooking, cleaning, and taking care of their husbands and children. They talked about adapting to be dependents and becoming perfect wives and mothers. Dependent status pushed them to draw on traditional tropes of marriage and their internalized gendered selves. They made do with their situation and learned to play the role of dependent spouse—the ideal wife and mother.

The women often flirted with their reproductive choices as a way to gain some agency. Some of the women used the borrowed time away from their careers to have children, to avoid interrupting careers when they would finally be able to go back to paid work. While this appears to be a choice, it also fulfills a heteronormative expectation for the women who do this, in keeping with a neoliberal, heterosexist logic of reproduction—"choosing" to have a child when there is the least disruption to paid work. Others resisted reproduction almost as a protest against adopting an even more dependent and restrictive status, in a small way defying heteronormative pressures.

Whatever coping mechanism the women adopted, most of them were not content as homemakers. The institutional policies of the visa regime failed to create the intended "stable families," though it compelled women to behave according to the societal expectations of an ideal migrant housewife. The institutional policy also relied on the unrecognized work of heterosexuality done by the women to make their husband's careers work in the United States. The women, however, were constantly in turmoil, forced to reconcile their "forced housewife" status with their desire for independence and aspirations for a professional career. They persisted in their attempt to disrupt the expectations of the role they dutifully, but unhappily, performed.

Husbands of Nurses

The dependent husbands of the nurses refused to take on any purely "wifely" or househusband role, but they were not resistant to adopting the role of a caregiver for the children. They adopted the role of the primary caregiver because the children needed care in the absence of the mother. The primary reason posited by most of the families for migration was a brighter future for the children. I argue that the men were reclaiming their protector and provider position in the home by becoming caring nurturers. The men inadvertently were undoing traditional gender by undertaking a kind of nurturing masculinity even when it was the only path for them to restore and negotiate patriarchal prowess in the home.

In all other respects, the dependent men asserted masculine privilege as heads of households. Most of their wives—the main breadwinners—held on to patriarchal tropes, so that the men could symbolically continue to claim their principal hierarchical position in the family. They carried and asserted internalized notions of what it meant to be a man in the context of a patriarchal family and struggled with the contradictory reality of being dependent husbands. To negotiate these contradictions, the husbands often performed hypermasculinity, sometimes involving heavy drinking. The dependent men in this study are reminiscent of the husbands of Sri Lankan domestic workers who emigrate to oil-rich countries, becoming breadwinners of their families, as described in anthropologist Michele Ruth Gamburd's[38] book on rural Sri Lankan women's emigration. The dependent men in those families also struggled to maintain their masculinity and often took to domestic violence and alcoholism. They held on to their masculinity by retaining the position of the "main decision maker and the head of the family,"[39] much like the men in this study 15 years later.

This becomes particularly clear when families with men on dependent visas are contrasted with families where the husbands were not on dependent visas, but their wives were still the primary earning member in the family. The family dynamics in those families were less gendered and more egalitarian, with husbands performing more of the household chores as well as childcare, and the nurses appreciating their husbands for being equal partners.

When comparing the experiences of women and men on dependent visas, I find that women were expected to adopt gendered performances of traditional femininities when they came on dependent visas and that most of them performed these roles well while actively resisting redefining themselves as just housewives. The men struggled much more, as their dependent position stood in opposition to their core identity of a provider. They felt humiliated and ashamed, and attempted to cover up the pain by asserting their masculinity—often in the most toxic ways; they refused to cook or clean despite being home all day. And yet, the visa regulations and institutional policies shaped how the dependent spouses live their daily lives, with women investing in traditional domesticity and men learning to become caregivers altering the material realities of each of their lives.

The Breadwinners: Tech-Workers and Nurses

The men tech workers, of all my participants, were the most comfortable in their visa-mandated role as the main breadwinner. They were, however, uncomfortable with and concerned about their wives' dependent status. Some of the men perhaps felt genuinely guilty because their wives had left their careers for the sake of being with them in the United States. But most often the concern did not emerge from their investment in a gender-egalitarian marriage. It was mostly because they were embarrassed that they could not afford to support their wives well enough to afford household help, which was incongruous to their class and caste status. This incongruity caused the tech workers to experience a loss of social status as their wives were forced into domestic labor. They saw this as a marker of downward mobility. Part of their unhappiness also emanated from the fact they were not able to spend enough time with their children or take leisure time; because they had a stay-at-home spouse, they could not ask for family time from their employers—it was assumed that the spouse at home would handle domestic duties.

The nurses and their husbands did not experience downward mobility, as they had emigrated from farming families in rural India. Their sense of dislocation was based more on the inability to maintain the patriarchal family structure headed, and financially supported, by the male head of household. The nurses emphasized that becoming a nurse was their way of escaping a life of poverty and patriarchal oppression in rural Kerala. But they believed that household work was women's work. They felt guilty for being the reason for their husband's migration as dependents. They also felt intensely unhappy at being employed mothers, with long and erratic work hours that made them absentee mothers in their children's lives. As the main breadwinners, they felt simultaneously compelled to abide by any and all demands of their employers, yet conflicted because such demands pulled them away from their equally important role as mothers and wives. The gendered identity of being a mother remained strong among nurses, who envied the time that the fathers had with the children. The nurses willingly did all the cooking on their days off, to show their children that they were good and caring mothers. While most nurses would have preferred that their husbands do more household labor, they acknowledged that for them to do so was emasculating, and so they refrained from demanding it. The dependent visa regime reinforced oppressive gendered outcomes in both households. But in the families of the nurses, the onus of managing these expectations fell squarely on the nurses' shoulders; on the surface, at the institutional level, the gender order was reversed, demonstrating that when a policy is designed on principles of dependency there are no positive outcomes even when it inadvertently creates circumstances where gender could hypothetically be undone.

Conclusion

In "Margin Becoming Centre," Raewyn Connell[40] contends that global capitalism and associated processes are responsible for reshaping and sometimes destabilizing masculinities in societies in the Global South and for creating "new forms of dependency and global power."[41] Connell calls these processes "coloniality of gender." Through the techniques of the visa regime, particularly where the dependent men were concerned, coloniality of gender was re-created in the Global North on Southern subjects through the capitalist project of controlling the migration experiences of professional workers of color and their families through an oppressive visa regime.[42]

The laws felt oppressive to both types of families. The societal expectations emerging from state-imposed dependence shaped the actions, behaviors, and everyday lives of the participants. The institutional constraints created economic dependency as well as legal dependency. They were forced to hold on to certain ideals, gendered and classed to make sense of their experiences as legally dependent subjects. The dependent spouses, whether men or women, used parenting as a way of finding self-worth. In the process, they transformed parenting, as will be explored in chapter 5.

In this chapter, it becomes clear how allegedly gender-neutral visa policies have oppressive and deeply gendered consequences within the homes. The analysis of how the families understand the gendered expectations shows the unintended consequences of the visa regime. Rather than creating stable families, the visa regime creates families rife with inequities, anxiety, and despair. This is a form of legal violence[43] that travels beyond the workplace and finds its way into the families of temporary immigrant workers.

5

Transcultural Cultivation

A New Form of Parenting

[The] H-4 visa has turned me into an H-4 mother.
—Anjali, participant

It was 11:00 a.m. on Sunday morning on a crisp autumn day in Chicago. I was on the Red Line of the Chicago transit system with Anjali and her two children, a son (three) and a daughter (seven). At the time, Anjali had been in the United States for four years on an H-4 visa. All of us were wearing traditional Indian attire. Anjali was wearing a blue and gold salwar kameez (a tunic with slacks), the kids were wearing gender-specific Indian clothes, and I was wearing a sari (traditional Indian attire for women that involves a long piece of fabric wrapped and draped around the body). We were on our way to the West Campus of the University of Illinois at Chicago, which hosts the annual Durga Puja (mentioned in chapter 3), one of the most popular regional Hindu religious festivals of India, to celebrate the harvest season and the annual descent of the goddess Durga to earth, as per Indian Hindu lore. Observed over an entire week in October in India, the celebration is held over a weekend in the United States. Anjali and her children were going to the festivities. She asked me to accompany them; her husband had been called into work, and in Anjali's words "it's hard to deal with two young children on transit." I was standing, while Anjali and the children were seated. The train stopped suddenly, and I nearly tripped over my sari. Anjali prevented me from falling and commented:

See, this is why I did not wear one of the scores of sari[s] in my closet. Saris are not practical when you have two young children to run after. If Rahul [her husband] came, I would wear a sari, but he could not. You had to go out of your way to come with us. I feel like I am a single mother most days, but especially on days like this. It is the Durga Puja after all. I don't know why we are doing this. This life really sucks.

"But Rahul is coming later to the event, yes?" I asked, and Anjali responded:

Yes, he is, in the evening, but it's not about that. It's about what kind of parents have we become. It's a lot harder to be parents these days than say when we were kids. The pressure to raise the perfect kid with all the skills and talents was not so intense. And it is especially hard in this country, you know. There is so much to consider. I would not, for anything, want my children to miss the Durga Puja, but I also want them to learn about Thanksgiving and salsa dancing, along with Bharatnatyam [Indian classical dance], while balancing the budget. But it's not easy—you get my drift. And when all of this falls on one parent mostly, it is exhausting. And I do it because I am on this stupid visa. [The] H-4 visa has turned me into an H-4 mother.

The trope of the "single mother" had come up multiple times when I explored questions about household work with the women on H-4 visas. Many saw themselves as single mothers because they felt as if they were the sole caregivers of their children; husbands, holding worker visas, did not have the ability to take much family time and be active caregivers. However, Anjali's concern was about the everyday work of raising children as middle-class immigrant parents in America forced to stay at home as primary parents to their children, as in Anjali's case. This everyday work of parenting, especially for the dependent parents (including dependent men/fathers), warrants more attention. Annette Lareau[1] has written extensively about how class affects parenting in white and Black Americans' homes. Given that most of the families in this book belonged to middle- and upper-middle-class families in India, and were living middle-class lifestyles in the United States while holding temporary migrant status and adjusting to transnational life, with the dependent spouse acting as the stay-at-home parent, how did these families parent? What did parenting involve? And what have visa policies to do with parenting at all?

Visa policies reconfigure gendered expectations and notions of the self for visa holders and impose constraints on relationships, family, work, belonging, and migration. In this chapter, I contend that visa laws also shape parenting expectations and practices. I examine how middle-class parenting might work in the context of Indian immigrant families in which one parent holds a professional job in the United States and the other is highly qualified but stays home because of visa restrictions. I specifically examine how the visa regime, transnational lives, and the parents' class status in this study interact to shape parenting styles.

One of the most influential studies in the United States on class-based parenting has been done by Lareau.[2] In her book *Unequal Childhoods*, Lareau uses a Bourdieuvian analysis of class in parenting. She used the class background of both white and Black parents as the central analytical category in defining what their parenting styles were and what might be the outcome of such parenting for the children's life chances. She proffered two distinct parenting practices across class locations: "concerted cultivation" as the kind of parenting done by Black and white middle-class parents, and the "accomplishment of natural growth" as the parenting path enacted by working-class parents.

In working-class households, the middle-school children she studied in the 1990s participated in very few organized activities and spent leisure time hanging out with kin and neighborhood friends. The work and economic lives of the parents did not afford them as much involvement in their children's lives. As a result, the way they parented was by issuing directives to their children. Parents in these households were authoritarian when speaking to children and created clear boundaries between adult and children's lives. The children were discouraged from questioning authority within and outside of the family. In the 2011 edition of *Unequal Childhoods*, a follow-up study shows that most of these working-class kids dropped out of college and had limited life chances. In addition, their parents were still less involved in their lives compared to the middle-class parents.

In sharp contrast, the middle-class parents who engaged in concerted cultivation of their middle-school children invested a large portion of their daily lives in developing their children's talents, organizing both leisure and learning activities, talking with their children in more discursive language that allowed for the development of negotiation skills, and actively interacting with and being involved in the institutions to which their children belonged. Lareau showed how deeply middle-class parents were involved in the lives of their children to motivate them as well as to organize their various leisure and extracurricular activities, often sacrificing their own leisure time to do so. The parents expended all this effort so that their children could have a secure future, primarily by supporting the preservation or even elevation of the children's class status. Lareau's 2011 edition revealed that almost all these children ended up finishing college, and many went to Ivy League schools. The parents remained involved in their children's lives and education, and if a child did not perform according to expectations, the parents often blamed themselves for not investing enough in the child's interests when the child was younger.

For Lareau, these two distinct paths emerge from class differences: Working-class parents do not enact concerted cultivation, while middle-class parents do not practice accomplishment of natural growth as parenting practice; these two diverging styles based on class then lead to the reproduction of parental class and habitus among children. When I first read Lareau's work as a graduate student, it revolutionized the way I thought about class and life chances. It allowed me to recognize that privilege and/or disadvantage begins with parenting acts. And yet, when I assigned *Unequal Childhoods* in my courses, the American and Canadian students emphatically nodded in agreement, while the first and second immigrant students shook their heads in disagreement. When questioned, the immigrant students would often tell me "parenting is not either/or." They said that they experienced both kinds of parenting in their households and experienced parental class mobility during their lifetimes as well.

This perspective is reflected in Pei-Chia Lan's[3] book in which she compares the parenting of professional/middle-class and working-class ethnic Chinese parents in Boston with the parenting of professional/middle-class and working-class Taiwanese parents in Taiwan. Lan adopts a transnational framework to analyze the emotional landscape of parenting across and within classes. In doing so, she dexterously captures the nuances of class-based parenting, unsettling the binarized parenting practices established in Lareau's work. Lan proposes a transnational relational approach to examine how parents, especially middle-class parents, develop parenting strategies, resources, a sense of (in)security, and "emotional experiences of childrearing"[4] in relation to other parents transnationally and across and within classes. Middle-class immigrant parents, in particular, engage in what Lan calls cultural mobility, in which they purchase and consume cultural goods and services locally and transnationally to shape their children's futures, while working-class parents invest heavily in their children's education to secure a safe future for them. In the process, these families experience gendered and racialized parenting, as mothers take on the main caregiving and educational roles and battle to protect their children from American racism by preparing them to be better than white Americans.

Similarly, Dawn Dow, in her book *Mothering While Black*, dismantles the assumption found in previous research, including Lareau's work, that, in middle-class parenting, class trumps race in shaping childrearing logics and practices. Using an intersectional approach, Dow shows that while middle- and upper-middle-class African American mothers do use their economic resources to create opportunities for their children—opportunities not available to working-class African American mothers—they also have to constantly navigate the racially unequal social landscape and gendered racism faced by their children. These mothers are left with little choice but to develop strategies and practices to protect their children and their children's futures in the face of unsurmountable structural racism, and as a result, for them, mothering is more intensive and time- and energy-consuming compared to white middle-class mothers.

The works by Lan and Dow and the reaction from my students inspired me to reanalyze my own data on middle-class Indians holding immigrant visas who were also parents. In so doing, I take on a transnational approach to understanding how middle-class parents in my sample deploy complex parenting strategies while navigating their liminal and restrictive legal statuses (which pose overwhelming structural constraint) even as they engage in some forms of concerted cultivation to ensure a secure future for their children. This chapter explores how dependent visa laws for middle-class families influence parenting in those families. I unpack the parenting practices in middle-class immigrant homes where the parents' legal statuses genders and racializes parenting, troubling a Lareautian understanding of middle-class parenting as unidimensional and undermining of other axes of marginalization.

What I present in this chapter are the consequences of the dependent visa status for parenting: the parenting practices of my participants lie squarely between concerted cultivation and accomplishment of natural growth because of how they implement transnational and transcultural parenting norms. I call this form of parenting "visa-regimented transcultural cultivation." In the remainder of the chapter, I build on the scholarship on transnational parenting, migration, concerted cultivation, and natural growth in order to theorize this concept.

Concerted Cultivation and Immigrant (Asian) Parenting

The West historically has stereotyped Asian parenting as authoritarian and solely focused on preparing children for educational success. Amy Chua's[5] controversial memoir *Battle Hymn of the Tiger Mom*, in which she alleged that Chinese mothers are superior to their Western counterparts, fed this stereotype. Lan[6] contends that ethnic Chinese parents in Boston and parents in Taiwan rejected this stereotype as a cultural heritage that was archaic and had to be discarded. Immigrant parents in Lan's study distanced themselves from Chua's controlling style of parenting while pointing out that Chua's child-rearing style was more indicative of her class privilege than her ethnic cultural inheritances.

In 2014, the Stanford psychologists Alyssa Fu and Hazel Markus[7] conducted an experimental study on middle-class European American high-school students and Asian American high-school students to assess how the Asian American students perceived their mothers' involvement in their lives. They concluded that, while the two groups of students differed in their interdependence level on their mothers, with Asian American students reporting more interdependence, both groups perceived their mothers' involvement as motivation toward academic achievement. Academic achievement was perceived by Asian American students as a team effort with their mothers, whereas the European American students saw it as a personal project motivated by their mothers. While Fu and Markus's research does not analyze class-based parenting styles, their research alludes to mothers' deep involvement in the academic lives of both groups of students, in line with the research on middle-class parenting styles.

Lareau[8] contends that class-based parenting perpetuates the cycle of class inequality: Working-class children are set up to fail in the competitive labor market because they do not receive the life skills necessary to succeed, whereas middle-class children are taught the skills to reproduce their class privilege. This is partly true because middle-class parents use discursive parenting, which helps their children develop effective negotiation skills, while working-class parents use authoritarian/directive parenting, which does not develop the same skills in their children, setting them back in their adult economic lives.

The wide range of social-scientific research on intergenerational relationships, between first- and second-generation immigrants, has confirmed the prevalence of authoritarian parenting in immigrant households. Psychological studies of parenting in first-generation immigrant families, including Caribbean, Chinese, East Indian, and Mexican families, have determined that these families enact authoritarian and directive parenting, where independence and individualism among children are discouraged.[9]

Sociological research has shown that the key source of intergenerational conflict and resentment in immigrant households emerges from what children perceive as authoritarian and directive parenting. For instance, second-generation Vietnamese and Korean college students desire what they see as the "normal American family" with more affective parent-child relationships that encourage open communication, flexibility, forgiveness, independence, and respect for individualism.[10] In contrast, they perceived their own families and parents as authoritarian and valuing obedience, respect toward elders, and collective interest as opposed to individual interest. Nancy Foner and Joanna Dreby,[11] in a review article on intergenerational relationships in immigrant families, also reaffirm the conflict highlighted by Karen Pyke[12] and several other researchers.[13] Foner and Dreby assert that "[i]mmigrant parents often expect a level of respect, deference, and obedience that their second-generation children view as authoritarian and domineering. The children have been raised in a U.S. cultural setting in which early independence is encouraged and childrearing norms are generally more permissive than in the parents' home country."[14] If we were to examine these parenting practices through Lareau's lens, we could postulate that these first-generation immigrant parents were at least in some respects engaged in the parental style that she calls "accomplishment of natural growth." However, calling our attention to another analytical frame, Lan[15] contends that, in a world where globalization dictates social and class mobility and neoliberalism directs educational outcomes for children, immigrant parents across the class spectrum engage in parenting practices that will help their children succeed in a globalized world through the use of transnational cultural resources, including discipline and care.

Other studies by immigration scholars that posit immigrant parenting as authoritarian showcase the complexities embedded in such parenting. Emotional closeness, interdependence, and support for educational achievement are also presented as hallmarks of immigrant parent-child interactions.[16] For instance, Asian Indian parents become more permissive with time and generation as families stay and establish themselves in host countries. Other researchers are of the opinion that what is interpreted as authoritarian is a monolithized view of parenting in other cultures as viewed through a Western lens.[17] Applying a Western lens assumes that modern European American parenting is the gold standard against which all other parenting practices must be measured. For instance, parenting by immigrant Chinese mothers in the United States is interpreted as authoritarian by researchers when they should instead be focusing on the social and cultural nuances and adjustments that these mothers are making while parenting in host societies as Jean Gorman shows in her study.[18] In her interview study with mostly middle-class Chinese mothers in the New York City area, she found that Chinese mothers were rarely confrontational or controlling of their children. Much of the parenting happened through discussions and conversations, but what was emphasized as important for children was culturally specific. For example, the Chinese mothers stressed to their children the importance of respect for elders, caring for others beyond the singular concern for one's own self, and being self-sufficient. The mothers warned them against the influences of the perceived ills of American adolescence such as drugs and sex, and ensured the children grew up bilingual. While these mothers did harbor some preconceived notions about American societies, Gorman[19] contends that their parenting should be perceived as more nuanced than just authoritarian.

While Gorman's description of Chinese American mothering does not fit the concerted cultivation model, a small body of scholarship maintains that immigrant parents, particularly Asian immigrant parents, undertake concerted cultivation.[20] For instance, Namita Manohar[21] shows that Indian Tamil immigrant mothers in the United States engaged heavily in concerted cultivation, much like the middle-class parents in Lareau's study. In another study with 13 middle-class immigrant parents, mostly of Asian descent in Britain, Archer[22] contends that these parents undoubtedly engaged in concerted cultivation. They did so by expressing the "desire for personalized education" for their children, being involved with schools and other institutions, climbing up the authority ladder in these institutions, and providing their children with various organized opportunities for skills development.[23] This work puts much more emphasis on race than Lareau did, arguing that, as a result of the racism in British institutions, immigrant parents needed to work extra hard so their children could reach their full potential. Likewise, Jennifer Lee and Min Zhou,[24] in their book investigating the achievement paradox of Asian Americans by focusing on 1.5-generation Chinese immigrants and Vietnamese refugees in the Los Angeles area, contend that Asian American immigrant children are saddled with a "success frame" in their lives. The success frame is really a cultural frame that is handed to Asian American children by their parents and establishes the expectations of doing well in school and preparing for white-collar professional jobs. The racialized model-minority framework also creates expectations held by teachers and other institutional actors of Asian American success and further feeds this success frame. The expectation leads to the pooling of resources and support in the schools, in the communities, and within the families, helping working-class Asian American children to be successful. This study shows that parenting in immigrant households mobilizes transnational cultural resources along with the concerted cultivation style, which extends beyond just middle-class parenting.

More recently, in a 2018 article, Pawan Dhingra asserts that affluent Asian Indian parents in the United States engage in a competitive form of concerted cultivation, particularly in the context of academic achievement and the enrichment education of their children. Dhingra contends that the motivation of the parents is rooted not only in their valuing of education or wanting to ensure social and class mobility of their children in the United States but also in an intense sense of competition. They want their children to stand out, and the clincher here is that this sense of competition is not only fostered in the United States but is also borrowed from the competitive education and economic systems in India where the parents were raised. In another ethnography of Indian American Malayalee Christian youth, Soulit Chacko also finds that the middle-class parents of her participants (many of whom were nurses, as in my study) engaged in strict achievement-based parenting. Similarly, in a 2015 article, Coe and Shani[25] analyzed parenting in middle-class immigrant Ghanaian parents in the United States. They show that Ghanaian parents use both social and institutional resources of the United States (educational resources) and Ghana (discipline and respect for elders) because they see both as important to parenting. What is clear from reviewing the scholarship is that immigrant parents across various groups used transnational resources, including ideologies, in parenting. These resources are often cultural in nature: respect and discipline are cultural constructs, and the sense of competitiveness as it existed in the old country is a social-cultural construct. The transnational parenting of middle-class parents therefore includes a specific engagement with cultural resources that straddles across two countries (homeland and the host country).

This literature seems to suggest that immigrant parenting includes elements of both authoritarian parenting and concerted cultivation. While the literature also suggests that cultural frames are important in shaping immigrant parenting, the complexity of parenting in middle-class immigrants is somewhat underanalyzed. The complexity is further deepened when the question changes to how visa policies—particularly any policy that forces highly educated, middle-class, new immigrant parents (women and men) to stay at home—affect parenting. How might the cultural context of the immigrant family further complicate parenting? My research provides answers to these questions based on the analysis of narratives and observations around the parenting styles of participants in my study, with special attention paid to those dependent H-4 status. It should be noted that, in the context of this analysis, I am using a Bourdieuvian[26] theorization of class, in which social class is interlinked and operationalized through distinctions achieved through cultural capital, which is defined as the knowledge of and access to social status–defining cultural resources that determine a person's exclusion and inclusion from garnering future economic resources and social prestige. In this formulation and in my analysis, unlike in Lareau's analysis, class in parenting does not exist in isolation and, as in Dow's work, does not trump gender or race. It intersects with gender, race, legal status, and transnational cultural experiences to frame parenting practices among the Indian migrant parents, much like in Lan's[27] analysis of the parenting practices of Chinese and Taiwanese parents.

Given what we know about immigrant families, especially Asian American families, and their racialization and parenting in the United States, I contend that we need a more nuanced understanding of their parenting styles because these do not fit neatly in the two distinct categories of class-based parenting that Lareau has provided us. However, drawing on Lareau's concepts of concerted cultivation and accomplishment of natural growth, and on Lan's approach of transnational relationality, I investigate how—along with class—culture, racialized expectations, and transnational experiences also shape parenting in the middle class–identified immigrant Indian parents, whose lives are decidedly shaped by visa laws.

Middle-Class Parenting: Transcultural Cultivation, Racialization, and the Visa Regime

A Different Kind of Concerted Cultivation

"'All happy families look alike.' Was it Tolstoy who said it?" The paraphrased quote and question were posed to me by Vani, a mother on an H-4 visa who was a manager at a financial firm in India before coming to the United States. "Yes, Vani," I responded to her rhetorical question as we watched her seven-year-old daughter perform a combination of ballet, salsa, and Bharatnatyam (Indian classical dance) to a peppy Hindi film song on Skype (a video chat platform) for her grandmother (Vani's mother) in India. It was about 11 a.m. on a Tuesday in Chicago and 10:30 p.m. in Chennai, India where Vani's mother lived. Vani's daughter had missed school that day because she had a Bharatnatyam recital in a Hindu temple in the suburbs of Chicago that afternoon and needed to prepare for it. As her daughter finished her short performance for her grandma and us, Vani continued:

Nothing can be farther from the truth. Not all happy families look alike. American parents don't have to constantly worry about their kids losing their culture. But we immigrant parents do. That makes our work so much harder. We are never sure if we are doing right by our kids. Are we putting too much pressure on our little one by having her learn three kinds of dance or are we just allowing her to learn more? Who knows!

Vani draws a distinction between American/nonimmigrant families with children and her own family by spotting the challenge of meeting transnational cultural expectations while ensuring that her child was receiving all the developmental opportunities. This concern for balancing the two aspects was shared by all the parents with whom I talked. Like the middle-class parents in Lareau's study, the parents in my sample spent a lot of time thinking, researching, and organizing leisure and developmental activities for their children, but the difference was that the Indian parents in my study were also actively and creatively thinking about how best to impart cultural knowledge to their children without alienating them from the host society. This effort was inextricably linked to their dependent status in multiple ways. Vani's next words bore testimony to this analysis:

> And you know I can invest this much time on the children because I am not working. Imagine if I had a job like my husband's—that would mean so much more work. But, we'd also have more resources . . . um, it's hard to tell—what would raising kids [look] like if I was not on a dependent visa . . . this issue of the visa never leaves, I keep wondering, what would life be like, parenting be like, if I did not have these shackles. There's so much to consider, our lives with these visas, and getting the parenting right, it's like a delicate dance.

The structure of the visa regime, even when it did not directly affect parenting, was always in the backdrop, as the parents, particularly the dependent mothers, tried to organize their children's lives such that they turned out to be culturally aware individuals who understood the cultural and social norms in both countries.

A poignant example of this delicate dance that parents had to perform came through in my interview with Mira. A copywriter of English commercials at a reputable international advertising firm in India before moving to the United States, Mira laid out her struggles in raising a seven-year-old boy who was born in the United States. She confessed to me her constant fear that her son, who spoke three Indian languages and was also learning Spanish in school, would be bullied and laughed at in school if he slipped into one of those languages because he was juggling so many linguistic complexities. Mira and her husband were from two different regions in India and spoke different languages. The languages they spoke did not include Hindi, the national language of India. Mira told me that, when her son was younger, she and her husband wanted to ensure that he was learning both their languages, and they spoke to him only in their own languages. They figured that their child would learn English in kindergarten and that they did not need to actively speak to him in English at home. After their son had been in school a year, they began to get a sense that he was being laughed at and isolated at day care because of what one of the day care teachers called "his wacky language skills." At home, he increasingly refused to speak any of the Indian languages and said he only wanted to speak languages he learned in school: English and Spanish. Devastated, Mira and her husband had multiple conversations with the day care teachers on how best to accommodate their son's cultural needs. This entailed Mira's volunteering at day care three days per week. And in consultation with other immigrant parents and kindergarten teachers, Mira began a Hindi language course with her son—a language she herself did not know—so that her son would learn to value Indian languages in the same way as English and Spanish. Mira also spent a considerable amount of time talking with her child about how to speak to his friends and his teachers in school about his own languages and culture without getting intimidated by their reaction. In a conversation with me, she revealed how fearful she was of bringing up the issue with day care teachers: "It was nerve-wracking to talk to my child's teachers. After all we are on visas here, and I don't even have a status beyond my husband's. What if the teacher complained we were creating trouble? We'd be thrown out of the country. But we had to persist for our child's sake."

This case reveals varied and complex aspects of immigrant parenting and parenting while being bound by visa laws. The time and effort invested by Mira to ensure that her son was learning the languages she felt were important for his bicultural existence are not required in the lives of middle-class nonimmigrant parents. While Mira and her husband engaged and interacted with institutions and had negotiation-based conversations with their child, much like the middle-class parents in Lareau's[28] study, in the case of Mira and other Indian parents, much of this effort was to protect their children from institutional and individual racism as in the case of Lan's[29] immigrant Taiwanese parents. The Black parents in Lareau's study also dealt with everyday racism. However, immigrant parents are often observed having to balance both racism and transnational cultural expectations while also being concerned about losing their legal status in the United States, and therefore they work to maintain and reproduce ethnic/cultural identity as well as class identity. In the immigrant families in my study, the parents felt it important to imbue their children with cultural knowledge through language, food, art, and religion. This was both part of social expectations and a marker of class status for immigrant parents in the transnational community. However, the children were subjected to everyday racism because of their performance of some of the cultural expectations; for instance, they were teased for having an accent or wearing clothing from their culture but different from US norms. The parents then had the additional task of strategizing how to counter the forms of everyday racism faced by their children while still emphasizing the importance of cultural learning. They also had to worry whether being their children's advocates could potentially jeopardize their legality in the country if the institution were to complain about them. Such concerns did not exist for the American parents in studies of middle-class parenting.

For immigrant parents of means, it mattered that their children grew up bilingual or multilingual, were well adjusted in the cultures of the home and host countries, and received all the support they needed to develop their talents and skills inside and outside their schools. This made the weekly schedules of both the children and the parents—particularly those parents responsible for the lion's share of the work—"as packed as the schedule of a company's CEO," as one mother said to me half-jokingly.

I asked to look at the weekly schedules of most of the children. On average, except for sleeping and taking an hour or so of leisure per day, the parents spent all their time on the children. I asked Mary and Joseph, a married couple with a 10-year-old daughter, to allow me to shadow them for a day during summer vacation. Mary was a nurse, and Joseph was here on a dependent visa. On the day I shadowed them, Mary had a two-shift workday, so Joseph was responsible for their daughter's schedule. I arrived at their suburban home at about 7:00 a.m. Mary was preparing breakfast. I ate breakfast with the family, and Mary gave me a rundown of what the day would look like. Joseph would take their daughter to the local Keralite/Malayalee ethnic church right after breakfast for an 8:30 a.m. children's choir group, followed by piano lessons in the town center at 10:00 a.m. That would be followed by a quick snack. After the snack we were to drive to Evanston, Illinois, about 30 minutes away from where Mary and Joseph lived. Joseph was taking their daughter to Northwestern University for a science summer-camp orientation that the child and a parent were supposed to attend together. I offered to wait in a café while they attended the orientation. After the orientation, the child was scheduled for an Indian classical-dance lesson for an hour, followed by a play date with her friends from dance class. The schedules of many other parents and children resembled the schedule that Mary, Joseph, and their daughter followed.

Church activities were a regular part of the children's schedules in the nurses' families. Gina, who had two children, aged eight and 10, told me why it was important to live near the church. She confirmed that sending them to church and getting them involved in church activities was the primary way that parents in her community imparted cultural knowledge to the children. The church offered classes in reading and writing Malayalee, the regional language of the nurses, and the priest taught catechism classes to the children in the same way. According to Gina, this is the way she had learned "Bible with local stories in our village in India." It was also important to the dependent fathers that their children had a regular church life, since they wanted to maintain their roles as leaders in the churches, as discussed in chapter 4.

The families of the tech workers, most of whom were Hindu, were less dependent on an organized religious institution for cultural transmission. This could be because most Hindu temples were located in the outer suburbs of the cities and most tech workers' families lived in the city, unlike the nurses' families, most of whom lived in neighborhoods near their ethnic churches. Given this fact, the parents in tech families generally imparted cultural knowledge through music, dance, language classes, religious gatherings and rituals at home, and activities organized with other Indian families and by ensuring that the children learned the rituals and customs of their parents' native culture.

However, the parents in both types of families, both Hindu (most tech workers) and Christian (all nurses), ensured that their children kept up in school and also developed skills that other American middle-class children acquired, such as playing the piano or participating in school sports. If that meant the children had to learn three languages, two dance forms, and both Indian and Western musical instruments, then the parents in these households did it all. As in the concerted cultivation style of parenting, the parents engaged with their children in dialogue and negotiations, often creating reward structures for accomplishments, and purposefully involved themselves in the institutions of their children. These parents, however, did more than just concerted cultivation. They also engaged in the kind of parenting that resembled what Lareau calls accomplishment of natural growth or what in Lan's work is expressed as transcultural relationality.

Accomplishment of Natural Growth or Simply Transcultural Parenting

I was attending a community event organized by Shija and Mathew, held in their suburban home near Chicago. There were five other nurses with their husbands and children at the event. The family had invited the priest of their church to hold a class on morality for the children. The event was organized as a potluck. It was a summer afternoon, and the hosts had laid out the food and chairs in the backyard, and most invitees were lounging outdoors. Most of the chairs were occupied by the adults, including me, while the children sat on the lawn or on the edges of the raised flower beds around the house. I walked into the kitchen to get myself some water, and when I walked out again, I found that my chair had been taken by one of the children. So, without thinking much about it, I sat down on the lawn with the children. But, two minutes later, I heard the very stern voice of one of the fathers telling the child to move from the chair and to let me sit. The child protested, and I—a little shocked and embarrassed—jumped to the defense of the child, saying I was perfectly fine sitting on the grass. At this point, the mother came up to the chair and, hovering over the child, said in a calm but cold voice: "Did you not hear Dad? When you are asked to move, you move—no questions. Miss Pallavi should not be sitting on the ground while you sit on the chair." She then turned to me and, stopping my protests, said: "You know how this is. They need to learn to respect their elders. They are growing up in America, but they cannot forget the respectful and the valuable lessons of our culture. Would you ever dare to do this when you were his age? No, right? He needs to learn. Also, he needs to listen to his dad." Later on, she whispered to me: "I don't ever want his dad to feel like he is not being listened to because he is mostly at home. So, I have to be extra strict with the children."

This interaction between the parents and the child can be analyzed as a good example of one aspect of Lareau's natural growth: authoritative and directive-oriented parenting, but in the nature of the disciplining they aligned more with the Taiwanese American parents[30] or Vietnamese and Korean American[31] parents. Yet, what differentiated the parents in this book was the undercurrent of the visa status in how it shaped the structure of authority in the household, especially in the nurses' homes. The nurses wanted to ensure that the fathers' voice of authority was respected and valued in the household given their perceptibly diminished legal status of being a dependent.

In the course of my fieldwork, I noticed other such interactions in almost all the families, along with other aspects of the natural growth or style of parenting. For instance, the children were often encouraged to negotiate play dates and sleepovers as a reward for good performance on educational and learning activities, but in day-to-day activities and when talking to authority figures, they were expected to follow orders and take directions. The parents gave strict directives about eating, sleeping, studying, and talking back. These orders issued by the parents, however, were almost always followed with an explanation about cultural expectations, often using the phrase "this is part of our culture."

The parents in both types of families told me they felt they had to be extra strict and authoritative with their children because of the visa situation. While many of the nurse mothers, like Gina, ensured that the children were respectful toward their fathers because of the role reversal, the dependent mothers worried that their children were not being disciplined enough because the fathers were not present in parenting on an everyday basis, as exemplified in the words of Radha, who said:

> I worry that I am too permissive. Sometimes I fear I am becoming an American parent. I don't believe in beating kids or anything, but it's also not okay for them to talk back and do whatever they want and disrespect people and family. I often let them talk back to me, and that is not good. There needs to be discipline [sic]. I wish Shankar [her husband] was around more—I strongly believe in the "good cop, bad cop strategy" for raising kids [*laughs*]. The fluffy, individualistic American parenting is no good. I like a healthy combo [*laughs*].

Radha's worry about being too permissive and becoming like an American parent, as well as her feeling the need for more authoritative parenting, are evidence that class is not always the predictor for the two parenting styles, as is apparent in Lan's work. Additionally, the absence of the father from everyday parenting shows how, even in the daily routine, the visa regime intrudes on how parents desire to raise their children. Radha's worry about developing overly individualistic children was also reflected in the views and parental approaches of other parents.

Much like the working-class children in Lareau's study, the children in the Indian immigrant households were also expected to spend time with their kin and extended families as part of their cultural training. If extended family, especially grandparents, were visiting from India—and these visits generally lasted about six months—they were put in charge of the children, who were expected to spend time with them. Parents did this both to take a break from parenting and to make sure the children were in touch with their transnational families and culture.

Additionally, the families, mainly the nonworking dependent spouses and children, often spent two to three months in India during the summers. During these trips, the children spent most of their days in unstructured leisure time with their kin. Taking these long vacations in India meant that the children missed out on summer-camp activities in which their middle-class American peers participated. But for the parents, this time spent with extended kin and family was important for transcultural learning.

The reasons why immigrant children spent time with their kin were different from the reasons expressed by the working-class children in Lareau's study. In her research, the children were spending time with kin in the neighborhood because their parents did not have the resources to organize other skill-developing activities for them. In the case of immigrant children, the parents actively insisted on time with extended families in India and in the United States. It must be noted that this was possible only because visa regulations forced one parent to stay home. The fact remains, however, that immigrant children spent unstructured time with family. Instead of being engaged in skill development all year, the children in my study might well be developing a sense of community with their kin and extended families by spending unstructured time with them, much in the same way as the working-class children did in Lareau's study.

The major difference between the concept of the accomplishment of natural growth as presented by Lareau for the working-class parents in her sample versus the parents in my study was that Lareau's participants parented in the way they did because they lacked the time, means, or know-how to engage in concerted cultivation. For the middle-class parents in my study, it was more a matter of ensuring the behavioral transmission of culture, which they feared would be lost in America. They achieved this through directive-oriented parenting, which also served to maintain the sanctity of parental authority given the complex visa statuses of the parents. Additionally, it is important to note that spending summers in India away from the regular after-school and extracurricular activities in the United States did not result in the loss of developmental enrichment among the children. The parents made sure to balance the developmental needs of the children along with the need to place the children in their home cultures during the summers.

Consequences of Transcultural Cultivation Parenting Practices

My analysis here reveals that the middle-class immigrant Indian parents practice both concerted cultivation and some form of the natural growth style of parenting. Yet, a question remains: What is at the heart of why and how they parent? I argue that these parents have a "success frame" for their children.[32] That is to say, they desire to raise children who fit the model-minority mold in the United States. This success frame also emerges from the cultural frame situated in the value of achievement handed down to children from their immigrant parents, but this frame is more hybrid in nature compared to that experienced, for example, by the Vietnamese and Chinese second-generation children in the literature.[33] This success frame includes a concerted effort toward the development of talents, skills, and achievement in school but within a transnational and transcultural context. It was very important for the parents that their children have a balanced upbringing with American as well as Indian middle-class material and cultural resources to make sure they excelled in school, grew up multilingual, acquired transnational cultural knowledge, developed artistic and other talents, and so on. That meant many extra hours of bicultural and talent development activities as well as a healthy dose of directive-based parenting and time with kin and extended families. What these parents were doing was converging Lareau's two parenting styles to fit within a cultural frame and aligning their parenting to the immigrant Taiwanese parents[34] and/or Black middle-class mothers.[35]

It is important to analyze these parenting styles because they have material meaning for the lives of the children. From Lareau's research, we know that these distinct parenting styles have widely divergent consequences for the children's life chances and social attributes. According to Lareau, middle-class children grow up to be more entitled and materially successful, while working-class children remain materially deprived but become more empathetic and relational people. What are the consequences for these Indian immigrant children? The children in my study definitely had a more communal upbringing ensconced in transcultural contexts. These children received even more organized talent- and skill-development activities than an average white or Black native-born American middle-class child. They experienced multiple institutions while growing up, learned to negotiate with parents and teachers, and fought institutional and individual racism with their parents as their advocates. At the same time, their parents imparted to them the value of extended family and the need to be respectful of elders. This combination of transcultural parenting and concerted cultivation is what I label "transcultural cultivation." However, such parenting also transpired under the shadow of the visa regime that structured the lives of the parents. In other words, transcultural cultivation could not help but be visa-regimented, which intensified fears and worries as the parents grappled with raising their children.

In the context of this research, transcultural cultivation does not happen in a vacuum. It has two strong influences: the gender of the parents and the visa status of the parents and the families. Complexities emerge when the analysis accounts for the visa status and the gender of the parent primarily responsible for raising the children, as will be explored in the next section.

Visa Laws, Gender, and Transcultural Cultivation

Gender—as to parents and parenting—is decidedly absent in Lareau's discussion. Yet we know from a host of research on the household division of labor that gender is central to parenting work and that the feminine/woman partner often takes on the major share of parenting duties.[36] Gender becomes even more relevant when the family is structured around having a breadwinner and a stay-at-home parent, as in the case of the families in my study. Is there a difference in the parenting approaches of middle-class stay-at-home fathers versus stay-at-home mothers who are legally forced by visa rules to take on the role of primary caregiver to their children? My analysis shows that there are definitely some material differences. Specifically, in my study, stay-at-home mothers were involved in all aspects of their children's lives with little help from their husbands, whereas stay-at-home fathers shared transcultural cultivation with their wives equally.

In the nurses' families, the dependent husbands took on most of the child care duties while the nurses themselves, as the breadwinners, still did most of the other housework.[37] In the context of child rearing and parenting done by the dependent fathers in comparison to dependent mothers, there were two identifiable patterns structured by the visa status of each parent: Dependent mothers were solely responsible for the work involved in parenting while their husbands managed the finances of parenting; in comparison, the nurses and the husbands shared the parenting work, but a gendered division of parenting existed nevertheless.

In the families of the tech workers, the wives—who were legally dependent and not allowed to work—did the bulk of parenting work. This included meeting the everyday emotional and material needs of the children, being involved in their school activities, identifying their talents, researching the range of activities available to the children, finding both leisure and developmental pursuits relevant to the specific ethnic culture of the family, planning events for the children, and carting the children to and from their activities. An additional task involved calculating the expenses related to the children's events and bringing a schedule of the activities to the breadwinner husband, who then determined the budget and where corners could be cut so that the needs of the children could be fulfilled. A notable concern in these families was affordability. Despite the middle-class professional status and identity of the families, the fact remained that only one person was permitted to work. With a single income, the families struggled to fulfill all the financial demands, including the transcultural cultivation of the children. It was the job of the wife to find affordable activities without compromising the quality of the service. This took quite an emotional toll on the mothers. Radhika ruefully shared her feelings with me regarding this:

> Sometimes it feels like my head will explode. You know, it's like asking someone who barely can swim to cross the ocean. I am still learning to live in this country, and I can't work, but I have the responsibility to give my child the best possible upbringing while maintaining all sides. It's very, very hard.

And, yet the mothers took on all of these responsibilities willingly because the fathers were mostly unavailable due to work demands. Additionally, transcultural cultivation had become part of the women's parental identity in the absence of a professional identity. It was a way for them to defy their dependent status. Anjali described her role as a parent in America as undertaking the "herculean task of parenting in a new country, the country that takes away your *gurud* [dignity] from you." Jaya, who used to be the chief accountant of a multinational corporation in India before moving to the United States on a dependent visa, best articulated what Anjali meant by this statement. Jaya told me:

> It felt like I had lost everything when I came to America as a dependent, and then I became A's [her son] mother, and I found this new vocation.

I have to give him the best despite all the constraints. And that best includes the best of India and America. For a long time, I felt worthless, but
the challenge of being a mother, who most of the time feels like a single
mother because Ravi [her husband] has to work so much, makes me feel
whole again, as paradoxical as it sounds. Some days it's too much, but
then I bring on my accountancy skills into this parenting thing and all is
right with the world [*laughs*].

What Anjali called a "herculean task" and Jaya called her new identity and vocation was the emotional work,[38] in addition to the physical
and mental labor required for the transcultural cultivation in which the
dependent mothers were engaging to cope with their legally dependent
status. The structure of the visa laws and the work demands on the men
made it easy for them not to be as involved in parenting responsibilities,
thus making parenting an intensively gendered process. Taken together,
the demands and pressures experienced by the dependent mothers to be
ideal mothers given they did not have a career anymore are an example
of intensive mothering ideology,[39] in which mothers feel they have to give
their all to their children's needs in order to be good mothers since that
is now their only productive task at hand. The struggle of the dependent
mothers is indicative of Hochschild's *time bind*[40] proposition; many mothers alluded to their past life where they were working professionals as less
stressful than being completely responsible for their children's development and well-being. This was especially apropos, as the fathers were min-
imally involved in the everyday because of the pressures of performing the
part of the ideal migrant worker at work as a result of their legal status.

In contrast, in the nurses' families, the dependent men appeared to be
as involved in parenting and even participating in the pleasures of caregiving, somewhat like the fathers in Dasgupta's[41] and Montes's[42] studies
where undocumented fathers separated from their children and transnational fathers (respectively) took pride in doing unpaid care labor for
their children to make up for lost time. However, for the fathers in this
book, a closer examination reveals that the men were doing only the
visible labor of transporting the children to various activities and being
engaged on an everyday basis in their lives. Much of the behind-the-
scenes work—researching, arranging activities, scheduling, and managing the expenses—was still being done by the mothers, who were the

main breadwinners in these families. Along with this work, the mothers were also responsible for cooking and cleaning and maintaining all transnational communications and relationships for the family.

The children in these families, however, were often more attached to their fathers because they were more present in their day-to-day lives, which induced guilt in the mothers. The mothers in these families repeatedly told me that the children were "closer to the fathers" than to them, which the fathers confirmed. One of the fathers told me that he was his children's "go-to person, not their mother." This forced these fathers to do some of the emotional labor of parenting.[43] Shija, one of the mothers, expanded on how exactly the attachment of children to the fathers manifested: "Whenever my daughter is upset, she runs to her dad. I am an afterthought. I think they forget that I am around because I am gone to work so much. It kills me. So, I make sure that I do as much for them when I am around." This guilt propelled the mothers to take on as much as they could of the work of transcultural cultivation.

Many of the nurses confirmed how difficult the parental dynamic was for them and how, as a result, they felt the need to be a cultural liaison. Rosy, in describing how she views her parenting responsibilities, said: "It's hard to be the only earner in the family, especially if you are a woman. My kids never see me because I am always at work. It's so hard. But as they grow, they will know how much their mother actually did. It's also about me feeling involved in their lives." The mothers also viewed themselves as cultural agents for their children. "It's the mother who passes on culture to the children" was common rhetoric among the nurses. This is an example of an internalized gendered cultural script[44] that the mothers in these families used to justify the transcultural cultivation style of parenting they took so seriously. They also engaged in the gendered work of extensive mothering[45] by delegating, unwillingly, some of the care obligations to the fathers while still assuming the major share of the responsibility for their children's well-being, provision, and cultural education—all the while juggling breadwinning responsibilities.

The dependent husbands took pride in being the main parent but eluded tasks such as cleaning, organizing schedules, and cooking, which were less rewarding. These fathers claimed a central fathering identity at the same time they downplayed their legal dependent status, in part because their role as head of the household was taken away.[46] However, the mothers who were the main breadwinners bore the load of parenting equally with fathers, if not a heavier load when both paid work and family demands were compounded.

Parents in both sets of families thought *transcultural parenting* was important because of the precariousness of their status in the United States. Naureen told me that she and her husband, Aasman, wanted to make sure that their children were not entirely out of touch with their Indianness in case they had to return to India, for instance, if Aasman lost his job and they lost their visa statuses. Many of the nurses also expressed similar concerns.

In both family types, women performed much of the transcultural parenting labor. We see some of the same trends in terms of parenting as gendered labor in studies done on nonimmigrant families in the United States.[47] What distinguishes the families in my research, however, is that, for the men and women who were forced to become stay-at-home parents because of their visa statuses, parenting became their main vocation. Unlike the stay-at-home fathers in Rehel's[48] study who transitioned seamlessly into a main caregiver role in the absence of workplace constraints, the stay-at-home fathers in my study resisted being viewed as mothers. They emphasized a fathering identity, especially to preserve their head-of-household status and alleviate the resentment over the loss of their provider status. The dependent parents in these ways saw the kind of intensive parenting they performed as a way of redefining their identities from being dependent parents to becoming transcultural parents.

As the analysis above shows, the visa laws unmistakably shape gendered parenting in the households of the Indian middle-class immigrant workers, and yet similar trends in both transcultural parenting and gendered parenting can be found in many immigrant families.[49] Perhaps a more focused study of parenting in immigrant households is required to expand on the class-based theory of parenting by using an intersectional framework given that the compounding effects of race, class, gender, sexualities, and immigration status on parenting styles are undeniable.

Conclusion

The middle-class Indian immigrants whose parenting I put under the microscope combine the approaches of concerted cultivation and natural growth with a strong emphasis on raising transcultural children. Their lives, including their parenting styles, are shaped by their visa statuses. For instance, if the dependent spouses had been able to enter the labor markets, either the parenting chores would have been more evenly distributed, or the range of activities would have had to be altered. Given that the parenting approaches of the Indian parents is a product not only of their class status but also their transnational lives and their legal immigration statuses, I call this parenting "visa-regimented transcultural cultivation." Additionally, much of what the parents did included the parenting styles that Lareau describes as well as the other nuances of transnational relationality that Lan posited. The immigrant parents engaged in a kind of cultivation that demanded equilibrium on various levels. The parents balanced their visa statuses with their identities as immigrant parents, balanced their children's activities by prioritizing the transnational context of their existence while ensuring they were acculturated in the United States as well, and balanced the gendered act of parenting. In effect, the Indian immigrant families' parenting choices lay at the intersection of class status, the gender of the parents, immigration status, the racialization of immigrants in the host society, and cultural practices.

The empirical examination of these intersections in the context of raising children helps us theorize parenting as a practice that is not simply molded by the class location of parents. Immigrant parents, especially those whose lives are heavily controlled by visa laws, negotiate multiple dimensions of their own and their children's lives while parenting to produce a type of cultivation that includes various transcultural elements. Does this kind of parenting affect the futures of immigrant children and/or contribute to the reproduction of class statuses? How does the application of intersectionality change the ways we think about parenting in minority households? These questions that arise from this chapter can become the topic of future inquiry.

But we can assume, given that Indian Americans are one of the most materially successful immigrant groups in the United States,[50] transcultural cultivation done by middle- to upper-middle-class Indian American parents reproduces, and will continue to reproduce, middle-class to upper-middle-class status for their adult children. That is, if these families were to stay in the United States—which the Trump presidency had made uncertain (as discussed in the conclusion), and another right-wing president in the future may do so again. There is no denying, however, that the middle-class immigrant parents and children have to work much harder than their American white counterparts to achieve similar levels of success.[51] The legal visa statuses of the parents intersect with their class status and their social and cultural expectations of parenting to make parenting a gendered process within the visa regime. The concept of *visa-regimented transcultural cultivation* I have introduced here can propel further exploration among and between other groups (e.g., Latinx families, Asian families that are not middle-class, rural families) on the topic. The possibilities for further research are many. What emerges clearly in this research is that the visa regime directly and indirectly shapes most experiences, even those as routine and personal as parenting.

Conclusion

Dismantling Dependence

When you come to this country, they tell you there's the
American Dream, and then you find out you need to get into
a very long queue to get to it. For us H-4 visa holders, that
queue seems to be unending and torturous.
—Neha Mahajan, H-4 activist and journalist

It was 6:00 a.m. on the morning of November 20, 2014. I woke to a flurry
of missed phone calls and voicemails from various women participants
of my research, journalists, and my partner at my hotel room in New
Jersey. I had a long and action-packed day ahead of me, given I was there
for a job interview. If these were messages and voicemails from any other
persons, I would have waited until the end of the day. But these were my
participants, and in a few hours, I would be talking about what they had
shared with me, in my research job talk. So, I had to listen to what they
had to say. I was also curious. The first voicemail I listened to was from
Jaya. Her excited and cheerful voice still rings in my ears. "Oh my god,
oh my god! Did you see the news? We did it. Obama will sign executive order offering EADs to H-4 holders.[1] And I kid you not, I cried big
tears—I never thought this would be true. Your op-ed[2] was cited as evidence for—it's on the White House website—how cool is that! Thank you.
Call me, call me." The next message was from my excited partner: "Hey,
your research is on the White House website." And so it went with the
other messages, voices welling up in elation, expressing a range of emotions, many sharing their happy tears with me. I was quite overwhelmed
to hear the news and deeply touched that so many of my participants had
called to share it. I was also skeptical until I had a chance to read the ruling, which had to wait until after the day was done. I will come back to
the ruling and its implications later in this conclusion.

When I first began this research in 2010, very few people outside the community of H-1B and H-4 visa holders knew much about these visas, especially the H-4 dependent visas, and their impact on people's lives. The women participants routinely told me how they were mistaken for undocumented people in their public interactions because they did not have any government-issued identification. Of the five legislators I spoke to for this research, only two had an in-depth understanding of how dependent visas worked. The women H-4 visa holders unequivocally said that this study was the only way for them to make their voices and their angst heard.

Dependent (H-4) visa holders had long felt invisible, ever since the creation of the category in 1952. Only after Barack Obama's election in 2008 would this change, as more and more women on H-4 visas used the power of the internet and social media, coupled with their social, human, and cultural capital, to tell the world their story. Some key figures among these women emerged as the lead voices of this online movement. The movement was further encouraged by President Obama's promises to "fix the broken immigration system" and the implementation of Deferred Action for Childhood Arrivals (DACA) in 2012. The leaders of the H-4 movement joined hands with another online movement, which was led mainly by Indian H-1B tech workers, to advocate for expediting the permanent residency process for Indians, and together these groups reached out to the Obama White House. In India and in the United States, the media began picking up these stories. In 2014, Obama ultimately signed an executive order that allowed H-4 visa holders to obtain a work permit; it went into effect in 2015.

Donald Trump, ever since taking office in 2016, threatened to rescind this executive order several times. A Google search on January 11, 2020, of "H-4 visa, dependent spouses" yielded more than 1.6 million results, including news reports, stories, and op-eds published on the topic. A quick scan of approximately 200 reports on the topic showed that most describe the situation of Indian women who come to the United States on H-4 dependent visas. Some also discuss the long wait for permanent residency that Indians on temporary visas must experience because of backlogs. More recent articles focus on children who will age out of their dependent status and will either have to get their own student visas or return to India.

Starkly absent from these movements and media reports are the voices of men holding H-4 visas. The tenor of reporting of the issues and the nature of the social action surrounding the issues further show how conversations about the legal status of skilled workers and their families are advertently and inadvertently engineered by a gendered and racialized visa regime.

This book has documented how visa policies for migrant skilled workers and their families represent a manifestation of the state power that, in conjunction with corporations that employ internationally mobile bodies as skilled workers, regulates and monitors these bodies configuring the formation of the visa regimes. The visa regime is designed to surveil and control the movement of legal nonimmigrant subjects in a country. When the nonimmigrant subjects are part of a racialized workforce, this control over their everyday lives—be it the interactions between spouses, or the raising of children, or the experience of discrimination and differentiation in the workplace or of uncomfortable public interactions, as in the case of the participants of this study—translates into the formation of a visa regime that is gendered and racialized.

The Making of a Gendered and Racialized Visa Regime

Over the years, as I have presented this research to various audiences, a comment I have often encountered is: "But the visas are not given to a particular gender or race—they are in fact gender- and race-neutral." While it is true that the H-1B visas are not meant for any racialized group of temporary workers and the H-4 visas are not meant only for women or women of color, the fact remains that, over the years, Indian men have become the largest recipients of H-1B visas and their wives the largest recipients of H-4 visas. The cumulative statistics on who arrives on these visas, the snowballing effect of the oppressive history of labor and family migration to the United States, and the contemporary impacts of these visas, have made them a tool for the gendered and racialized oppression of migrant subjects.

The mechanisms that produce a coherent system of oppressive structures through the visa laws, which I argue take the form of a gendered and racialized visa regime, are to be understood through two parallel and distinct levels of governmentality. On one level, the visa regime draws its power from coercive forms of domination embedded in the state-corporation nexus. This nexus manifests in three ways: (1) the temporally uncertain and unstable nature of legal status associated with being on a temporary visa with a seemingly unending wait toward permanent residency; (2) the ever-present, continual threat of delegalization and deportation; and (3) the power given to corporations by the state to control the visa statuses of the lead migrant and her family.

On another level, the "techniques of the self" come into play; these are the means by which migrant families and migrant individuals negotiate their visa statuses and adjust to their new lives. These negotiations happen in the everyday lives of the migrant subjects and are rooted in: (1) gendered negotiations with spouses in the family; (2) parenting in a context in which the class status of the parents is undermined by their legal and racialized status in the United States; and (3) struggles with the self in reconciling premigration independent status with the postmigration dependent status and the experience of overtly discriminatory public interactions. All of these are filtered through the intersections of gender and legal status, meaning that men on work visas and women on work visas have distinct experiences based on their gender and race. Likewise, men on dependent visas and women on dependent visas have different experiences of oppression and agency based on their gender and legal status. These two levels lead to the formation of a visa-based governmentality that is gendered and racialized and that governs the lives of my participants in every way while they remain on these visas.

Therefore, legal status, the gender of the person, and the racialized experiences in the public sphere that co-constitute the experiential conditions they must negotiate in order to navigate their new lives in the United States all create an invisible web of dependence that becomes binding for all my participants—dependent visa holders as well as their work visa–holding spouses.

Consequences of Living Under a Gendered and Racialized Visa Regime

Dependent visa policies that regulate the migration of temporary professional workers and their families are often touted as a way to build stable migrant families through family reunification provisions, and the policies do use gender- and race-neutral legal language, but at their core they are framed by gendered assumptions that view work and family as two separate, binary spheres: the men as provider and the women as homemaker/caretaker.

I showed in chapter 5 that the dependent visa regime is interpreted through a gendered lens by the families of migrant workers even when the policies fostering such migration have gender-neutral language. In migrant families where women are dependent spouses, the visa structure successfully builds on and enforces an internalized gendered understanding of what it means to be a dependent wife. Even when the women disavow their dependent positions and express angst at the idea of being a dependent, they still perform most of the household and child-care responsibilities. They perform femininities beyond the call of household duty and call it "learning to be dependent." While most women are resentful of such gendered performances, a handful embrace it as a way to justify their dependence and to claim agency in their dependent lives.

The dependent husbands do not have a gendered script to fall back on to explain their dependence. In fact, state-imposed dependence delegitimizes all their cultural beliefs about what it means to be a man in the context of the family. In order to cope with this loss of status, dependent men use different strategies to reassert masculinity. Some refuse to migrate on dependent visas, leaving their nurse wives in the lurch. When they do come over, they express resentment, sometimes by excessive drinking or by not doing their full share of household work. Their way of resisting "learning to be dependent" is to protect male privilege within the household against the dependency enforced by their visa statuses. However, in the realm of child care, these men perform caretaking roles and often represent themselves as fathers who make sacrifices to support their children's lives.

Lead migrants also participate in gendered behaviors. Nurses overcompensate or perform compensatory femininities to make their husbands feel in charge of the family. Tech workers excuse themselves from household responsibilities completely, except on weekends when they engage in some child-care duties. These men often cite the demands of their work life for "missing out" on being involved in their children's lives, but the net result is a family life modeled after a 1950s version of the American nuclear family. Gender-neutral visas do not significantly reverse gendered performances and expectations within either family type, with the exception of dependent fathers assuming the role of primary caregivers of their children.

In various chapters, I also demonstrate that, despite the constraints of the visa regime, the participants exhibited strong reflexive agency as they expressed their dissent and resentment against the power of the state. Most participants were not in a position to act collectively on their dissent. It is important to note, however, that these men and women actively resisted the disciplining of their selves by the visa regime and sought out different avenues to express their agency. My research challenges the self-disciplining aspect of Foucault's theory by providing evidence that individuals resist disciplining themselves even when state power is binding and coercive, as in the case of visa structures. I call these resistances "acts of disruption."

Nonetheless, I have shown that visa laws are oppressive for both family forms (men as breadwinners and women as breadwinners). Women in both family forms—the wives of tech workers and the nurses—seem to be more severely disadvantaged as a consequence of the visa policies: the wives of tech workers assume all family responsibilities and therefore feel dehumanized. The nurses are overworked, as they do both their paid work and most of the housework. Male dependents also suffer but find ways of reasserting their male privilege.

My research shows that visa policies have clearly failed to implement "stable immigrant families." Instead, they have created highly gendered family environments with anxious, overworked, self-doubting, and unhappy individuals. This is not unusual when it comes to US policies touted as profamily. For instance, the stated goal of the 1996 welfare reforms was not poverty reduction but to encourage marriage and alleviate rates of single parenthood among communities of color, especially Black and Latinx communities. Subsequently this became a heteropaternalistic project that punished the poor people of color by propogating moral values that eulogize heterosexual marriages and pronatalism in dual parenthood.[3] The Family and Medical Leave Act (FMLA) was another piece of legislation presented as profamily; it allowed eligible workers to take up to 12 weeks of leave—unpaid, in most cases—to care for a child or a sick family member. Under FMLA, workers who take this leave have peace of mind, knowing that they will continue to receive employee health benefits and won't lose their job for taking leave. However, temporary workers, as with the workers in this study, and low-wage workers are not eligible under FMLA, and most eligible employees cannot afford 12 weeks of unpaid leave; it is therefore almost impossible for them to take FMLA leave, making this a failed policy that disproportionately impacts women's health and careers.[4] These examples show how the US neoliberal state in late capitalism institutes policies that almost always harm the most marginalized, despite the proclaimed progressive goals. The "family-friendly" visa policies are no exception: they become tools of coercion and impose model-minority behavior on temporary migrant families of color. They insist on gendered and heterosexist family arrangements and racialized experiences at work, leaving the families deeply distressed and vulnerable to uncertainties. If the US government is truly concerned with the interests of migrant families and their stability, then visa laws must be seriously reconsidered even in their current manifestation.

Visa-Based Governmentality and the Gendered and Racialized Visa Regime

The Opportunity Trap shows how dependent and work visas regulate, control, and encompass the lives of migrants. Visas affect the construction of self, family configurations, workplace experiences, and the public interactions of visa holders. The coercive nature of visa laws, along with their effect on the subjectivities of migrants, produces what I call "visa-based governmentality." Even when the migrant subjects display reflexive agency in their criticism of the visa laws, their actions are still governed by the visa structures, which have gendered and racialized consequences. Dependent visas and skilled-worker visas have distinctly different consequences for the men and women in my study.

Dependent visas create continual conflict for visa holders. The nature of these conflicts, however, differs by gender. Women find that they are forced to reconstruct their identities upon migration: their previous identity of an independent professional woman clashes with the new identity of a dependent housewife. This recalibration of identity is complicated further because of the dissonance between a premigration imagination of the United States as a land of opportunity and the material realities encountered upon arrival. Men, in contrast, are more reconciled to their economic dependency. Most of them are not as highly qualified as the women dependents or their wives. Yet, they struggle with the loss of social status as they reformulate their identities in response to their dependent status.

In the sphere of public interaction, dependent visa holders feel marginalized, disenfranchised, and constricted. Men as well as women feel a deep sense of humiliation. The gendered nature of dependent visas is clearer in the public discourse, as men are largely absent from public policy conversations. Most discussions presume the economic and social dependence of Indian women as normative. This public understanding is problematic because it effectively erases the struggles of visa holders across genders.

The experiences of the tech workers and the nurses at work support my argument about the racialized, gendered nature of labor migration.[5] My analysis in chapter 4 showed that visa status allows exploitation of migrant workers in the workplace. Tech workers and nurses gave accounts of the ways in which coercive aspects of visa regimes were used to extract more labor time from them compared to their fellow employees. The lead migrants felt their treatment in the workplace hinged on the successful construction of the identity of an "ideal migrant worker"—skilled, obedient, with no family responsibilities, and with unlimited availability for work. The construction of this image was entirely predicated on having a dependent visa holder as a stay-at-home spouse. A grand narrative that emerged among lead migrants was that their employers also owned their spouse's labor. Their spouse's labor allowed employers to extract more labor time from the lead migrants, who felt as though they were "always on call."

While tech workers and nurses felt exploited at work, nurses experienced discrimination at the intersection of race and gender. As migrant women of color in a feminized profession, they faced multiple disadvantages. The "ideal worker" identity for the nurses carried the same meaning as it did for the tech workers, but it also included being docile, obedient, nurturing, and caring. The nurses also faced more blatant racism at work and a far higher glass ceiling compared to the male tech workers.

The visa regimes constructed multiple layers of dependence in the lives of the participants. This challenges the popular perception (which several immigrant experts in the study held) that "highly skilled" migrant workers and their families are significantly better off than other guest workers and possess near-equal status to American counterparts in terms of opportunities and life chances.[6] Even when the migrant subject "submits to power relations . . . and hegemony of the state"[7] by making desperate efforts to project the ideal worker and ideal family image, they are far from achieving cultural or political citizenship. Instead, they continue to straddle the tenuous identities of "aliens" and "model minorities"[8] encumbered by visa status.

The visa regime is constructed and consolidated by *visa-based governmentality*, the racialization and gendering of visa holders at work and in public interactions, the reconstruction of the self to be malleable to the state-imposed dependence, and the households that become deeply gendered because of the visa enforced division of labor. These aspects of the visa regime form the orbs of the invisible web of dependence structure for all visa holders. The visa policies may not be written in gendered or racialized language but are nevertheless part of the larger picture of gendered and racialized structural inequalities in the United States that disenfranchise minorities and migrant workers. The work visas allow tech corporations to control the lives of workers and their families by relying on a racialized, controlling image of the "ideal migrant worker" and the gendered and racialized image of an "ideal Third World dependent wife/spouse." Further, dependent visas control the lives of the dependent spouses and lead migrants by enforcing distinct spheres of work for each spouse.

Despite the rigid structures of dependence, the participants in this study, especially the dependent-visa holders, resisted being made into passive victims. They challenged the web of dependence by engaging in small and sometimes big *acts of disruption* and broke the web. Many women dependents tried changing their situations by volunteering, by going back to college, by telling their stories and organizing online, and even by leaving their husbands in the United States and returning to India. Men often refused to come to America on dependent visas. Many men and women dependents worked in the informal economy, jeopardizing their spouses' jobs and the visa status of the family by doing so.[9] Such acts of disruption challenged the notion of "stable families" put forth in defense of dependent visas by public officials. Starting in 2012, women on H-4 visas played a prominent part in raising awareness and advocating for themselves using the new media, as described in the next section. On a theoretical level, these acts of disruption also challenge the self-disciplining aspect of Foucault's[10] concept of governmentality.

Resistance, Activism, and Privilege in an Oppressive Visa Regime

Chandra Mohanty[11] has argued for creating "communities of dissent" to counter racist, heterosexist, classist, and capitalist structures of power. When I began my research, there was no formal or informal forum for advocacy, or even a place for sharing and building solidarity among holders of dependent visas. Many of the women on dependent visas believed that this research was their only means of activism. They felt they had no other way to make their voices heard. Many participants expressed a desire to find ways of creating awareness about their situations. I often proposed ways of forming "communities of support" to help prospective and current dependent visa holders negotiate the experience of being a migrant dependent. I recommended that participants holding H-4 visas develop a website with information relevant to the lived experiences of visa holders. This would also establish lines of communication between current visa holders and prospective visa applicants. All the available "immigration help" websites at the time listed the processes for procuring a visa, but there was no systematic forum that provided information about the actual experiences of H-4 visa holders in the United States.

With the precedent of global and national collective actions such as the 2010 Arab Spring and 2011 Occupy Wall Street movements, whose organizational successes were linked to the use of social media,[12] my suggestion that the H-4 participants in the study create virtual support groups of Indian women on dependent visas was soon acted upon. Deploying their social, cultural, and class capital, women on H-4 visas, especially on the coasts, gradually started organizing themselves on social media. By the second half of 2012, women H-4 visa holders, a couple of whom were in my study and others who were not, launched websites and blogs to share the experiences of dependency. One Facebook page, titled "H-4 Visa—A Curse," that later became a blog was started by Rashi Bhatnagar, an H-4 visa holder who had been a journalist in India; it became one of the most visible repositories of resources for and stories of women on the H-4 visa. The blog, managed by Bhatnagar, also listed research, some of which was conducted by Bhatnagar herself, to demonstrate the injustice of this aspect of the visa laws. When I interviewed Bhatnagar and the other two H-4 activists named here, they insisted I use their real names in the book. Bhatnagar told me: "I just could not sit quietly. I had to do something. Nobody knew what this H-4 visa was, and I thought, why not use the Internet to spread our story and our message." Bhatnagar, who is heralded as one of the first H-4 activists by the Indian community of H-4 visa holders, charted the path for other activists, including Meghna Damani, who filmed a 2014 documentary about H-4 visa holders, including herself as well as other women on these visas as subjects. The documentary also featured Neha Mahajan, who was a television journalist in India and became the voice of H-4 visa holders in the press and media post-migration. It was no accident that all three of these women activists had been journalists or media figures in their past lives. In my interviews with them, all three reported that they wanted to use their skills to raise their voices against the oppressive law that had "put their lives on hold," as Damani said. These women, each in their own way, mobilized other H-4 women with the goal of making their voices heard.

In a very moving and passionate interview, Neha Mahajan told me that, when she migrated to the United States on an H-4 visa, she was aware she could not work but thought to herself at the time, "How bad can it be? I am going to New York City, and I am a journalist; surely, I will find something." When her dreams of restarting a career in the United States were shattered, she sought out communities of support and decided to speak up. She responded to media calls for interviews on the issue of H-4 visas and voluntarily participated in research on the topic. She added: "When you come to this country, they tell you there's the American Dream, and then you find out you need to get into a very long queue to get to it. For us H-4 visa holders, that queue seems to be unending and torturous. So, I decided not to be afraid and speak out. How long can one be duped and remain silent?" Neha insightfully elucidates that the promise of hope that frames the American dream and sustains the model-minority myth for Indian skilled workers is largely false, given the seeming impossibility for immigrants of color of fulfilling that dream.

It is important to note here that the absence of the nurses and their husbands from all forms of advocacy was striking. I did not ask the nurses and their families why that might be, so I can only speculate that, given that the overall number of dependent men is lower than the number of dependent women, the men were opposed to making their dependency an explicit issue. They lacked the strength of the collective that the women had. Also, it is possible that the two communities—tech workers and nurses—did not overlap socially and they were socially distanced by class locations and the occupation of their spouses. Consequently, H-4 women became the main voices of advocacy for employment authorization, while the H-1B men led the charge on advocacy efforts for green card backlogs.

The three salient phenomena present in the unsilencing project led by the women on H-4 visas speak to the larger context in which the visa regime operates. First, the wives of the men H-1B visa holders squarely took up the charge of online organizing to spread information on the plight of H-4 visa holders. Very few men whose wives were on work visas (especially the husbands of the nurses) participated or took leadership in the matter. Second, most of the women who led the charge were upper-middle-class to upper-class in India, belonged to Hindu upper castes, were highly educated, had careers in public engagement, and had come to the United States after 2005, at the precipice of the social-media revolution. And third, the women activists deployed a narrative of self-actualization and unsilencing of the self when explaining their decision to engage in online and news media–related activism on the issue of visa-based dependency.

The three elements I underscore speak to the governmentality under which the activism was taking shape. The issue of dependent visas was presented both by the press/media and the government as an issue primarily connected to women. The formulation of the issue of visa-based dependency as a feminized problem excluded the experiences of men who were on these visas and the relational consequences for the spouses of H-4 visa holders, reifying the binarized gendered ideologies insisting that it was women who had to fight for freedom from the confines of home and caregiving. It is important to acknowledge that, given the upper-class and -caste demographics of the population who are the recipients of H1-B and H-4 visas from India, activism for independence from state-imposed dependence becomes a movement of the relatively privileged, much like the white middle-class second-wave feminist movement in the West. However, the story of state-imposed dependence is more complex. It is also a fact that most spouses on dependent visas are people of color and are bound to the home and given very few of the rights offered to legal residents of the United States because of a visa policy that mainly affects bodies of color. This demographic specificity makes the online organizing by only the women H-4 holders a reactive and a gendered one against the multifaceted disenfranchisement that all dependent visa holders experience under the racialized and gendered visa regime.

I will unpack the pitfalls of such a reactive movement below, but when it comes to the stories of self-actualization as activism, we get a peek into a neoliberal discourse of social action. The discourse shifts from calling for collective action to actualizing the self and individualizing the struggle to realize the mythical American Dream. This individualization also appears in how the movement coalesced with the H-1B advocacy group during the Trump era, also discussed below; however, the power of the H-4 women's action also lay in the individual stories shared on virtual platforms that, along with the research on the topic, became the final push for Obama's 2014 executive order, which would offer Employment Authorization Documents to some H-4 visa holders.

The Obama-Era Ruling on H-4 Visas and Critiques

Regardless of the structural climate in which H-4 activism was germinating, the initiatives by the H-4 activists realized the creation of virtual support groups as a grassroots support system for H-4 visa holders. When I first began this research in 2007, H-4 visa holders, many of whom came here in the late 1990s and early 2000s, seemed to have no support or resources to cope with the deep mental agony they were experiencing. The online support groups established more recently provided a space for dependent visa holders to seek support in coping with the frustrations and depression of being forced into a life of dependency. These spaces have also become a place for mobilizing advocacy to change the law. In time, the women activists (especially Bhatnagar and Mahajan) made connections with another online advocacy group, Skilled Immigrants In America (SIIA), created mainly by men H-1B workers to advocate for resolving the green card backlog for Indians[13] in the United States.

Bhatnagar mobilized H-4 visa holders on her blog and Facebook page to write letters to senators and lawmakers seeking employment authorization for H-4 visa holders. In a report[14] released by the Department of Homeland Security on January 31, 2012, on how to attract and retain highly skilled workers in the United States, especially those in the global market, one of the strategies was a proposal to allow some H-4 spouses to work. This led the Department of Labor to consider allowing H-4 holders whose spouses' employers have filed for permanent residency to find paid employment. The US government was forced to recognize spousal dependency as a major hindrance to the recruitment and retention of highly skilled workers, and the Obama White House published a website to collect public opinion on "Allowing Employment Authorization for H-4 Dependent Spouses."[15] In 2014, when the Department of Homeland Security opened a forum for public comment on the proposed rule, Bhatnagar mobilized the H-4 community, and 13,000 people responded within 60 days. A compilation of stories of H-4 visa holders and research, including my own, was presented to the White House following the public commentary period. President Obama responded with an executive order in November 2014 allowing some H-4 visa holders to receive employment authorization; this order permitted what was popularly known as the "H-4 EAD rule," which was finalized by Homeland Security in February 2015 and went into effect on May 26, 2015.[16] The first sentence of the H-4 EAD ruling in the Federal Register, at page 10284,[17] states:

> This final rule amends Department of Homeland Security . . . regulations by extending eligibility for employment authorization to certain H-4 dependent spouses of H-1B nonimmigrants who are seeking employment-based lawful permanent resident ("LPR") status."

This ruling was the first attempt at reforming the H-4 visa law since it was first passed, allowing some dependent spouses to obtain work authorization. The ruling came on the heels of a serious economic crisis and an unemployment rate of nearly 10 percent. The policy change was possibly driven by a dynamic and demanding global economy with constantly shifting labor markets and new destinations for global labor, affecting the import and export of global labor.[18] The policy change was perhaps also prompted by the emerging trend of Indian tech workers in the United States returning to India, men married to nurses refusing to come to the United States on dependent visas, women H-4 visa holders leaving the United States to go back home, and tech workers and nurses seeking jobs in other parts of the world. Whatever the reasons, this ruling was an important step in the right direction.

The change expediting the process of acquiring work authorization for H-4 spouses was projected to have had positive effects on the lives of 179,600 H-4 visa holders in the first year of its implementation (and more than 55,000 every year thereafter, according to United States Citizenship and Immigration Services[19] estimates) on two levels: at the individual level and at the family level. On the individual level, being able to obtain work authorization helped alleviate the sense of shame, humiliation, and loss of self-esteem and personhood that many of the highly educated spouses (mostly women) of H1-B visa holders experienced because of their dependent status. On the family level, it predictably would make for happier, more stable families if spouses have the option to work and have an equitable economic standing in the family. The policy change may also disrupt the strict gendered division of labor that I saw in many of the families a topic perhaps for the future research. I think that the action may also prevent—or at least make some room to address—domestic violence and abuse in families where that is an issue. In particular, women with work authorization could have the economic agency to walk away from abusive relationships.

However, it is important to note that, while this legislation improved conditions for some, it does not guarantee a better future. A staggering number of spouses of H-1B workers have been on H-4 visas for years now and thus have been kept out of the labor market. We know from past research[20] that the longer that individuals are out of the labor market in the United States, particularly if they are women, the harder it is for them to get jobs commensurate with their qualifications. My interviews with those who have acquired H-4 EADs shows that it has been extremely difficult for them to reenter the labor market after their forced hiatus. One H-4 EAD holder said: "[The] only companies that were ready to hire me were owned by Indians and they treated me like shit because they knew my vulnerable status."

Additionally, the rule itself does not solve the problems of most incoming H-4 visa holders, for it stipulates that only the spouses of those H-1B holders who have applied for employment-based lawful permanent residency and whose I-140s (the first step of approval for LPR) have been approved will be eligible for the H-4 EAD. This means that new H-4 visas holders coming to the United States must go without work authorization for at least six years (the length of H-1B/H-4 visas), if not more, holding them hostage to the visa laws until then. Moreover, employment-based LPRs are contingent on an employer sponsoring their employees. If an employer refuses to apply for an LPR for its H-1B employee, the H-4 visa holder is legally not allowed to work or have credit cards or, in some states, drive for the entirety of their stay in the United States. Further, the H-4 visa is still tied to and dependent on the H1-B visa that the lead migrant holds. The H-4 EAD ruling only makes it possible for the spouses to get permission to work a few years earlier than they previously could. In addition to these pitfalls, President Trump had threatened to rescind this Obama-era ruling and had suspended the processing of new H-4 EADs, which had galvanized new advocacy among the H-1B and H-4 visa holders to save the H-4 EADs.

Given that the issue of H-4 dependency has supposedly been resolved in the Obama era, the focus of advocacy in the Trump era had shifted to saving the H-4 EAD rather than overhauling the visa policy. My concern is that, given the reactive and shifting focus of advocacy, H-4 visa holders who are still waiting in line to get H-4 EADs (i.e., the vast number of H-4 spouses who are in the pre-I-140 stage) will be forgotten by their peers and by the state, which has largely been the trend in the first year of Joe Biden's presidency.

Beyond the issue of H-4 EADs, another concern has emerged among the H-4 visa holders: the fear of children aging out of dependent status and losing their H-4 status. Many families I interviewed had young children who were H-4 visa holders as legal dependents. As these children turn 18—and many, at the time of my interviews, were only a couple years away from legal adulthood—they no longer remain legal dependents and need to get their own student or work visa or return to India.

This possibility has created widespread panic in the Indian temporary worker households and, starting in 2018, led to youth-led advocacy in the community, which is calling itself "H-4 Dreamers," inspired by the name of the Dreamers movement (the young people fighting for the Development, Relief, and Education for Alien Minors Act, or DREAM Act)[21] that resulted in the DACA program.[22]

Clearly, the Obama-era ruling did not solve the core issues related to state-imposed dependency. Instead, the ruling led to new concerns and created new structures of inequality while retaining the problems of the visa regime. It has also created new divisiveness among immigrants by bolstering the rhetoric of deserving and underserving immigrants. The only way forward is a total overhaul of the visa regime.

Suggestions for Overhauling the Visa Regime

Since 1965, the US government has incrementally revised the laws for family migration. These revisions changed some parts of the law but have not overhauled the policy substantially. The Obama-era ruling was a miniscule improvement in the overall situation of H-4 visa holders, and as an executive order it faces the threat of being rescinded by any future administration that decides to act on it as Trump had threatened to do. Any overhaul must begin with the H-1B visa program, because the H-4 is an appendage of the H-1B program, as the activist Neha Mahajan pointed out in my interview with her. She relayed her dissatisfaction saying: "The H-1B visa program is a version of modern-day slavery. Either change the entire H-1B program to fix the problems of both skilled workers and their dependents or scrap these programs because it is *not* right to continuously play with people's lives and keep them in constant limbo." Again, I exercise caution when using analogies of slavery for migrant skilled workers, given the horrific history of slavery in the United States and its enduring oppressive fallouts for the enslaved people. I do, however concur that, based on this research, migrant skilled workers and their families are an exploited group whose labor is indentured through the visa program and whose experiences are mostly invisibilized in the immigration discourse. As suggested by Mahajan, I offer suggestions for the complete overhaul of the entire visa system for skilled workers and their families.

Suggestions and Reasons for Reforming Skilled Worker Visa Laws

To achieve substantial improvement in the lived experiences of the families that come to the United States on the highly skilled temporary visa program, the entire program needs to be rethought. My research demonstrates how the experiences of lead migrants at work are intrinsically tied to the legal status of their spouses at home. Their visa status too often allows their exploitation as migrant workers, mainly because they are expected to have little familial responsibility, turning them into extreme versions of Joan Acker's and Joan Williams' ideal workers—expected to have no family obligations whatsoever. Listed below are some policy recommendations to assuage the effects of the visa regime on the lead migrants and their families:

1. Visas should be tied to the employee rather than the employer. The employee should have the opportunity to change jobs and to transfer their visas and their LPR applications to their new job. They should not have to leave the country to acquire a new job. I recommend that the migrant employee be given at least six months to look for a job after leaving or losing one before they must return to their own country. In other words, employers should not have the power to immediately delegitimize the visas and have the lead migrant deported simply by firing them. This step would ensure that H-1B holders are not indentured to their employers because of their legal status, and it would be an important move toward a more equitable visa structure.

2. Corporations in the tech industry or the health care industry that are major employers of temporary migrant workers should be regulated by the government such that they are required to adopt family-friendly policies covering both American and temporary workers alike. This would create conditions for more gender-equitable lives for the families of highly skilled immigrant workers in the United States.

3. Skilled workers should have the right to file grievances with the Department of Labor for discrimination and exploitation at work without fearing deportation to ensure better labor conditions for immigrant workers.

4. And finally, the US government must take immediate action to clear the green card/LPR backlogs for Indian applicants, given that the current wait times (upward of 20 years) are making a travesty of the LPR process. Resolving the green card backlog will solve many of the issues mentioned here and throughout the book.

Suggestions and Reasons for Reforming H-4 (Dependent) Visa Laws

The quick fix that is the Obama-era ruling has clearly not solved many of the problems faced by H-4 visa holders. Those with work authorization experience discrimination in hiring and in the workplace because they have been out of the labor market for years. Of the eight H-4 visa holders with EADs I interviewed, at the end of 2018 and early 2019, four had given up on finding a job that matched their qualifications and in which they were not underemployed. Newly arrived H-4 visa holders are likely to wait at least six years before they can apply for an H-4 EAD and are likely to have similar lived realities as those on H-4 visas interviewed in this study. Legal employment still emerges as the main issue for dependent visa holders. Based on the accounts of my participants and given the negative consequences of the dependent visa on them, their family lives, and material realities, I recommend that the US government allow dependent visa holders to seek employment soon after they arrive in the United States. The argument put forth by the congresswoman quoted in chapter 3 (allowing a dependent-visa holder to look for a job is a "two-for-one situation") is logically flawed, as the dependent spouse does not come to the United States with a job in hand. I contend that dependent visa holders should be eligible to look for a job based on their qualifications, experience, and credentials. The forced hiatus that H-4 visa–holding spouses must take from the labor markets has ripple effects on their lives. As the immigration lawyer, H-4 expert, and activist Shivali Shah points out, if dependent spouses were allowed a work permit, it would level the playing field for them, and they would be able to find a job in line with their qualifications. This would provide them the option of looking for work.

Many public officials have put forward two main arguments against allowing H-4 visa holders (read: women) to obtain work authorization: (1) This would further privilege an already privileged group of women;

and (2) taking into account high rates of unemployment, this would dis-advantage American workers in the labor markets.

I contend that both these arguments are logically flawed. Arguing that allowing H-4 visa holders to work will further privilege already privileged women makes the heterosexist assumption that, if a husband has a privileged position, then the wife automatically shares the same privileged position. This overlooks the situations of abuse and dependency encouraged by this visa status. Shah contends that many H-4 women find themselves trapped in situations of domestic violence because their visa renders them helpless without financial or social re-sources. Even when the violence is not explicit, as some H-4 visa hold-ers say, "[T]he set-up itself is abusive, whether [this] is intended or not."[23]

Men H-4 visa holders have been mostly absent from the public con-versation about jobs. In my interviews with public officials, I tried to steer the conversation toward the men, but such attempts were largely ignored. Officials say that very few men arrive in the United States on dependent visas, thereby discounting their situations of dependence. In my conversations with the dependent men, they indicated that they often worked part-time in the "informal market," such as Indian-owned gas stations, motels, grocery stores, and other co-ethnic businesses. But, as in all undocumented work, this creates exploitative circumstances. They struggled with low pay, risky work, and the fear of being reported to authorities.

One of the key reasons that H-4 visa holders should be allowed the opportunity to seek employment is to prevent them from being en-snared in situations of abuse because they are economically dependent on a spouse. As a nation that has built its global image on championing the ideals of freedom, liberty, and equality, the US government should assume responsibility to protect the families of the skilled workers that it seeks to recruit from situations of abuse at home or in the informal economy.

Much like the congresswoman in the PBS panel discussion, one might still argue that allowing H-4 visa holders to work poses compe-tition to other American workers, which is a problem when there are high rates of unemployment, especially among minorities. This argu-ment can easily be countered. First, the number of dependent spouses seeking employment is very small: it is estimated to be less than 50,000 individuals cumulatively, which is less than 0.2% of all employable adults in the United States. Moreover, economists such as Chiswick et al.[24] and Peri[25] have shown that immigrants do not reduce native employment rates. Rather, they increase productivity, especially in the long run. Peri has shown mathematically that, even in the short run and in times of economic downturn, immigrants do not have a negative effect on the employment rates of US workers, though the net gains from immigrant employment are slow in times of economic downturn.[26]

Following a market-driven logic, prohibiting employment for H-4 visa holders during any stage of their stay in the United States is detrimental to the economy for several reasons.

1. Men on H-4 visas already work in the informal economy, mainly in low-paying jobs, while some H-4 women periodically enter into self-employment.[27] Because they work in informal economies, they do not contribute to the economy through taxes or to resources such as Social Security. Allowing these men and women to work legally would help them find employment commensurate with their qualifications and allow them to contribute taxes and to Social Security.
2. Dependent visas do not make lead migrants more productive through the creation of stable families, as lawmakers envisioned. Instead, dependency creates fragile families. In families led by men, the wives are depressed and often return home to India to reclaim their independence. Many marriages in my sample ended up in divorce simply because of the visa situation. In the families of women nurses, the husbands are resentful and often refuse to come to the United States on dependent visas, creating unstable and unhappy families as a result.
3. Allowing dependent spouses to work is not unprecedented. Spouses on short-term dependent visas such as L-2 or J-2 who come to the United States with their "highly skilled" spouses are allowed to work.

My participants highlighted other issues they faced as dependent visa holders that contribute to other oppressive experiences. Shah said: "For these dependent visa women, it is like they are always without their wallets." My participants also offered suggestions for change.

All my participants discussed the many disadvantages of not having a valid ID other than their passports. This does not change even with H-4 EADs. My participants feared carrying their passports everywhere because losing a passport would mean losing one's visa along with it. To be denied a valid ID (beyond the passport) issued in the United States prevents these spouses from accessing resources available to most legal residents—immigrants and citizens—of the United States. I recommend that dependent visa holders be permitted to have a state ID valid for identification or that their driving licenses, which at present state "Not Valid for Identification," be made valid for identification.

Dependents should be allowed to get a driver's license in all states. Many states, including Alabama, Arkansas, Arizona, Idaho, Wyoming, North and South Dakota, South Carolina, and Mississippi, do not allow dependent visa holders to obtain a driver's license because they do not have a Social Security Number. Also, the process of obtaining a license should be the same for H-4 visas holders as for all other applicants in states that allow dependent visa holders to obtain a license. Having to go through a different process and a special DMV office only adds to the harassment and humiliation.

H-4 visa holders should be able to acquire a Social Security Number (SSN) when they arrive and not have to wait until they have their EADs to get one. As long as H-4 visa holders are not allowed to work, they are barred from procuring an SSN. Along with preventing H-4 visa holders from seeking legal employment, not having an SSN also prevents them from having basic benefits, such as a bank account, credit card, cell phone, and credit history. I contend that dependent spouses should be allowed on arrival to apply for an SSN or some other form of identification that will allow them to access basic rights, even if they are not allowed to work immediately. Last, I argue that the H-4 EAD should be made into a permanent policy that cannot be rescinded by executive order under later administrations.

While there are compelling reasons to allow H-4 visa holders to work and have access to other benefits that they are currently denied, a few more important issues need to be addressed. As a feminist immigration sociologist, it is my responsibility to prioritize the voices of my participants who unequivocally talk about the loss of dignity and personhood that comes with the loss of employed status. Further, the uncertainty around H-4 EADs causes deep anxiety for the families about their futures in the United States. The question of children aging out of H-4 is another significant concern that warrants a study of its own. *The Opportunity Trap* presents the unintended negative impacts that dependent visas have on migrating individuals. I provide evidence for the need to reform the visa policies. However, the most radical and desirable solution would be to remove the dependency clause from H-4 visas and issue an independent visa for the family members of skilled workers and move them into permanent residency status after five years. This would ensure a secure future for all temporary workers and their families in the United States—although that appears to be a distant dream.

A Trumpian Future

Trump is no longer in office, but the present and the future remain Trumpian.[28] The discursive core of American politics has shifted to become more populist, combative, nativist and antiminority,[29] which has impacted all people of color, including all categories of immigrants of color. As president of the United States, Donald Trump had, in both words and action, *attempted* to upend the future of immigrants in America, including the tech workers I interviewed. In February 2017, soon after Trump's Muslim Ban, the online news outlet Vox had leaked an unsigned executive order dated January 23, 2017, in which Trump had threatened to overhaul the skilled migration process and make it more restrictive. Amid protests from immigrant skilled workers' advocacy groups, Trump kept delaying formalizing the order and had finally promised to sign it in March 2020. This was postponed because of the COVID-19 pandemic, which took grip in United States in March 2020; it remained unsigned before Trump was voted out and left office in January 2021. This executive order was designed to restructure highly skilled migration to the United States and clamp down on the H-1B visa program. The order proposed to rescind President Obama's actions allowing spouses of H-1B workers to obtain work permits and to place the program under heavier scrutiny.[30]

Trump had also initiated programs such as "Buy American, Hire American." This program empowered the Department of Homeland Security to exercise further scrutiny on H-1B visa processing for workers and employers. One impact of this policy on the H-1B program had been the suspension of provisions for new highly skilled workers to bring their families to the United States and stopping the processing of new H-4 EADs. Other legal actions, such as unannounced random checks in IT firms to evaluate immigrant IT workers, unfair detentions, potential deportation, and family separations, had become regular occurrences as well. Trump had also suggested an expansion of the merit-based immigration program at the cost of other immigration programs, such as refugee and resettlement programs.

The inconsistency of Trump's proposals, I contend, was a bait-and-switch strategy that sent mixed messages to those on temporary highly skilled visas, producing a condition of instability and precarity and exacerbating the legal liminality of their position. Trump's strategy of keeping temporary workers and their families on edge at all times leveraged what the sociologist Eduardo Bonilla Silva calls "racialized emotions."[31] Racialized emotions are group-based feelings and emotions predicated on a kind of human rationality that normalizes the feelings of the dominant race as legitimate while undermining and dismissing the feelings of the racial subaltern, thereby allowing the dominant race to impose its racist anger, enact violence, and enforce segregation on the subaltern. Trump had effectively used these emotions since the early days of his campaign to pander to feelings of white supremacy while sending mixed signals to the more privileged immigrants such as my participants.

This strategy led to widespread panic among immigrant IT workers in the United States, the main beneficiaries of the H-1B visa program. In follow-up interviews after Trump's election, some of my participants who received H-4 EADs expressed deep concerns about their futures. Piyu, the wife of one Indian tech worker, said: "I have lost sleep since Trump came to power. We are constantly afraid that we'll be asked to leave anytime. My kid who came here with us when she was two and is now 11, what do I tell her if we have to leave?" Vani, who received an H-4 EAD early in 2019, said: "[Trump's] election has completely rattled us—meaning the entire community. We feel very uncertain about our fate in the United States. We are considering returning to India. We can't live in fear all the time."

These statements indicate the fear and uncertainty that immigrant tech workers felt under the Trump administration. The realities of downward mobility, fear of deportation, family separation, marital strife, and long-term anxiety and/or depression are some of the most worrying outcomes that these workers faced due to their legal status as temporary workers. I contend that the downward economic path and the anxiety/depression that result from the backlogs and complicated stipulations of the laws obstruct the benefits that these workers' education and professional experiences may have granted them.

A more insidious outcome of Trump's panic-mongering politics was the divisiveness it created among minorities and the sense of desperation it instilled. Trump's bait-and-switch strategy led some of the highly skilled workers on visas and in the green card queue to take the technocratic stance that they possess superior technical skills[32] and to align with right-wing groups such as the Hindus for Trump/Republican Hindu Coalition—a US-based group that supports right-wing Hindu nationalist politics in India and Trumpism in the United States.

Early in 2019, when the information about the possible rescinding of H-4 EADs by the Trump administration flooded the news, a couple of hundred highly skilled Indians from across the United States rallied in Washington, DC, in support of Trump's merit-based immigration program instead of protesting the administration's position on H-4 EADs. This was because most people who rallied belonged to Hindus for Trump/Republican Hindu Coalition. There were, however, others who did not necessarily agree with the politics of the group who also joined the rally. One of my participants, Nilu, who joined the rally, told me:

> I really don't see eye to eye with the Hindus for Trump nonsense—they are too crazy for me, but you know my back is against the wall. My kid will age out in a couple of years; I might lose my right to work again. We may have to uproot our family and return to India, or worse, our family might be separated. We stand to lose a lot, so I decided to go to the rally even if I was uncomfortable. It's good news that Trump supports merit-based immigration. So, if I have to show my face with these people to encourage that and stop him from rescinding H-4 EAD, so be it.

Nilu's justification for joining the rally exuded desperation and despair. It also provided a peek into how bait-and-switch politics peddles fear and plays on the insecurities of an otherwise privileged group and thereby evokes the drive for vested group interests—a strategy used by imperial colonialists as a technique of domination against the colonized. This strategy from the colonial playbook in turn reifies the categories of deserving and undeserving immigrants and minorities. The rally displayed signs such as "DALCA before DACA" (indicating that children who had entered the United States legally should be given priority for permanent residency before the Dreamers) and "DACA—charge fees for building wall"; these are emblematic of the construction of Indians as deserving immigrants and of the othering and vilification of immigrants seen by conservatives as undeserving in the United States. The rally also sported slogans that positioned Indian IT and other knowledge workers as more deserving of permanent residency and citizenship than those perceived as lower-skilled workers, many of whom are thought to be undocumented, thereby reifying the myth of model minorities with a technocratic claim to American citizenship.

The COVID-19 global pandemic revealed the many deep-seated intersectional and systemic inequities festering in our social systems, including imperialism, colonialism, racism, white supremacy, gender-based violence, xenophobia, and many more such ills. Migration has become a hot-button issue across the world, especially after most governments moved to shut down their borders for noncitizens soon after the World Health Organization declared COVID-19 to be a global pandemic.[33] The pandemic became putty in the hands of the Trump administration to be molded to further its racist and anti-immigration policies. On June 22, 2020, Trump ordered the suspension of new work visas for temporary workers until October, including highly skilled workers who would enter on the H-1B visa.[34] Trump's actions were in line with his racist, anti-immigrant, white nationalist agenda,[35] given that temporary workers are disproportionately people of color[36] and more than 75 percent of them come from the Global South. Additionally, 60 percent of H-1B positions certified by the Department of Labor are assigned wage levels well below the local median wage, and major American firms, including Amazon, Microsoft, Facebook, Apple, and Google, take advantage of this system of lower pay.[37] And H-1B visa holders pay much more in taxes than they receive in federal benefits. These funds go toward supporting Social Security, Medicare, STEM research, and workforce preparedness programs.[38] By suspending the H-1B visa program, Trump had also effectively suspended this revenue stream. The loss of support for STEM research was particularly striking at a time when scientific research was critical to fighting the pandemic.

It would not have been surprising if Trump had decided to follow through with his threat and stop the issuance of work permits to the spouses of existing H-1B visa holders. As my earlier research shows, this would have had drastic repercussions for the families of temporary workers and the recovering economy.[39] While these moves may have solidified Trump's support among his voting base, it likely came at the expense of the US economy and STEM research. For Trump, the marginal value of suspending work visas lay in its ideological alignment with the white nationalist rhetoric he regularly espoused.[40] This decision seemingly sought to tap into the same racist furor mobilized against Latinx and Muslim immigrants that was instrumental in getting him elected in 2016.[41]

Trump's America was designed to make the already marginalized even more defenseless so as to drive a wedge between minority groups. Under Trump, the possibilities of new forms of legal violence made the positions of migrant temporary workers and their families even more precarious than ever before while further distancing them from the possibility of solidarity with other oppressed minorities. Now that Trump is out of office, we must remember that these dangerous policies may be reenacted if Trump, or someone such as Trump, were to be elected again, elevating the risk of legal violence for all immigrants of color.

The Need for Caution When Demanding Change

The rallies attended by Indian highly skilled workers, with a conspicuous presence of Indian tech workers, organized by Hindus for Trump in Washington in early 2019 left me flummoxed and devastated. The standpoint dilemma that I have experienced throughout this project was clamping down on me. While I was still committed to analytically dismantling the oppressive visa regime, I was conflicted about how I could advocate for a group of people who were associated with what I considered to be a majoritarian fascist ideology—Hindu nationalism—aligning with Trump against undocumented immigrants to push forward a technocratic policy favoring merit-based immigration. This was especially difficult because most of the tech-worker families I interviewed were upper-caste/upper-class Hindus in India, which showered them with an array of privileges. I was deeply troubled and saddened by the absence of reflexivity among this group both about their own privileges and the oppressions they shared with other people and immigrants of color in the United States. And yet, there is no denying that the gendered and racialized visa regime that governs the lives of the families in this study, including the nurses' families, marginalizes them in the United States by creating oppressive structures of dependency. And those still warrant being made visible and demand the critical attention that this book offers.

The visa regime creates competing identities for migrants as they struggle to adapt to its policy restrictions, and therefore it produces deep pain, suffering, and humiliation in these migrants despite their legal status. In negotiating contradictory selfhoods and navigating the structures of inequality, migrant families find themselves ensnared in webs of dependence that have become a part of their material reality. While men dependents also undergo mental suffering, the women participants of this study (the nurses and the wives of the tech workers) are harmed by this structure in more ways compared to the men participants (tech workers and dependent husbands). Their mental agonies are compounded by the nonstop physical and emotional labor they put into the household work and caregiving that were often evaded by the men. We all know of two Indian men who came to the United States on H-1B visas and who ascended to the top of the tech industry, breaking the racialized glass ceiling: Satya Nadella, CEO of Microsoft, and Sundar Pichai, CEO of Google. We rarely have such examples of women immigrants breaking the gendered and racialized glass ceilings. This reaffirms Mohanty's thesis that the Euro-American state, through its heterosexist, gendered, and racialized immigration policies, operates to disenfranchise Third World women in both the public and private spheres. The stories of these women need to be told. This state also effectively creates divisive politics by offering a false sense of power to relatively privileged minorities—in this case, Indians—by encouraging them to internalize the model-minority myth. Given this reality, I want to conclude this book with a word of caution. It is imperative that immigrants and migrants of color who come to the United States with relative privilege, such as upper-caste/upper-class Hindu Indians, must think long and hard about how they position themselves as a group and about which institutions they align with in the racialized landscape of the United States.

As Audre Lorde famously said: "The master's tools will never dismantle the master's house." The only way that the gendered and racialized visa regime can be dismantled is if Indian immigrants, instead of aligning with the oppressors to consolidate power, choose to align with other oppressed immigrant communities of color and build solidarities with them in order to decenter power. As Naureen, who was a lawyer in India and who was one of the very few Muslim participants in my study, said: "As someone who grew up with wealth, but [was] a religious minority in India and now [am] a racial, religious and immigration-status minority in the United States, I quickly learned that the only power I have is to fight for what's right for everyone and not just me."

ACKNOWLEDGMENTS

The cover of this book has one name on it, but books are never written alone. They carry with them words, ideas, intellectual labor, and care of many who help the author give voice to their thoughts. This book is no exception. While the limitations and flaws in this book are mine alone, I owe gratitude to many people across many parts of the world for enriching it and for walking with me for nearly a decade to bring the book to life.

I am ever so grateful to everyone who participated in this study, because without their unconditional support this project would not have been possible. I do not have enough words to thank the families who opened up their hearts, lives, and homes to me. This book is as much yours as it is mine.

Writing this book made me realize how crucial the role of editors is to the writing process. I am thankful to my editor, Ilene Kalish, at New York University Press for her unwavering support of me and my project. I am especially grateful for her patience, as it took longer for me to finish this book than we predicted. I would also like to thank Sonia Tsuruoka, Assistant Editor for Social Sciences at New York University Press, whose support was key in the completion process. The four brilliant anonymous reviewers Ilene picked provided excellent and extensive feedback. The book is so much better for their feedback.

I would like to acknowledge that a handful of the quoted material and arguments in chapter 5 appeared in a book chapter titled "When Men Stay Home: Household Labor and Parenthood in Female-Led Families of Indian Migrant Nurses" in the anthology *Families as They Really Are*, vol. 2 (New York: Norton, 2015), edited by Barbara Risman and Virginia Rutter. Additionally, some arguments and quoted materials that appeared in chapter 6 have been adapted from another edited volume, "What Do Visas Have to Do with Parenting? Middle-Class Dependent Visa Holders and Transcultural Parenting," in *Contemporary Parenting and Parenthood: From News Headlines to New Research*, edited by Michelle Janning (New York: Praeger/ABC-CLIO, 2018).

This book greatly benefited from readings of drafts, editorial help by, and conversations with several people along the way. The first person who always was at the brunt of all demands concerning the book was my partner in life, my colleague, and my sharpest and most supportive critic, Pratim Sengupta. Thank you for reading, listening, and engaging with this project in the most nurturing ways possible. Long-time friends from graduate school Amy Brainer and Georgiann Davis are the next two people I would like to thank, not only for steadfastly believing in my book and pushing me when I wanted to give up but also for reading early and late drafts and offering valuable feedback and deepening my insights. Thank you, Rachel Allision and Courtney Carter, also graduate school friends and writing group buddies, for reading early drafts of the book, and Courtney for your support and love of my intellectual work through the best and worst of times. To my colleagues in sociology at Vanderbilt University Laura Carpenter, Dan Cornfield, and Holly McCammon: your thoughtful comments during the proposal writing stages is deeply appreciated. My writing group at Vanderbilt University, Marzia Milazzo, Michelle Murray, and LaTonya Trotter, read early drafts and helped me find what is good in the book. To my current writing group, Melissa Abad, Sharla Alegria, Adilia James, Ethel Mickey and Megan Tobais Neely, thank you for reading drafts of many chapters and providing important feedback. To my departmental colleagues Ariel Ducey, Naomi Lightman, Matt Patterson, and Jean Wallace, thank you for reading and engaging with one of the many drafts of some chapters along the way. And to Soulit Chacko, I can never thank you enough for all that you have given to this project, including reading many, many drafts of each chapter, offering deep feedback, editorial help, and for being my most ardent supporter as I plodded through the writing process. Students in my graduate courses over the years provided me some of the best insights on draft chapters. You taught me more than you will know. Thank you, Santanu Dutta and Megha Sanyal, for your thoughtful insights and help with the last iteration of this project. To Debika Chatterjee, thank you for your invaluable inputs early on in this process. And thanks to Kristy Johnson, Dennis Lee, and Anya Litviniuc for editorial help and to Shazia Iftkhar for being the best editor friend and for that last push I needed to get this done and off my desk.

Special shout-outs to Shweta Adur, Anustup Basu, Manisha Basu, Hae Yeon Choo, Kiana Cox, Tatiana Filimonova, Ayush Gupta, Epsita Halder, Sheba Karim, Beaumie Kim, Ratoola Kundu, Riyaz Latif, Neda Maghbouleh, Safaneh Mohaghegh Neyshabouri, Namita Manohar, Ghassan Moussawi, Nicole Mottier, Ulrike Muench, Michael Rodriguez Muniz, Carla Pfeffer, Jennifer Randles, Ranita Ray, Lina Rincon, Ipsita Sapra, Tahseen Shams, Evren Savci, Miwa Takeuchi, Anand V. Taneja, and Anton Tenser, scholars and writers all, who are friends and co-conspirators, who make radical writing and scholarship possible and exciting and who in so many ways inspired me on this journey of book-writing.

People outside academia who supported and sustained me in the writing process by being brilliant in what they do include my friends Cynthia Aoki, Tapo Banerjee, Sulagana Biswas (you inspire me to write and think better every day), Moumita Ghosh, and Bernice Weissbourd; and family who are also close friends, Priyanka Bhaduri and Krishnakali Sengupta—thank you all for being there. And the next generation of little troublemakers I have known closely, who made me smile several times during writing—Aurho, Inu, Jarul, Kiaan, Lillah, Omar, Ritwik, and Vasya—here's to you changing the world.

At the University of Calgary, I am grateful to my past and current department heads, Erin Gibbs Van Brunschot and Fiona Nelson, respectively, for protecting my time so I had time for writing. Thanks to those departmental colleagues and colleagues/friends outside of the department and all the Sociology Office staff who have supported me over the past five years. To my undergraduate mentees over the years, Auska Adhikari, Rupinder Brar, Juliana Castillo, Kennedy Novak, and Sophia Thraya, your passion for making the world better was so refreshing as I muddled through the writing. To my graduate students Sepideh Borzoo, Isabel Fandino, Melanie Jong, Chetna Khandelwal, Pedrom Nasiri, Negin Saheb Javaher, Tanner Short and Carieta Thomas, I owe some of my most profound thoughts about this project to you all.

One mentor I am ever grateful to is Bandana Purkayastha, who has showed me new ways of looking at my work, supported me unconditionally, and provided the intellectual guidance I needed to grow as a scholar through writing this book. Thank you for believing in me. I would also like to extend my gratitude to Shibaji Bandopadyay, Raewyn Connell, Patricia Hill Collins, Manisha Desai, Milian Kang, Nazli Kibria, Cecilia Menjívar, Joya Misra, Chandra Talpade Mohanty, Mignon Moore Salvador Ortiz-Vidal, Rhacel Salzar Parrenas, Mary Romero, and Zulema Valdez for the critical articulations in their scholarship and for the dialogical space they have created that allowed me to enrich and deepen my thoughts about my research.

My everlasting gratitude to my teachers and mentors at the University of Illinois at Chicago who were foundational in shaping the ideas in this book. This research and eventually this book came to be because of my dissertation chair and adviser Barbara Risman's unconditional and unwavering support, for believing in me, and for helping me grow the kernel of an idea I had many summers back. For that I will be forever grateful. To the members of my dissertation committee, Bill Beilby, Nilda Flores Gonzales, Anna Romina Guevarra, Chandra Mohanty, and R. Stephen Warner, thank you for making me the scholar I am. You all will always remain an integral part of who I am as a sociologist. I would also like to thank Sharon Collins for her support throughout my graduate school life and Lorena Garcia for being one of the kindest and the most brilliant professors I have met. I aspire to be like you. Beyond being on my dissertation committee, Anna Guevarra was that mentor who nurtured my strengths but never allowed me to become complacent in them, an invaluable lesson in growing as a scholar that I will always carry with me.

I thank my mother, whose love and dreams sustain me always, and my father, who, when he lived in this world, specialized in embarrassing the teenage me by being my most loud and enthusiastic champion and cheerleader; he must be smiling down from the skies. I thank my grandparents, Manu and Didibhai, for creating a charming world of love and joy where reading and writing were always fun. I thank my parents-in-law, Biplabi and Prabir Sengupta, for always cheering me on as I wrote this book and for bringing my anchor and my wings, Pratim, into this world.

This book literally would not be written if it were not for Pratim. From dreaming big for and with me, creating magic, to gentle and hard nudges as required so I don't give up on the book, to doing all the carework to keep me and our household afloat, this book would not be there without you. So, thank you! And finally, I am grateful for our little baby, Chuli, whose cuddles, meows, and head butts are all I needed on days when nothing else made sense.

Demographics of 25 Families of Tech Workers

TABLE A.1. Demographics of 25 Families of tech workers (50 participants)

# of families	Pseudonym	Visa status	Age	Regional identities	Religion	Year of arrival to United States	Highest education	Current occupation	Family income/ annually
1	Jaya	H4-EAD	33	Tamil	Hindu	2006	CPA	Dependent	81–100K
	Akash	H-1B	37	Tamil	Hindu	2005	MBA	IT professional	
2	Tona	H-4	36	Bengali	Hindu	2004	PhD	Dependent	81–100K
	Kaushik	H-1B	36	Bengali	Hindu	2002	BTech	IT professional	
3	Mia	H-4	29	Bengali	Hindu	2007	MBA	Dependent	120K above
	Rocky	H-1B	33	Bengali	Hindu	2003	MBA	Financial Consultant	
4	Survi	H-4	31	Uttari	Hindu	2006	BCA	Dependent	61–80K
	Satya	H-1B	33	Uttari	Hindu	2004	BTech	IT professional	
5	Piyali	H-4	26	Bengali	Hindu	2007	MCA*	Dependent	41–60K
	Jeet	H-1B	30	Bengali	Hindu	2000	PhD	Research Scientist	
6	Suchitra	H-4	32	Andhra	Hindu	2003	PhD	Dependent	120K above
	Sawan	H-1B	35	Andhra	Hindu	1997	MS	Financial Consultant	
7	Anjali	H-4	26	Oriya	Hindu	2006	MCA	Dependent/ Student	120K above
	Rahul	H-1B	33	Oriya	Hindu	2000	PhD	Research Scientist	
8	Titash	H-4	28	Bengali	Hindu	2008	MCA	Dependent	41–60K
	Gopal	H-1B	33	Bengali	Hindu	2004	PhD	Research Scientist	
9	Poonam	H-4	31	Mararthi	Hindu	2005	MPhil	Dependent	41–60K
	Shri	H-1B	35	Mararthi	Hindu	2001	PhD	Research Scientist	
10	Naureen	H-4	41	Mararthi	Muslim	1996	J.D, MBA	Dependent	81–100K
	Asman	H-1B	45	Mararthi	Muslim	1999	BTech	IT professional	
11	Mili	H-4	31	Malayalee	Christian	2004	BCom	Dependent/ Student	101–120K
	Ravish	H-1B	35	Gujarati	Hindu	1998	MS	Financial Consultant	
12	Radhika	H4-EAD	36	Punjabi	Hindu	1999	MS & MBA	Dependent	81–100K
	Geet	H-1B	38	Tamil	Hindu	1997	BTech	IT professional	
13	Anushree	H-4	27	Bihari	Hindu	2002	MCA	Dependent	81–100K
	Satish	H-1B	29	Bihari	Hindu	2007	PhD	Research Scientist	
14	Jasleen	H-4	35	Punjabi	Sikh	2003	MCA	Dependent	101–120K
	Shobhit	H-1B	37	Punjabi	Sikh	1998	MBA	IT professional	
15	Ria	H-4	33	Bengali	Hindu	2003	MA	Dependent	81–100K
	Sumit	H-1B	41	Bengali	Hindu	2002	BTech	IT professional	

Table A.1. (cont.)

# of families	Pseudonym	Visa status	Age	Regional identities	Religion	Year of arrival to United States	Highest education	Current occupation	Family income/ annually
16	Karuna	H-4	33	Bihari	Hindu	2005	MSW	Dependent	101–120K
	Aniket	H-1B	36	Marathi	Hindu	2005	PhD	Research Scientist	
17	Antara	H-4	28	Bengali	Hindu	2001	MBA	Dependent	81–100K
	Anik	H-1B	39	Bengali	Hindu	1999	BTech	IT professional	
18	Nisha	H-4	34	Bihari	Hindu	1999	MA	Dependent	81–100K
	Ranveer	H-1B	39	Bihari	Hindu	1997	MBA	IT professional	
19	Radha	H-4	33	Bengali	Hindu	2000	BEd	Dependent	101–120K
	Shankar	H-1B	33	Bengali	Hindu	2001	PhD	Tech Financial Consultant	
20	Alka	H-4	45	Assamese	Hindu	2006	MA	Dependent	81–100K
	Sambit	H-1B	38	Assamese	Hindu	2000	BTech	IT professional	
21	Vani	H-4	45	Tamil	Hindu	2009	MSc	Dependent	61–70K
	Karthick	H-1B	38	Tamil	Hindu	2009	MTech.	Auto Engineer	
22	Piyali	**H-4 EAD	45	Bengali	Hindu	2016	MSc	Dependent	51–60K
	Shubham	H-1B	38	Bengali	Hindu	2014	BSc	IT professional	
23	Afiya	H-4	45	Delhi	Muslim	2010	MBA	Dependent	61–70K
	Arif	H-1B	38	Uttari	Muslim	2010	MTech	IT professional	
24	Rachita	***LPR	45	Marathi	Hindu	1995	BEd	Kindergarten Teacher	81–100K
	Rajiv	LPR	38	Gujarati	Hindu	1992	BTech	IT professional	
25	Mira	H-4	45	Tamil	Hindu	2013	MA	Dependent	71–90K
	Kapil	H-1B	38	Punjabi	Hindu	2010	BTech	IT professional	

*MCA: Masters in Computer Applications; **H-4 EAD—Those who have gotten H-4 EAD due to the Obama Era Ruling; ***LPR— lawful permanent resident status received after the interview

Note: This table only includes couples' interviewees. I also interviewed an additional 15 individuals in this category who were not part of a family unit but were individual interviewees and hence not included in this list.

APPENDIX B

Demographics of 30 Families of Nurses

TABLE B.1. Demographics of 30 families of nurses (60 participants) Families where the man is on a dependent visa

# of families	Pseudonym	Visa status	Age	Regional identities	Religion	Year of first arrival to United States	Highest education	Current occupation	Range of family income/ annually	Age of children (years)
1	Joseph	H-4	38	Kerela	Christian	2001	High School	Dependent	41–60K	10
	Mary	H-1B	35	Kerela	Christian	2001	BSN	Nurse		
2	Thomas	H-4	31	Kerela	Christian	2003	Vocational	Dependent	41–60K	4
	Lily	H-1B	28	Kerela	Christian	2003	BSN	Nurse		
3	Jejo	H-4	35	Kerela	Christian	2004	B.A	Dependent	41–60K	6
	Nancy	H-1B	33	Kerela	Christian	2004	BSN	Nurse		
4	Rocky	H-4	40	Kerela	Christian	2002	Vocational	Dependent	41–60K	8
	Rosy	H-1B	37	Kerela	Christian	2002	BSN	Nurse		
5	George	*H-4:EAD	37	Kerela	Christian	2000	Some College	Dependent	61–80K	8 and 10
	Gina	H-1B	36	Kerela	Christian	2000	BSN	Nurse		
6	Daniel	H-4	36	Kerela	Christian	2006	Some College	Dependent	41–60K	3
	Alba	H-1B	32	Kerela	Christian	2004	BSN	Nurse		
7	Charlie	*H-4:EAD	42	Kerela	Christian	2010	Some College	Dependent	61–80K	7 and 5
	Clara	H-1B	35	Kerela	Christian	2008	BSN	Nurse		
8	Philip	H-4	45	Kerela	Christian	2005	Some College	Dependent	41–60K	12 and 5
	Aju	H-1B	40	Kerela	Christian	2004	BSN	Nurse		
9	Joshua	H-4	42	Kerela	Christian	2004	Some College	Dependent	41–60K	10
	Jenny	H-1B	43	Kerela	Christian	2004	BSN	Nurse		
10	Mathai (Mat)	H4-EAD	39	Kerela	Christian	2011	Some College	Dependent	61–80K	2, 5, and 8
	Maira	H-1B	36	Kerela	Christian	2010	BSN	Nurse		

TABLE B.1. (*cont.*)
Families where the man is on a dependent visa

# of families	Pseudonym	Visa status	Age	Regional identities	Religion	Year of first arrival to United States	Highest education	Current occupation	Range of family income/annually	Age of children (years)
11	Joel	H-4:EAD	32	Kerela	Christian	2003	High School	Unemployed	61–80K	5
	Maria	H-1B	30	Kerela	Christian	2001	BSN	Nurse		
12	Arun	H-4 (previous transnational arrangement)	40	Kerela	Christian	2003	Some College	Mail Sorting in Post office	61–80K	10
	Missy	H-B	36	Kerela	Christian	1999	BSN	Nurse		
13	Rueben	Still in India	31	Kerela	Christian		B.A	Business owner in India	41–60K	4
	Rose	H1B	28	Kerela	Christian	1997	BSN	Nurse		
14	Themba	Still in India	32	Kerela	Christian		Vocational	Business owner in India	41–60K	4 months
	Jiya	H1B	25	Kerela	Christian	2010	BSN	Nurse		

TABLE B.1. (*cont.*)
Families where the nurses and her family came on immigrant visas but men were still dependents

# of families	Pseudonym	Visa status	Age	Regional identities	Religion	Year of first arrival to United States	Highest education	Current occupation	Range of family income/ annually	Age of children (years)
15	Shijo	E34	33	Kerela	Christian	2008	High School	Unemployed	41–60K	3
	Shelly	EB-3	32	Kerela	Christian	2004	BSN	Nurse		
16	Mathew	LPR	35	Kerela	Christian	2010	Some College	Insurance Agent	61–80k	5
	Shija	LPR	33	Kerela	Christian	2009	BSN	Nurse		
17	John	LPR	40	Kerela	Christian	2005	MSW	State Social Services	61–80k	11 and 4
	Josi	LPR	36	Kerela	Christian	2001	MSN	Nurse		
18	Sally	EB-3	33	Kerela	Christian	2006	BSN	Nurse	81–100k	4 and 7
	Patrick	E34	37	Kerela	Christian	2006	BA	Self Employed		
19	Christian	EAD	36	Kerela	Christian	2003	BSc	Medical Technician	81–100k	5
	Alma	EB-3	31	Kerela	Christian	1998	BSN	Nurse		
20	Peter	E34	37	Kerela	Christian	2003	Vocational	Warehouse loader	81–100k	6
	Patricia	EB-3	35	Kerela	Christian	2002	BSN	Nurse		
21	Paola	EB-3	37	Kerela	Christian	2001	BSN	Nurse	81–100k	8 6
	Thomas	E34:EAD	35	Kerela	Christian	1990	Some College	Respiratory Therapist Assistant		

TABLE B.1. (cont.)
Families where the man came as sponsored by other family members to avoid being on dependent visas

# of families	Pseudonym	Visa status	Age	Regional identities	Religion	Year of first arrival to United States	Highest Education	Current Occupation	Range of Family Income/ annually	Age of children (years)
22	Amy	Citizen	40	Kerela	Christian	1999	BSN	Nurse	61–80K	8, 14, and 17
	Samuel	Citizen	45	Kerela	Christian	1982	10th Grade	Hospital cleaning staff		
23	Rebecca	Citizen	39	Kerela	Christian	2001	BSN	Nurse	61–80K	13
	Roth	Citizen	42	Kerela	Christian	1980	High School	Works in a gas station		
24	Sheila	LPR	33	Kerela	Christian	2005	BSN	Nurse	61–80K	4 years and 6 months
	Jacob	LPR	39	Kerela	Christian	1999	Some College	Works in a gas station		
25	Carolyn	Citizen	43	Kerela	Christian	1999	MSN	Nurse Practitioner	61–80K	8, 10, and 14
	Benny	Citizen	45	Kerela	Christian	1991	High School	Hospital staff		
26	Susie	Citizen	36	Kerela	Christian	2003	BSN	Nurse	120K and above	12
	Mamooty	Citizen	45	Kerela	Christian	1991	10th Grade	Own gas station		
27	Rosa	LPR	37	Kerela	Christian	1994	MSN	Nurse Practitioner	81–100K	9
	Alex	LPR	38	Kerela	Christian	2000	High School	Self Employed		
28	Usha	Citizen	36	Kerela	Christian	2002	BSN	Nurse	61–80K	5 and 8
	Madhav	Citizen	44	Kerela	Christian	1989	Some College	Part-time in grocery store		
29	Rakesh	LPR	39	Kerela	Christian	1999	MSW	State social services	61–80K	8 and 3
	Preeti	LPR	36	Kerela	Christian	1996	BSN	Nurse		
30	Sweety	Citizen	41	Kerela	Christian	2001	BSN	Nurse	61–80K	11 and 7

APPENDIX C

The Four Main Visa Categories

H1-B (TEMPORARY WORKER) VISA STATUS

H1-B is a nonimmigrant temporary visa status held by "alien profession-als who will fill a specialized knowledge position in the United States" (Papa, Homeland Security Act of 2002). The basic eligibility for the H1-B status requires that the job being proffered is categorized as "specialty occupation," meaning that it requires "theoretical and practical appli-cation of a body of highly specialized knowledge in a field of human endeavor including but not limited to but not limited to, architecture, engineering, mathematics, physical sciences, social sciences, medicine and health, education, law, accounting, business specialties, theology, and the arts" (Congressional Research Service; Wasem 2006, 1). In order to qualify for any position, employees must meet one of the three catego-ries to qualify for H1-B classification: A bachelor's degree or equivalent is the minimum requirement for entry in a particular position; the nature and specific duties of the position to be held is so complex that the knowledge required to perform the job is associated with the degree attained; and such degree requirement is common in parallel positions among similar organization or the position calls for a specialized degree (Papa, Homeland Security Act of 2005). The employer must demonstrate that an H1-B status holder will be paid at least 95 percent of the prevail-ing wage for a similar position in a particular metropolitan area. The H1-B usually has a three-year term and can be extended to another three years, after which the H1-B holder is required to leave the United States for one year before being eligible for H1-B status again. Further, "an alien with an H1-B approval may not move to a new work location or different employer without first applying for a new or amended H1-B approval from the Citizenship and Immigration Services" (Papa, Homeland Secu-rity Act of 2005, 284). It is important to note that this process requires an official release from the current employer. H1-B is a nonimmigrant visa but has a pathway to citizenship via the permanent residency program. The employer can petition for lawful permanent residency for an H1-B holder through one of the employment-based categories (Congressional Research Service; Wasem 2006, 5). This can take anywhere between five and 10 years. The H-1 nonimmigrant visa for "aliens of distinguished merit and ability" was introduced in the Immigration and Naturalization Act of 1952. Congress has made several revisions to the visa since then. The H1-B category in its current form was introduced in the Immigration Act of 1990. The demand for and inflow of H-1B workers have escalated since the 1990s. Starting in 1990, immigration law allows for a total of 85,000 new H-1B visas to be made available each government fiscal year.

H-4 (DEPENDENT) VISA STATUS

The family reunion clause of the Immigration Act of 1965 led to the facilitation of the "dependent visa status" for spouses and children of temporary skilled workers and was revised to its current form to include spouses of foreign students per the Immigration Act of 1990 (Naujoks 2009). H-4 status can apply to dependents of temporary workers of any H category, as well as F-2 (foreign students), J-2 (exchange scholars), L-2 (intracompany transferees), and P-2 (artists). Of the all the dependent visas, the H-4 and F-2 versions do not include a work permit. The H-4 dependent visa—the visa status that all the dependent spouses in my study held—allows the dependent spouse and children of any principal H-class visa holder entry to the United States and free travel in and out of the country. The H-4 visa holder is dependent on the principal H visa holder and will lose their status when the H visa holder loses their status, usually at the end of a period of employment. H-4 Dependent visa holders may accompany any of the following temporary workers to the United States: H1-B specialty occupations, H2-A temporary agricultural workers, H-2B temporary workers (semiskilled and unskilled), and H-3 workers who are trainees (Immigration Fundamentals, Rel. #31. 10/10). According to United States Citizenship and Immigration Services, descriptions of nonimmigrant temporary visa dependents on H-4 visas are not permitted to be employed or receive compensation from any US source. They may volunteer only if the position they are interested in has always been a volunteer position and always will be. The Department of Labor does not allow a dependent to volunteer for a position and then begin to receive payment for performing the same duties once a change of immigration status is approved. It is possible for the dependent to be offered a paid position and apply for a change of status to an appropriate visa that allows employment. These opportunities are rare, however, and certain qualifications dictated by the visa type must be met before the visa status change is approved. In addition, employment may not commence until the Citizenship and Immigration Services approves the change, which can take up to six months. As H-4 visa holders often include dependent children under the age of 21, studying is permitted, but a H-4 visa holder is strictly prohibited from working in the United States. However, studying on an H-4 does not make the student eligible for any kind of scholarship, fellowship, or financial aid unless they change their status to that of an international student on a student (F-1) visa. It may also be possible for a H-4 visa holder to change status to another visa that will allow them to work in the United States, but without that, working on H-4 visa may cause main visa holder—that is, the highly skilled spouse—to lose their job, and the family may even face deportation (Immigration Fundamentals, Rel. #31. 10/10). Statistics released by the Department of Homeland Security in 2010 show that there were a total of 141,575 people in the United States on the H-4 dependent visa category in 2010; 55,335 of those were Indian citizens. The exact gender data is not available, but the Department of Homeland Security Reports on visa issuances in the last 10 years state that the majority of dependent H-4 visas go to women, followed by children; a small percentage go to men.

EB-3 VISA STATUS FOR NURSES

Like high-tech workers, nurses can also hold H1-B status because they fall under the "specialty occupation" category. However, due to the known shortage of nurses in the United States, immigrant nurses can bypass the H1-B nonimmigrant visa process and apply for an employment-based immigration visa—the third preference known as EB-3. Due to the shortage of nurses, the employer is exempt from filing "labor certification," a step in the employment-based immigration visa process that often takes a long time. The EB-3 opens up a straight path to permanent residency for the immigrant worker. The spouses of EB-3 holder may be admitted to the United States in the E34 (spouse of a "skilled worker" or "professional") or EW4 (spouse of an "other worker") categories. During the process when the immigrant nurse or the EB-3 holder is applying for permanent resident status (status as a green card holder), the spouse is eligible to file for an Employment Authorization Document. Minor children (under the age of 18) of nurses or EB-3 holders may be admitted as E35 (child of a "skilled worker" or "professional") or EW5 (child of an "other worker") (U.S. Citizenship and Immigration Services Memo, 2010). The caveat here is that it is often easier to get approval for H1-B status than a EB-3 status, and when the quota for immigrant labor from a particular country is met, the EB-3 category is stalled or frozen (called "retrogression") for several years, which is not the case for H1-B visas.

EMPLOYMENT-BASED PERMANENT RESIDENCY (GREEN CARD)
Every fiscal year (October 1—September 30), approximately 140,000 employment-based immigrant visas are made available to qualified applicants from all national origins under the provisions of US immigration law. Employment-based immigrant visas are divided into five preference categories—EB-1 to EB-5, which includes skilled and specialized workers of different categories. Spouses and children of certain preference categories are allowed to accompany (or follow to join) employment-based immigrants. To be considered for an immigrant visa under some of the employment-based preference categories, the applicant's prospective employer or agent must first obtain a Labor Certification approval from the Department of Labor. Once labor certification (if required) is received, the employer can then file for an "Immigrant Petition for an Alien Worker" with Citizenship and Immigration Services for the appropriate preference category. President Joseph Biden is planning to replace the word "Alien" with "Non-Citizen" as a gesture to root out systemic racism. After Citizenship and Immigration Services approves the petition, it is sent to the National Visa Center. There are several steps thereafter, the first being a wait for processing of applications, which may take from three months to several years depending on the preference category; once the application is processed, there are other steps such as medical examination, vaccination, and an interview with the

National Visa Center before permanent residency is granted, which then opens up the pathway to citizenship (U.S. Citizenship and Immigration Services Memo, 2010). Several of the H1-B holders in my study had petitioned for permanent residency through their employers and were waiting for approval.

NOTES

INTRODUCTION

Epigraph: George .W. Bush, 2006, Transcript, "Bush's Speech on Immigration," *New York Times* (Presidential Address on Immigration); The White House, Obama Administration, 2014, "Remarks by the President in Address to the Nation on Immigration" (Presidential Address on Immigration).

1 The relationship between the visa regime and household labor is discussed in detail in chapter 5.

2 Kurtas are long traditional shirts worn by Indian men in most regions in India.

3 Temporary highly skilled workers who arrive on work visas are referred to as "nonimmigrants" because they do not occupy an immigrant status but are eligible for lawful permanent residency and eventual citizenship in time.

4 Collins 1990; Pallavi Banerjee 2018.

5 Salter 2006.

6 Salter 2006: 175.

7 Salter 2006: 184.

8 Jachimowicz and Meyers 2002; Zong and Batalova 2017.

9 Kirkegaard 2019 (www.piie.com).

10 Brader et al. 2008; Jachimowicz and Meyers 2002; B. Smith 2011; Surowiecki 2012; Zong and Batalova 2017.

11 George 2005.

12 The "H-1B Non-Immigrant Work Visa may be issued to applicants seeking temporary work in a "Specialty Occupation," which requires the skills of a professional. "Specialty Occupations" include: accounting, computer analysts, programmers, database administrators, web designers, engineers, financial analysts, doctors, scientists, architects, and lawyers. H-1B/H-1C visas are issued to foreign nurses going to the United States to perform nursing services in medically underserved areas for a temporary period up to three years, extendable to six years (www.uscis. gov).

13 Copeland and Norell, 2002; De Verthelyi 1995, Hardill and MacDonald, 1998; Kim 2006; Meares 2010.

14 Bhatt 2018; Manohar 2019.

15 Hollifield 2004; Koslowski 2006; Salter 2004: 169; 2006.

16 Derrida 2000; Kalm 2005; Salter 2006.

17 Foucault 1991: 103.

18 Ong 2006: xvi.
19 Foucault 1988.
20 Lazzarato 2000; Lemke 2007: 219.
21 Lemke 2007.
22 Menjívar 2006.
23 Menjívar and Abrego 2011.
24 Bevir 1999; McKee 2009; Rose et al. 2006.
25 Collins 1990.
26 Acker 2006; Connell 1987; Patricia Martin 2004; Risman, 2004, 2018.
27 Manalansan 2006; Rich 1980.
28 Acosta 2007; Cantú Jr. 2009; Luibhéid 2008; Manalansan 2003; Ward and Schneider 2009.
29 Connell 2005: 6.
30 Risman 2004, 2018.
31 Risman 2004: 432.
32 Glenn 2002; Mohanty 2003; Ong 1999.
33 Mohanty 2003.
34 Mohanty 1988, 2003b. Mohanty, Russo, and Torres, eds. 1991.
35 Mohanty 1991: 28.
36 Mohanty 1988: 64
37 Mohanty 1988: 64.
38 Abrego and Menjívar 2011; Golash-Boza 2015; Menjívar 1999, 2006; Romero and Valdez 2016.
39 Abrego and Menjívar 2011.
40 Pallavi Banerjee 2012; Bhatt 2018; Manohar 2019; Purkayastha 2005.
41 Guevarra 2010; Rodriguez 2010.
42 Payal Banerjee 2006; Chakravartty 2006; Mahalingam and Ramakrishnan 2002; Rudrappa 2009; D. Sharma 2015.
43 Irani 2019; Mahalingam and Leu 2005; Walton-Roberts 2015.
44 Banerjee 2006; Philip and Sengupta 2020; D. Sharma 2015.
45 Bhatia 2007.
46 Payal Banerjee 2006.
47 Payal Banerjee 2006: 432.
48 Payal Banerjee 2006.
49 Payal Banerjee 2006: 441.
50 Payal Banerjee 2006: 38.
51 George 2005.
52 Salzinger 2003.
53 Ong and Collier 2005.
54 Guevarra 2006.
55 Chakravartty 2006.
56 Shah 2007.
57 Bhatt 2018.

58 Manohar 2019.

59 Kim 2006: 163.

60 Kim 2006.

61 Collins 1990; Haraway 1988; B. Smith 2011; Sprague 2016.

62 Malayalam is a Dravidian language (as opposed to Indo-European) that many of the northern Indian languages have roots in.

63 Beoku-Betts 1994: 414.

64 Aguilar 1981; Bolak 1996; Haraway 1988; Zinn 1979.

65 DeVault 1999.

66 Haberman 2016.

1. THE VISA REGIME

Epigraph: Aniket, participant.

1 Munoz and Zients 2016; Thibodeau 2017.

2 Gass 2016.

3 In the 1960s, Indians made up less than 0.5 percent of the overall immigrant population of the United States. This percentage swelled exponentially after the Immigration and Nationality Act of 1965. The act abolished national origins quotas and made it possible for highly skilled immigrants from across the world to gain permanent residency and bring their family members to the United States. According to Kaushal and Fix's Migration Policy Institute report: "Since the early 1970s, the source of high-skilled foreign-born workers in the United States has shifted from Europe to Asia. Within Asia, an increasing number of immigrants come from South Asia and China." Kaushal and Fix 2006, 7.

4 Batalova et al. 2021.

5 The number of Indian immigrants rose from 27,000 to 85,000 between 1986 and 2005. In the same period, the proportion of Indians in the United States rose from 4.4 to 7.4 percent of total immigration. Indian citizens accounted for 5.7 percent of all persons obtaining lawful permanent resident status in 2008. Economist B. Lindsay Lowell observed that the number of Indian H-1B visa holders grew fivefold between 1989 and 1999 and peaked in 2001 with 160,000 visas issued. In 2001, 82 percent of all computer industry–related H-1B visas were given to Indians, and 85 percent of all Indian H-1B beneficiaries were for tech-related jobs. In addition to tech workers, India also accounts for a large percentage of the international students who migrate to the United States. Many of these students obtain H-1B visas upon graduation.

6 A term coined by sociologist William Pettersen 1966 in an article for a New York Times Magazine article titled "Success Story: Japanese-American Style" to explain how the Japanese deployed strong family values and cultural emphasis on hard work to overcome the discrimination they faced in the United States to succeed economically and educationally. Pettersen 1966.

7 Guevarra 2010; Jacoby 1979; Jensen 1988; Takaki 1989.

8 Lowe 1996; Ngai 2004.

9 Hernandez 2021; www.latimes.com.

10 See the introduction to *Immigrant Acts: On Asian American Cultural Politics* (1996) by Lisa Lowe.

11 Baldoz 2004; Lowe 1996; Mohanty 2003.

12 Lowe 1996: 172.

13 Ngai 2004.

14 Bagoria 2009.

15 Jacoby 1979; Jensen 1988.

16 Gonzales Jr. 1986.

17 Takaki 1989.

18 Bagoria 2009.

19 Chishti and Yale-Loehr 2016; Donato 2010.

20 Manohar and Banerjee 2016.

21 Balgamwalla 2014: 56; Kelkar 2011.

22 Quoted in Abrams 2012: 10.

23 Immigration and Nationality Act of 1952, Pub. L. 82–414, § 203(d), 66 Stat. 163 (codified as amended at 8 U.S.C. § 1153(d) (2012)).

24 Hawkes et al. 2009; Khadria 2002, 2007.

25 Xiang 2007.

26 Xiang 2007: 4.

27 Xiang 2007: 5.

28 Payal Banerjee 2006; Chakravartty 2006; Manohar 2009; Radhakrishnan 2011.

29 Sahoo et al. 2010.

30 Payal Banerjee 2006; Chakravartty 2006; Xiang 2007.

31 Glenn 2002.

32 Payal Banerjee 2006; Pallavi Banerjee 2012; Xiang 2011.

33 Salzinger 2003.

34 Salzinger 2003.

35 Pallavi Banerjee 2012; Dicicco-Bloom 2004; Purkayastha 2005.

36 Raghuram and Kofman 2004, 2006.

37 Raghuram and Kofman 2004.

38 Ball 2004.

39 Pallavi Banerjee 2015b; George 2005; R. Sharma 2011.

40 Masselink and Jones 2014.

41 George 2005.

42 R. Sharma 2011.

43 Dicicco-Bloom 2004.

44 Stiglitz 2003.

45 Appadurai 1996; Urry 2000; Kellner 2002.

46 Kellner 2002: 297.

47 Eisenstein 2005; Guevarra 2010; Kellner 2002; Mohanty 2009; Ngai 2004; Ong 1999; Parreñas 2001; Rodriguez 2010; Sassen 1996, 2008.

48 Misra et al. 2006.

49 Purkayastha 2018: 179.

50 Mohanty 2003; Sassen 1996.

51 Sassen 1996; Ong 1999, 2003; Parreñas 2001; Rodriguez 2010; Guevarra 2006, 2010.

52 Carla Freeman 2001; Kofman and Raghuram 2006; Parreñas 2015; Romero 2018.

53 Sassen 2003: 45.

54 Sassen 2003: 51, 55.

55 Sassen 2003: 56.

56 Sassen 2008.

57 Eisenstein 2005; Desai 2007.

58 Eisenstein 2005; Salzinger 2003.

59 Ahmed 2007.

60 Walsh 2014.

61 U.S. Department of Homeland Security, "Lawful Permanent Residents."

62 Internal Revenue Service, "Resident Aliens."

63 Homeland Security, "Nonimmigrant Admission," www.dhs.gov.

64 Rangarajan 2019.

65 Naujoks 2009.

66 Immigration Fundamentals, Rel. #31. 10/10

67 Xiang (2008) provides a detailed description of the recruitment and emigration process of Indian tech workers, particularly information technology (tech) workers from India, to US firms as well as to other parts of the world.

68 The official State Department current cutoff for hiring of H-1B workers from India is capped at 65,000 per year.

69 Xiang 2007.

70 All the major cities in India have a regional US consulate.

71 The few reasons put forth by my participants for denial of visas are: (1) qualifications of applicants do not match the job description; (2) the paperwork from the hiring company or the sending company is incomplete or unsatisfactory; (3) Contradictory of shifty responses to interview questions; and (4) visa officer in bad mood.

72 Aiken 2007.

73 Nair and Percot 2007.

74 Khadria 2007.

75 Pittman et al. 2010.

76 Khadria 2007 (see Table 1 for number of registered nurses).

77 Khadria 2007.

78 National Council of State Boards of Nursing (NCSBN) 2016; Thompson and Walton-Roberts 2019.

79 Pittman et al. 2010.

80 Pittman et al. 2000.

81 US embassy, New Delhi website: http://newdelhi.usembassy.gov.

82 The NCLEX-RN is the examination that registered nurses are required to pass in order to obtain a nursing license in the United States. This examination is administered at certain international locations, including in New Delhi, since 2005.

83 CGFNS International website: www.cgfns.org.

84 George 2005; Khadria 2007; Walton-Roberts 2015; Timmons et al. 2016.

85 Kurien 2002; Timmons et al. 2016.

86 George 2005; Healey 2008; Wells 2013.

87 Garner et al. 2015; Reddy 2008; Wells 2013.

88 Zia Haq, 2021

89 George 2005; Kurien 2001, 2002; Walton-Roberts 2012.

90 Turner and Espinoza 2021

91 Adur 2020

92 Pallavi Banerjee 2015b, 2018; Banerjee et al. 2020; Espiritu 2003; Glenn 2002; Hondagneu-Sotelo and Avila; Manohar 2019.

93 Pallavi Banerjee 2015b; George 2005; Pedraza 1991; Pessar 1986.

94 Espiritu 2003; George 2005; Pessar 1986.

95 Purkayastha 2005.

96 Purkayastha 2002: 186.

2. MODEL MIGRANTS AND IDEAL WORKERS

Epigraph: Jose Antonio Vargas, 2014, "Why I Made 'Documented,'" CNN online, www.cnn.com.

1 Coontz 2011.

2 Fanon 1968.

3 Foucault 1988.

4 Hall and Gay 1996.

5 Goffman 1959.

6 Mead 1934.

7 Harvey 2007; Larner 2000; Lemke 2002; Rose et al. 2006.

8 Foucault 1977.

9 Salter 2004, 2006.

10 Agamben 1998.

11 Salter 2006.

12 Agamben 1998.

13 Salter 2006: 171.

14 Salter 2006: 179.

15 Salter 2004, 2006; Hollifield 2004; Koslowski 2004, 2006.

16 Mohanty 2003.

17 Beoku-Betts 2004; Gurung 2015; Purkayastha 2010.

18 Mohanty 2003.

19 Balgamwalla 2014.

20 Engzell and Ichou 2019.

21 Kofman and Raghuram 2006.

22 Ngai 2014; Ahmed 2007.

23 Agamben 1998.

24 Butler 2004.

25 Connell 2016; Escobar 1995; Sassen 2000; Spivak 1988.

26 George 2005; Hoang 2015; Montes 2013.

27 George 2005; Kurien 2001; Warner and Wittner 1998; Walton-Roberts 2015.

28 Puar 2013.

29 Butler 2004.

30 Rich 1980.

31 Hochschild 2012; Pfeffer 2017.

32 Erikson 1976.

33 Mohanty 2003.

34 A. Pande 2017: 384.

35 Patricia Martin 2001.

36 Messner and Montez de Oca 2005.

37 Darwin 2018.

38 Bridges 2009.

39 Rose et al. 2006, building on Foucault (1991).

40 Harvey 2007; Guevarra 2010; Rodriguez 2010.

41 Foucault 1977.

42 Coontz 2011.

43 Mohanty 2003.

44 Mohanty 2006.

3. BEHOLDEN TO EMPLOYERS

Epigraph: Remarks by President Obama on comprehensive immigration reform. Barack Obama, 2013, Transcript, "Obama's Immigration Remarks (transcript)," *POLITICO* online, www.politico.com.

1 Menjívar 2006.

2 Menjívar 2006.

3 Acker 2006.

4 Glenn 2002.

5 Payal Banerjee 2006; Lowell 2000.

6 Lowell 2000: 18.

7 H-1B visas are offered for a maximum for six year; when an employer applies for permanent residency (green card) for the employee, the H-1B can be extended until the permanent residency is processed, which can take up to 15 years. One important aspect of the green card is that, once the employer applies for the migrant employee and after the first processing stage, the dependents—spouses and children—are automatically included in the application.

8 Salzinger 2003.

9 Lowell 2000; Xiang 2011.

10 Payal Banerjee 2006; Chakravartty 2006; Xiang 2007.

11 Payal Banerjee 2006: 422.

12 Rajas 2015.

13 Richwine 2009.

14 Lee and Zhou 2015; Pettersen 1966.

15 Bonilla-Silva 2019; Du Bois 1903; Omi and Winant 2014; Ray 2017.

16 Payal Banerjee 2006; Lee and Zhou 2015; Lowe 1996; Purkayastha 2005; Rudrappa 2009; Wu 2003.

17 Payal Banerjee 2006; Chakravartty 2006; Chekuri and Muppidi 2003; Lee and Zhou 2015; Rudrappa 2009.

18 Burch 2017.

19 Acker 2006; Pettersen 1966.

20 Warren and Twine 1997.

21 Evans 2004; Sassen 2000; Wingfield 2009.

22 Wooten and Branch 2012.

23 Alegria 2019.

24 The Development, Relief, and Education for Alien Minors (DREAM) Act, introduced in 2001, allows current, former, and future undocumented high-school graduates and GED recipients a three-step pathway to US citizenship through college, work, or the armed services.

25 Loewen 1988.

26 Guglielmo 2003.

27 Roediger 2018.

28 Philip and Sengupta 2020.

29 Cooper 2000.

30 Cooper 2000: 403.

31 Hacker 2017; Webster 2014.

32 Acker 2006.

33 Pettersen 1966.

34 Payal Banerjee 2006.

35 Xiang 2007.

36 See www.bsnedu.org, an independent group of web publishers committed to developing user-friendly resources on health care education.

37 See www.bsnedu.org.

38 George 2005; Glenn 2002; Guevarra 2010.

39 Wingfield 2019.

40 McElmurry et al. 2006; Percot and Rajan 2007; Pittman et al. 2010.

41 Jacox 2003; Walani 2015.

42 Dreby 2010; Guevarra 2010; Hondagneu-Sotelo and Avila 1997; Parreñas 2001.

43 Guevarra 2010.

44 Cooper 2000.

45 Bhatia 2007; Lowe 1996; Ngai 2014; Radhakrishnan 2011.

46 Jacobs and Gerson 2004; Williams 2000.

47 Clawson and Gerstel 2014.

48 Payal Banerjee 2006, 2010; Xiang 2007.

49 Glenn 2009.

4. AT HOME

Epigraph: Hillary Clinton, presidential campaign speech in Las Vegas. Hillary Clinton, 2015, Transcript, "Road to the White House 2016: Presidential Candidate Hillary Clinton Campaign Rally in Las Vegas," *C-SPAN* online, www.c-span.org.

1 Arvin et al. 2013.

2 Acker 2004; Carrington 1999; Collins 2009; DeVault 1994; Hochschild 1989; Moore 2011; Pfeffer 2017.

3 DeVault 1994.

4 Hochschild 2012.

5 Acker 1998.

6 Collins 2009.

7 Carrington 1999; Moore 2011; Pfeffer 2017.

8 Carrington 1999.

9 Moore 2011.

10 Pfeffer 2017.

11 According to Adrienne Rich (1990), "compulsory heterosexuality" is the hegemony of heterosexuality that makes heterosexual relationships and men's access to women's bodies the norm and all other types of relationships deviant.

12 Acosta 2007; Adur 2018; Adur 2020; Arvin et al 2013; Carrillo 2018; Luibhéid 2018.

13 Risman 2004, 2018.

14 Connell 2005.

15 Mohanty 1988.

16 Coltrane 1989; England 2005; Hochschild 1989

17 The definitions are taken from United States Immigration and Citizenship Services website: www.uscis.gov.

18 Xiang 2011.

19 Pallavi Banerjee 2012; Dicicco-Bloom 2004; George 2005; Khadria 2007.

20 The proposal was to add fixed quotas of H-1Bs for each sending country, limiting the number of years on the visa to three years, with the possibility of continuation for three years, and making the process of procuring H-4 dependent visas easier.

21 Dasgupta 1998; Espiritu 2003; Schmalzbauer 2009.

22 I call Mili's excerpt "thick descriptions" as defined by Geertz (1973) because she provides a minutely detailed description of her daily routine as an example of what she interprets as being "just a wife."

23 Coontz 2011.

24 Bano et al. 2021; M. Gupta 1987; R. Pande 2003.

25 Mahmood 2005.

26 Hochschild 1989.
27 Agarwal 1994.
28 Walton-Roberts 2012.
29 Greenstein 1996; S. Gupta 1999; Young et al. 2015.
30 Kanter 2008.
31 Brines 1994.
32 Most nurses had similarly designed suburban houses and had similar wood furniture ornately designed and bought from a generic suburban furniture store.
33 I usually did not address most of the nurses by their first names. I added *chechi* (the Malayalam term for "big sister") after their first names for the women and *chettan* (the Malayalam term for "big brother") for the men. The community viewed me as a younger woman, though I was not markedly younger than most of the women and men I interviewed. But I learned quickly that it was disrespectful to address my participants by their first names. This was not an issue in the families of the tech workers.
34 George 2005.
35 Walton-Roberts 2012.
36 George 2005.
37 Ranson 2010; Rehel 2014.
38 Gamburd 2000.
39 Gamburd 2000: 202.
40 Connell 2014.
41 Connell 2014: 10.
42 Banerjee and Connell 2018.
43 Menjívar and Abrego 2012.

5. TRANSCULTURAL CULTIVATION

Epigraph: Anjali, participant.
1 Lareau 2003, 2011.
2 Lareau 2003, 2011.
3 Lan 2018.
4 Lan 2018: 4.
5 Chua 2011.
6 Lan 2018.
7 Fu and Markus 2014.
8 Lareau 2003, 2011.
9 Cheah et al. 2009; Driscoll et al. 2008; Farver et al. 2007; Roopnarine et al. 2006.
10 Pyke 2000.
11 Foner and Dreby 2011.
12 Pyke 2000.

13 Foner 2009; Foner and Kasinitz 2007; Manohar 2008; Portes and Fernández-Kelly 2008; C. Suárez-Orozco and M. Suárez-Orozco 2002; Zhou 2009.

14 Foner and Dreby 2011: 527.

15 Lan 2018.

16 Lopez 2003; Manohar 2008; R. Smith 2006; Zhou 2009.

17 Mohanty 1988.

18 Gorman 1998.

19 Gorman 1998.

20 Archer 2010; Cross-Barnet and McDonald 2015; Lee and Zhou 2015; Manohar 2013.

21 Manohar 2013.

22 Archer 2010.

23 Archer 2010: 465.

24 Lee and Zhou 2015.

25 Chacko 2013; Coe and Shani 2015.

26 Bourdieu 1987.

27 Lan 2018.

28 Lareau 2011.

29 Lan 2018.

30 Lan 2018.

31 Pyke 2000.

32 Lee and Zhou 2015.

33 Lee and Zhou 2015.

34 Lan 2018.

35 Dow 2019.

36 Pallavi Banerjee 2015b; Hays 1996; Hochschild and Machung 2012; Moore 2011; Purkayastha 2005; Risman 1998.

37 Pallavi Banerjee 2015b.

38 Hochschild 1979; Milkie and Peltola 1999.

39 Hays 1996.

40 Hochschild 1989.

41 Das Gupta 2014.

42 Montes 2013.

43 Pfeffer 2017; Hochschild 1979.

44 Ridgeway and Correll 2004.

45 Christopher 2012.

46 Pallavi Banerjee 2015b.

47 Bobel 2002; Christopher 2012; Coltrane 1989; Hays 1996; Hochschild 2012; Pfeffer 2017; Wade 2013, 2016.

48 Rehel 2014.

49 Archer 2010; Pallavi Banerjee 2012; Foner 2009; Lan 2018.

50 Chakravorty et al. 2016.

51 Gorman 1998.

CONCLUSION

Epigraph: Neha Mahajan, H-4 activist and journalist.

1 Lind 2014.
2 Pallavi Banerjee 2015a.
3 Cohen 2019.
4 Frothingham and Glynn 2016.
5 Acker 2004; Payal Banerjee 2006; Guevarra 2010; Glenn 2010.
6 Ruark and Graham 2011.
7 Ong et al. 1996: 738.
8 Lowe 1996.
9 Pallavi Banerjee 2018.
10 Foucault 1977.
11 Mohanty 2009.
12 Khondker 2011; Kavada 2015.
13 SIIA claims that Indian have to wait 7 to 30 years to obtain an employer-sponsored green card in the United States, whereas applicants from all other countries can get a green card in one to four years. This directly affects the life chances of H-4 visa holders.
14 U.S. Department of Homeland Security 2012.
15 The White House, Obama Administration, "Tell Us What You Think about . . ."
16 U.S. Department of Homeland Security, "Employment Authorization for Certain H-4 Dependent Spouses."
17 U.S. Department of Homeland Security, "Employment Authorization for Certain H-4 Dependent Spouses."
18 Martin et al. 2006; Ong 2006; Rodriguez 2010.
19 U.S. Department of Homeland Security, "Employment Authorization for Certain H-4 Dependent Spouses."
20 Lovejoy and Stone 2012; Weisshaar 2018.
21 Anti-Defamation League 2020, "What Is DACA and Who Are the DREAMers?"
22 Paul 2018.
23 Shah 2007.
24 Chiswick et al. 1997.
25 Peri 2010.
26 Peri 2010.
27 Pallavi Banerjee 2019.
28 Menkel-Meadow 2019.
29 Holland and Fermor 2020.
30 Banerjee and Rincón 2019.
31 Bonilla-Silva 2019.
32 Philip and Sengupta, 2020.
33 Connor 2020.
34 U.S. President, Proclamation 10052 of June 22, 2020.

35 Holpuch 2019.
36 U.S. Citizenship and Immigration Services 2018.
37 Costa and Hira 2020.
38 Holen 2009.
39 Banerjee and Rincón 2019.
40 Banerjee and Sengupta 2020.
41 Reny et al. 2019.

BIBLIOGRAPHY

Abraham, Margaret. 1995. "Ethnicity, Gender, and Marital Violence: South Asian Women's Organizations in the United States." *Gender & Society* 9(4): 450–68.

Abrams, Kerry. 2012. "What Makes the Family Special?" *University of Chicago Law Review* 80(1): 7–27.

Abrego, Leisy J., and Cecilia Menjívar. 2011. "Immigrant Latina Mothers as Targets of Legal Violence." *International Journal of Sociology of the Family* 37(1): 9–26.

Acker, Joan. 1998. "The Future of 'Gender and Organizations': Connections and Boundaries." *Gender, Work & Organization* 5(4): 195–206. doi:10.1111/1468–0432.00057.

———. 2004. "Gender, Capitalism and Globalization." *Critical Sociology* 30(1): 17–41.

———. 2006. "Inequality Regimes: Gender, Class, and Race in Organizations." *Gender & Society* 20(4): 441–64.

Acosta, Katie L. 2007. "'Everything Would Be Solved If Only We Could Marry': Queer Marriages and US Immigration Policy." Pp. 21–40 in *Sexual Politics of Desire and Belonging*, edited by Alejandro Cervantes-Carson and Nick Rumens. Amsterdam: Brill | Rodopi.

Adur, Shweta M. 2018. "In Pursuit of Love: 'Safe Passages', Migration and Queer South Asians in the US." *Current Sociology* 66(2): 320–34.

———. 2020. "Sexuality and Migration." Companion to Sexuality Studies. 357–70.

Agamben, Giorgio. 1998. *Homo Sacer: Sovereign Power and Bare Life*. Palo Alto: Stanford University Press.

Agarwal, Bina. 1994. *A Field of One's Own: Gender and Land Rights in South Asia*. Cambridge: Cambridge University Press.

Aguilar, John L. 1981. "Insider Research: An Ethnography of a Debate." Pp. 15–26 in *Anthropologists at Home in North America: Methods and Issues in the Study of One's Own Society*, edited by Donald A. Messerschmidt. Cambridge: Cambridge University Press.

Ahmed, Sara. 2007. "A Phenomenology of Whiteness." *Feminist Theory* 8(2): 149–68.

Aiken, Linda H. 2007. "U.S. Nurse Labor Market Dynamics Are Key to Global Nurse Sufficiency." *Health Services Research* 42(3p2): 1299–320.

Alegria, Sharla. 2019. "Escalator or Step Stool? Gendered Labor and Token Processes in Tech Work." *Gender & Society* 33(5): 722–45. doi:10.1177/0891243219835737.

Anti-Defamation League (ADL). 2020. "What Is DACA and Who Are the DREAMers?" www.adl.org/education.

Appadurai, Arjun. 1996. *Modernity at Large: Cultural Dimensions of Globalization*. Minneapolis: University of Minnesota Press.

Archer, Louise. 2010. "'We Raised It with the Head': The Educational Practices of Minority Ethnic, Middle-Class Families." *British Journal of Sociology of Education* 31(4): 449–69.

Arvin, Maile, Eve Tuck, and Angie Morrill. 2013. "Decolonizing Feminism: Challenging Connections between Settler Colonialism and Heteropatriarchy." *Feminist Formations* 25(1): 8–34.

Ayers, Kristen N., and Scott D. Syfert. 2001. "U.S. Visa Options and Strategies for the Information Technology Industry." *North Carolina Journal of International Law and Commercial Regulation* 27(2): 301–34.

Ayyub, Ruksana. 2000. "Domestic Violence in the South Asian Muslim Immigrant Population in the United States." *Journal of Social Distress and the Homeless* 9(3): 237–48.

Bagoria, Mukesh. 2009. "Tracing the Historical Migration of Indians to the United States." *Proceedings of the Indian History Congress* 70: 894–904.

Baldoz, Rick. 2004. "Valorizing Racial Boundaries: Hegemony and Conflict in the Racialization of Filipino Migrant Labour in the United States." *Ethnic and Racial Studies* 27(6): 969–86.

Balgamwalla, Sabrina. 2014. "Bride and Prejudice: How U.S. Immigration Law Discriminates against Spousal Visa Holders." *Berkeley Journal of Gender, Law & Justice* 29(1): 25–71.

Ball, Rochelle E. 2004. "Divergent Development, Racialised Rights: Globalised Labour Markets and the Trade of Nurses—The Case of the Philippines." *Women's Studies International Forum* 27(2): 119–33.

Baluja, Kaari F. 2003. *Gender Roles at Home and Abroad: The Adaptation of Bangladeshi Immigrants*. New York: LFB Scholarly.

Banerjee, Pallavi. 2008. "Religious Gathering of Immigrant Bangladeshi Muslim Women in Chicago." Master's thesis, Department of Sociology, University of Illinois at Chicago.

———. 2012. "Constructing Dependence: Visa Regimes and Gendered Migration in Families of Indian Professional Workers." PhD diss., Department of Sociology, University of Illinois at Chicago.

———. 2015a. "New Visa Policy Allows Immigrant Spouses to Hold Jobs." *Ms. Magazine* Blog. https://msmagazine.com.

———. 2015b. "When Men Stay Home: Household Labor and Parenthood in Female-Led Families of Indian Migrant Nurses." Pp. 500–17 in *Families as They Really Are*, edited by B. J. Risman and V. Rutter. 2nd ed. New York: W. W. Norton.

———. 2018. "What Do Visas Have to Do with Parenting? Middle-Class Dependent Visa Holders and Transcultural Parenting." Pp. 237–57 in *Contemporary Parenting and Parenthood: From News Headlines to New Research*, edited by Michelle Janning. New York: Praeger/ABC-CLIO.

———. 2019. "Subversive Self-Employment: Intersectionality and Self-Employment among Dependent Visas Holders in the United States." *American Behavioral Scientist* 63(2): 186–207.

Banerjee, Pallavi, and Lina Rincón. 2019. "Trouble in Tech Paradise." *Contexts* 18(2): 24–29. doi:10.1177/1536504219854714.

Banerjee, Pallavi, and Raewyn Connell. 2018. "Gender Theory as Southern Theory." Pp. 57–68 in *The Handbook of the Sociology of Gender*, edited by Barbara Risman, Carrissa Froyum, and William Scarborough. 2nd ed. New York: Springer Press.

Banerjee, Pallavi, and Pratim Sengupta. 2020. "Trump's Suspension of H-1B Visas Is a Racist Attack on Immigrants—and a Bad Move for the Economy." The Conversation. June 30. https://theconversation.com.

Banerjee, Pallavi, Soulit Chacko, and Bhumika Piya. 2020. "Paradoxes of Being and Becoming South Asian Single-Mothers: The Enclave Economy, Patriarchy and Migration." *Women, Gender, and Families of Color* 8(1):5–39.

Banerjee, Payal. 2006. "Indian Information Technology Workers in the United States: The H-1B Visa, Flexible Production, and the Racialization of Labor." *Critical Sociology* 32(2–3): 425–45.

———. 2010. "Transnational Subcontracting, Indian IT Workers, and the US Visa System." *Women's Studies Quarterly* 38(1/2): 89–110.

Bano, Naaz, Asif Beg, Arti Kumari, and Rajesh Dahiya. 2021. "A Critical Review: Problem of Female Feoticide and Female Infanticide in India." *Pharma Innovation Journal* 10(3): 243–48.

Basu, Anustup. 2008. "Hindutva and Informatic Modernization." *boundary 2* 35(3): 239–50.

Batalova, Jeanne, Brittany Blizzard, and Jessica Bolter. 2021. "Frequently Requested Statistics on Immigrants and Immigration in the United States." *Migration Information Source*. www.migrationpolicy.org.

Becker, Howard S. 1992. "Cases, Causes. Conjunctures. Stories and Imagery." Pp. 205–07 in *What Is a Case? Exploring the Foundations of Social Inquiry*, edited by H. Becker and C. Ragin. Cambridge: Cambridge University Press.

———. 1998. "Sampling." Pp. 67–108 in *Tricks of the Trade: How to Think about Your Research While You're Doing It*. Chicago: University of Chicago Press.

Beoku-Betts, Josephine. 1994. "When Black Is Not Enough: Doing Field Research among Gullah Women." *NWSA Journal* 6(3): 413–33.

———. 2004. "African Women Pursuing Graduate Studies in the Sciences: Racism, Gender Bias, and Third World Marginality." *NWSA Journal* 16(1): 116–35.

Bevir, Mark. 1999. "Foucault and Critique: Deploying Agency against Autonomy." *Political Theory* 27(1): 65–84.

Bhatia, Sunil. 2007. *American Karma: Race, Culture, and Identity in the Indian Diaspora*. New York: New York University Press.

Bhatt, Amy. 2018. *High-Tech Housewives: Indian IT Workers, Gendered Labor, and Transmigration*. Seattle: University of Washington Press.

Bielby, William T., and Denise D. Bielby. 1989. "Family Ties: Balancing Commitments to Work and Family in Dual Earner Households." *American Sociological Review* 54(5): 776–89.

———. 1992. "I Will Follow Him: Family Ties, Gender-Role Beliefs, and Reluctance to Relocate for a Better Job." *American Journal of Sociology* 97(5): 1241–67.

Biernacki, Patrick, and Dan Waldorf. 1981. "Snowball Sampling: Problems and Techniques of Chain Referral Sampling." *Sociological Methods & Research* 10(2): 141–63.

Bobel, Chris. 2002. *The Paradox of Natural Mothering*. Philadelphia: Temple University Press.

Bolak, Hale C. 1996. "Studying One's Own in the Middle East: Negotiating Gender and Self-Other Dynamics in the Field." *Qualitative Sociology* 19(1): 107–30.

Bonacich, Edna, Lucie Cheng, Norma Chinchilla, Nora Hamilton, and Paul Ong, eds. 1994. *Global Production: The Apparel Industry in the Pacific Rim*. Philadelphia: Temple University Press.

Bonilla-Silva, Eduardo. 2019. "Feeling Race: Theorizing the Racial Economy of Emotions." *American Sociological Review* 84(1): 1–25.

Bourdieu, Pierre. 1987. "What Makes a Social Class? On the theoretical and Practical Existence of Groups." *Berkeley Journal of Sociology* 32: 1–17.

Brader, Ted, Nicholas A. Valentino, and Elizabeth Suhay. 2008. "What Triggers Public Opposition to Immigration? Anxiety, Group Cues, and Immigration Threat." *American Journal of Political Science* 52(4): 959–78.

Bridges, Tristan. S. 2009. "Gender Capital and Male Bodybuilders." *Body & Society* 15(1): 83–107.

Brines, Julie. 1994. "Economic Dependency, Gender, and the Division of Labor at Home." *American Journal of Sociology* 100(3): 652–88.

Brush, Barbara L., and Julie Sochalski. 2007. "International Nurse Migration: Lessons from the Philippines." *Policy, Politics & Nursing Practice* 8(1): 37–46.

BSNedu.org. N.d. "About BSNedu.org." www.bsnedu.org.

Burch, Audra D. S. 2017. "He Became a Hate Crime Victim. She Became a Widow." *New York Times*. www.nytimes.com.

Burchell, Graham, Colin Gordon, and Peter Miller, eds. 1991. *The Foucault Effect: Studies in Governmentality*. Chicago: University of Chicago Press.

Bush, George W. 2006. Transcript. "Bush's Speech on Immigration." *New York Times*. www.nytimes.com.

Butler, Judith. 2004. *Undoing Gender*. New York: Routledge.

Cancian, Francesca M., and Stacey J. Oliker. 1999. *Caring and Gender*. Walnut Creek, CA. AltaMira Press.

Cantú Jr., Lionel. 2009. *The Sexuality of Migration: Border Crossings and Mexican Immigrant Men*, edited by N. A. Naples and S. Vidal-Ortiz. New York: New York University Press.

Carrillo, Hector. 2018. *Pathways of Desire: The Sexual Migration of Mexican Gay Men*. Chicago: University of Chicago Press.

Carrington, Christopher. 1999. *No Place Like Home: Relationships and Family Life among Lesbians and Gay Men.* Chicago: University of Chicago Press.

Castells, Manuel. 1975. "Immigrant Workers and Class Struggles in Advanced Capitalism: The Western European Experience." *Politics & Society* 5(1): 33–66.

———. 1999. *The Information Age: Economy, Society and Culture.* Vols. 1–3. Hoboken, NJ: Wiley-Blackwell.

CGFNS International. N.d. "VisaScreen®: Visa Credentials Assessment." www.cgfns .org.

Chacko, Soulit, 2013. "Treading Identities: Second-Generation Christian Indian Americans Negotiating Race, Ethnicity and Religion in America." Master's thesis, Department of Sociology, Loyola University Chicago. https://ecommons.luc.edu.

Chakravartty, Paula. 2006. "Symbolic Analysts or Indentured Servants? Indian High-Tech Migrants in America's Information Economy." *Knowledge, Technology & Policy* 19(3): 27–43.

Chakravorty, Sanjoy, Devesh Kapur, and Nirvikar Singh. 2016. *The Other One Percent: Indians in America.* New York: Oxford University Press.

Chanana, Karuna. 2007. "Globalisation, Higher Education and Gender: Changing Subject Choices of Indian Women Students." *Economic and Political Weekly* 42(7): 590–98.

Cheah, Charissa S. L., Christy YY Leung, Madiha Tahseen, and David Schultz. 2009. "Authoritative Parenting among Immigrant Chinese Mothers of Preschoolers." *Journal of Family Psychology* 23(3): 311–20.

Chekuri, Christopher, and Himadeep Muppidi. 2003. "Diasporas Before and After the Nation." *Interventions* 5(1):45–57.

Chishti, Muzaffar. 2007. "The Rise in Remittances to India: A Closer Look." *Migration Information Source.* www.migrationpolicy.org.

Chishti, Muzaffar, and Stephen Yale-Loehr. 2016. *The Immigration Act of 1990: Unfinished Business a Quarter-Century Later.* Washington, DC: Migration Policy Institute. www.immigrationresearch.org.

Chiswick, Barry R., Yinon Cohen, and Tzippi Zach. 1997. "The Labor Market Status of Immigrants: Effects of the Unemployment Rate at Arrival and Duration of Residence." *Industrial and Labor Relations Review* 50(2): 289–303.

Chodorow, Nancy J. 1999. *The Reproduction of Mothering: Psychoanalysis and the Sociology of Gender.* Berkeley: University of California Press.

Christopher, Karen. 2012. "Extensive Mothering: Employed Mothers' Constructions of the Good Mother." *Gender & Society* 26(1): 73–96.

Chua, Amy. 2011. *Battle Hymn of the Tiger Mother.* New York: Bloomsbury.

Clawson, Dan, and Naomi Gerstel. 2014. *Unequal Time: Gender, Class, and Family in Employment Schedules.* New York: Russell Sage Foundation.

Clinton, Hillary. 2015. Transcript. "Road to the White House 2016: Presidential Candidate Hillary Clinton Campaign Rally in Las Vegas." *C-SPAN* online. www.c-span .org.

Coe, Cati, and Serah Shani. 2015. "Cultural Capital and Transnational Parenting: The Case of Ghanaian Migrants in the United States." *Harvard Educational Review* 85(4): 562–86.

Cohen, Philip. 2019. "American Policy Fails at Reducing Child Poverty Because It Aims to Fix the Poor." *Washington Post*. www.washingtonpost.com.

Collins, Patricia Hill. 2009. *Black Feminist Thought: Knowledge, Consciousness, and the Politics of Empowerment*. New York: Routledge.

Coltrane, Scott. 1989. "Household Labor and the Routine Production of Gender." *Social Problems* 36: 473–90.

Connell, Raewyn. W. 1987. *Gender and Power: Society, the Person, and Sexual Politics*. Palo Alto: Stanford University Press.

———. 2005. "Advancing Gender Reform in Large-Scale Organisations: A New Approach for Practitioners and Researchers." *Policy and Society* 24(4): 5–24.

———. 2007. "The Northern Theory of Globalization." *Sociological Theory* 25(4): 368–85. doi:10.1111/j.1467–9558.2007.00314.x.

———. 2014. "Margin Becoming Centre: For a World-Centred Rethinking of Masculinities." *NORMA: International Journal for Masculinity Studies* 9(4): 217–31.

———. 2016. "Masculinities in Global Perspective: Hegemony, Contestation, and Changing Structures of Power." *Theory and Society* 45(4): 303–18.

Connor, Phillip. 2020. "More Than Nine-in-Ten People Worldwide Live in Countries with Travel Restrictions amid COVID-19." *Pew Research Center*. www.pewresearch.org.

Coontz, Stephanie. 2011. *A Strange Stirring: The Feminine Mystique and American Women at the Dawn of the 1960s*. New York: Basic Books.

Cooper, Marianne. 2000. "Being the 'Go-To Guy': Fatherhood, Masculinity, and the Organization of Work in Silicon Valley." *Qualitative Sociology* 23(4): 379–405.

Copeland, Anne P., and Sara K. Norell. 2002. "Spousal Adjustment on International Assignments: The Role of Social Support." *International Journal of Intercultural Relations* 26(3): 255–72.

Costa, Daniel, and Ron Hira. 2020. *H-1B Visas and Prevailing Wage Levels, a Majority of H-1B Employers—Including Major U.S. Tech Firms—Use the Program to Pay Migrant Workers Well Below Market Wages*. Washington, DC: Economic Policy Institute. www.epi.org.

Council of Graduate Schools (CGS). 2009. *Findings from the 2009 CGS International Graduate Admissions Survey Phase II: Final Applications and Initial Offers of Admission*. Washington, DC: Council of Graduate Schools. https://cgsnet.org.

Cross-Barnet, Caitlin, and Katrina Bell McDonald. 2015. "It's All about the Children: An Intersectional Perspective on Parenting Values among Black Married Couples in the United States." *Societies* 5(4): 855–71.

Darwin, Helana. 2018. "Omnivorous Masculinity: Gender Capital and Cultural Legitimacy in Craft Beer Culture." *Social Currents* 5(3): 301–16. doi:10.1177/2329496517748336.

Das Gupta, Monisha. 2014. "'Don't Deport Our Daddies': Gendering State Deportation Practices and Immigrant Organizing." *Gender & Society* 28(1): 83–109.

Dasgupta, Shamita D., and Sujata Warrier. 1996. "In the Footsteps of 'Arundhati': Asian Indian Women's Experience of Domestic Violence in the United States." *Violence Against Women* 2(3): 238–59.

———., ed. 1998. *A Patchwork Shawl: Chronicles of South Asian Women in America.* New Brunswick, NJ: Rutgers University Press.

———. 1998. "Gender Roles and Cultural Continuity in the Asian Indian Immigrant Community in the US." *Sex Roles* 38(11): 953–74.

De Verthelyi, Renata F. 1995. "International Students' Spouses: Invisible Sojourners in the Culture Shock Literature." *International Journal of Intercultural Relations* 19(3): 387–411.

Derrida, Jacques. 2000. "Foreigner Question." Pp. 3–74 in *Of Hospitality,* translated by Rachel Bowlby. Palo Alto: Stanford University Press.

Desai, Manisha. 2007. "The Messy Relationship between Feminisms and Globalizations." *Gender & Society* 21(6): 797–803.

Deutsch, Francine. 1999. *Halving It All: How Equally Shared Parenting Works.* Cambridge, MA: Harvard University Press.

DeVault, Marjorie L. 1994. *Feeding the Family: The Social Organization of Caring as Gendered Work.* Chicago: University of Chicago Press.

———. 1999. "Talking and Listening from Women's Standpoint." Pp. 59–83 in *Liberating Method: Feminism and Social Research.* Philadelphia: Temple University Press.

Dhingra, Pawan. 2018. "What Asian Americans Really Care about When They Care about Education." *Sociological Quarterly* 59(2): 301–19. doi:10.1080/00380253.2018.1 436944.

Dicicco-Bloom, Barbara. 2004. "The Racial and Gendered Experiences of Immigrant Nurses from Kerala, India." *Journal of Transcultural Nursing* 15(1): 26–33.

Donato, Katharine. M. 2010. "U.S. Migration from Latin America: Gendered Patterns and Shifts." *Annals of the American Academy of Political and Social Science* 630(1): 78–92. doi:10.1177/0002716210368104.

Doucet, Andrea, and Laura Merla. 2007. "Stay-at-Home Fathering: A Strategy for Balancing Work and Home in Canadian and Belgian Families." *Community, Work and Family* 10(4): 455–73.

Dow, Dawn. M. 2019. *Mothering While Black: Boundaries and Burdens of Middle-Class Parenthood.* Oakland: University of California Press.

Dreby, Joanna. 2010. *Divided by Borders: Mexican Migrants and Their Children.* Berkeley: University of California Press.

Driscoll, Anne K., Stephen T. Russell, and Lisa J. Crockett. 2008. "Parenting Styles and Youth Well-being Across Immigrant Generations." *Journal of Family Issues* 29(2): 185–209.

Du Bois, W. E. Burghardt. 1903. *The Souls of Black Folk; Essays and Sketches.* Chicago: A. G. McClurg.

Eisenstein, Hester. 2005. "A Dangerous Liaison? Feminism and Corporate Globalization." *Science & Society* 69(3): 487–518.

England, Paula. 2005 "Emerging Theories of Care Work." *Annual Review of Sociology* 31: 381–99.

Engzell, Per, and Mathieu Ichou. 2019. "Status Loss: The Burden of Positively Selected Immigrants." *International Migration Review.* doi:10.1177/0197918319850756.

Erikson, Kai T. 1976. *Everything in Its Path: Destruction of Community in the Buffalo Creek Flood.* New York: Simon & Schuster.

Escobar, Arturo. 1995. *Encountering Development: The Making and Unmaking of the Third World.* Princeton: Princeton University Press.

Espiritu, Yen Le. 1999. "Gender and Labor in Asian Immigrant Families." *American Behavioral Scientist* 42(4): 628–47.

———. 2003. *Home Bound: Filipino American Lives across Cultures, Communities, and Countries.* Berkeley: University of California Press.

Evans, Joan. 2004. "Men Nurses: A Historical and Feminist Perspective." *Journal of Advanced Nursing* 47(3): 321–28.

Fanon, Frantz. 1968. *Black Skin, White Masks.* New York: Grove Press.

Farver, Jo Ann M., Yiyuan Xu, Bakhtawar R. Bhadha, Sonia Narang, and Eli Lieber. 2007. "Ethnic Identity, Acculturation, Parenting Beliefs, and Adolescent Adjustment: A Comparison of Asian Indian and European American Families." *Merrill-Palmer Quarterly* 53(2): 184–215.

Ferree, Myra M. 1990. "Beyond Separate Spheres: Feminism and Family Research." *Journal of Marriage and Family* 52(4): 866–84.

Flores, William V., and Rina Benmayor. 1997. *Latino Cultural Citizenship: Claiming Identity, Space, and Rights.* Boston: Beacon Press.

Foner, Nancy, ed. 2009. *Across Generations: Immigrant Families in America.* New York: New York University Press.

Foner, Nancy, and Joanna Dreby. 2011. "Relations between the Generations in Immigrant Families." *Annual Review of Sociology* 37: 545–64.

Foner, Nancy, and Philip Kasinitz. 2007. "The Second Generation." Pp. 270–82 in *The New Americans: A Guide to Immigration Since 1965*, edited by Mary C. Waters, Reed Ueda, and Helen B. Marrow. Cambridge: Harvard University Press.

Fong, Timothy P. 1998. *The Contemporary Asian American Experience: Beyond the Model Minority.* Upper Saddle River, NJ: Prentice Hall.

Foucault, Michel. 1977. *Discipline and Punish: The Birth of the Prison.* London: Allen Lane.

———. 1988. *Technologies of the Self: A Seminar with Michel Foucault*, edited by L. H. Martin, H. Gutman, and P. H. Hutton. Amherst: University of Massachusetts Press.

———. 1991. "Governmentality." Pp. 87–104 in *The Foucault Effect: Studies in Governmentality*, edited by G. Burchell, C. Gordon, and M. Foucault. London: Harvester, Wheatsheaf.

———. 2000. *Essential Works of Foucault, 1954–1984.* Vol. 3, *Power*, edited by Paul Rabinow and James D. Faubion, translated by Robert Hurley and others. New York: New Press.

Freeman, Carla. 2001. "Is Local: Global as Feminine: Masculine? Rethinking the Gender of Globalization." *Journal of Women in Culture and Society* 26(4): 1007–37.

Frothingham, Sunny, and Sarah Jane Glynn. 2016. *Rhetoric vs. Reality: Paid Family and Medical Leave*. Washington, DC: Center for American Progress. www.american-progress.org.

Fu, Alyssa S., and Hazel Rose Markus. 2014. "My Mother and Me: Why Tiger Mothers Motivate Asian Americans but Not European Americans." *Personality and Social Psychology Bulletin* 40(6): 739–49.

Gamburd, Michele. R. 2000. *The Kitchen Spoon's Handle: Transnationalism and Sri Lanka's Migrant Housemaids*. Ithaca: Cornell University Press.

Garfinkel, Harold. 1967. *Studies in Ethnomethodology*. Cambridge: Polity Press.

Garner, Shelby L., Shelley F. Conroy, and Susan Gerding Bader. 2015. "Nurse Migration from India: A Literature Review." *International Journal of Nursing Studies* 52 (12): 1879–90.

Gass, Nick. 2016. "Trump Softens Opposition to H1B Visas." *Politico* Blogs. www.politico.com.

Geertz, Clifford. 1973. "Thick Description: Toward an Interpretive Theory of Culture." Pp. 143–68 in *Turning Points in Qualitative Research: Tying Knots in a Handkerchief*, edited by Yvonna S. Lincoln and Norman K. Denzin. Walnut Creek, CA: AltaMira Press.

George, Sheba. 2000. "Dirty Nurses and Men Who Play: Gender and Class." In *Global Ethnography: Forces, Connections, and Imaginations in a Postmodern World*. Berkeley: University of California Press.

———. 2005. *When Women Come First: Gender and Class in Transnational Migration*. Berkeley: University of California Press.

Giddens, Anthony. 1986. *The Constitution of Society: Outline of the Theory of Structuration*. Berkeley: University of California Press.

———. 1990. *The Consequences of Modernity*. Palo Alto: Stanford University Press.

Glenn, Evelyn N. 1990. "Cleaning Up/Kept Down: A Historical Perspective on Racial Inequality in Women's Work." *Stanford Law Review* 43(6): 1333–56.

———. 2002. *Unequal Freedom: How Race and Gender Shaped American Citizenship and Labor*. Cambridge, MA: Harvard University Press.

———. 2010. *Forced to Care: Coercion and Caregiving in America*. Cambridge, MA: Harvard University Press.

Goffman, Erving. 1959. *The Presentation of Self in Everyday Life*. Garden City, NY: Doubleday.

Golash-Boza, Tanya M. 2015. *Latina/o Sociology*. Vol. 6, *Deported: Immigrant Policing, Disposable Labor and Global Capitalism*. New York: New York University Press.

Gonzales Jr., Juan L. 1986. "Asian Indian Immigration Patterns: The Origins of the Sikh Community in California." *International Migration Review* 20(1): 40–54.

Gorman, Jean Cheng. 1998. "Parenting Attitudes and Practices of Immigrant Chinese Mothers of Adolescents." *Family Relations* 47(1): 73–80. doi:10.2307/584853.

Greenstein, Theodore N. 1996. "Gender Ideology and Perceptions of the Fairness of the Division of Household Labor: Effects on Marital Quality." *Social Forces* 74(3): 1029–42.

Guevarra, Anna R. 2006a. "The Balikbayan Researcher: Negotiating Vulnerability in Fieldwork with Filipino Labor Brokers." *Journal of Contemporary Ethnography* 35(5): 526–51.

———.2006b. "Managing 'Vulnerabilities' and 'Empowering' Migrant FILIPINA Workers: The Philippines' Overseas Employment Program." *Social Identities* 12(5): 523–41.

———. 2010. *Marketing Dreams, Manufacturing Heroes: The Transnational Labor Brokering of Filipino Workers*. New Brunswick, NJ: Rutgers University Press.

Guglielmo, Thomas A. 2003. *White on Arrival: Italians, Race, Color, and Power in Chicago, 1890–1945*. New York: Oxford University Press.

Gupta, Monica. D. 1987. "Selective Discrimination against Female Children in Rural Punjab, India." *Population and Development Review* 13(1): 77–100.

Gupta, Sanjiv. 1999. "The Effects of Transitions in Marital Status on Men's Performance of Housework." *Journal of Marriage and the Family* 61(3): 700–711.

Gurung, Shobha. H. 2015. *Nepali Migrant Women: Resistance and Survival in America*. Syracuse: Syracuse University Press.

Haberman, Maggie. 2016. "Donald Trump Says He's a 'Big Fan' of Hindus." *New York Times*. www.nytimes.com.

Hacker, S. 2017. *Pleasure, Power and Technology: Some Tales of Gender, Engineering, and the Cooperative Workplace*. New York: Routledge.

Hall, Stuart, and Paul Du Gay, eds. 1996. *Questions of Cultural Identity*. London: Sage. doi:10.4135/9781446221907.

Haraway, Donna. 1988. "Situated Knowledges: The Science Question in Feminism and the Privilege of Partial Perspective." *Feminist Studies* 14(3): 575–99.

Hardill, Irene, and Sandra Macdonald. 1998. "Choosing to Relocate: An Examination of the Impact of Expatriate Work on Dual-Career Households." *Women's Studies International Forum* 21(1): 21–29.

Harvey, David. 2007. *A Brief History of Neoliberalism*. New York: Oxford University Press.

Hawkes, Michael, Mary Kolenko, Michelle Shockness, and Krishna Diwaker. 2009. "Nursing Brain Drain from India." *Human Resources for Health* 7(1): 5.

Hays, Sharon. 1996. *The Cultural Contradictions of Motherhood*. New Haven: Yale University Press.m

Haq, Zia. 2021. "How Kerala's Economy Has Fared under LDF Rule." *Hindustan Times*. March 30, 2021. www.hindustantimes.com.

Healey, Madelaine. 2008. "Seeds That May Have Been Planted May Take Root: International Aid Nurses and Projects of Professionalism in Postindependence India, 1947–1965." *Nursing History Review* 16(1): 58–90.

Hernandez, Daniel. 2021. "From 'Alien' to 'Noncitizen': Why the Biden Word Change Matters in the Immigration Debate." *Los Angeles Times*. www.latimes.com.

Hoang, Kimberly. K. 2015. *Dealing in Desire: Asian Ascendancy, Western Decline, and the Hidden Currencies of Global Sex Work*. Berkeley: University of California Press.

Hochschild, Arlie R. 1979. "Emotion Work, Feeling Rules and Social Structure." *American Journal of Sociology* 85(3): 551–75

———. 1997. *The Time Bind: When Work Becomes Home and Home Becomes Work*. New York: Metropolitan Books.

———. 2000. "Global Care Chains and Emotional Surplus Value." Pp. 130–46 in *On the Edge: Living with Global Capitalism*, edited by A. Giddens and W. Hutton. London: Vintage.

———. 2012. *The Managed Heart: Commercialization of Human Feeling*. Berkeley: University of California Press.

Hochschild, Arlie, and Anne Machung. 2012. *The Second Shift: Working Families and the Revolution at Home*. London: Penguin Books.

Holen, Arlene. 2009. *The Budgetary Effects of High-Skilled Immigration Reform*. Washington, DC: Technology Policy Institute. https://techpolicyinstitute.org.

Holland, Jack, and Ben Fermor. 2021. "The Discursive Hegemony of Trump's Jacksonian Populism: Race, Class, and Gender in Constructions and Contestations of US National Identity, 2016–2018." *Politics* 41(1): 64–79.

Hollifield, James F. 2004. "The Emerging Migration State 1." *International Migration Review* 38(3): 885–912.

Holpuch, Amanda. 2019. "Stephen Miller: Why Is Trump's White Nationalist Aide Untouchable?" *The Guardian*. www.theguardian.com.

Hondagneu-Sotelo, Pierrette, and Ernestine Avila. 1997. "'I'm Here, but I'm There:' The Meanings of Latina Transnational Motherhood." *Gender & Society* 11(5): 548–71.

Hune, Shirley, and Gail M. Nomura, eds. 2003. *Asian/Pacific Islander American Women: A Historical Anthology*. New York: New York University Press.

Hurh, Won M., and Kwang C. Kim. 1990. "Religious Participation of Korean Immigrants in the United States." *Journal for the Scientific Study of Religion* 29(1): 19–34.

Internal Revenue Service. N.d. "Resident Aliens." www.irs.gov.

Irani, Lily, 2019. *Chasing Innovation: Making Entrepreneurial Citizens in Modern India*. Princeton: Princeton University Press.

Jachimowicz, Maia, and Deborah W. Meyers. 2002. "Temporary High-Skilled Migration." *Migration Information Source*. www.migrationpolicy.org.

Jacobs, Jerry A., and Kathleen Gerson. 2004. *The Time Divide: Work, Family, and Gender Inequality*. Cambridge, MA: Harvard University Press.

Jacoby, Harold. 1979. "Some Demographic and Social Aspects of Early East Indian Life in the United States." Pp. 159–71 in *Sikh Studies: Comparative Perspectives on a Changing Tradition*, edited by M. Juergensmeyer and N. G. Barrier. Berkeley: Graduate Theological Union.

Jacox, A. K. 2003. "Barbara Nichols on Professional Nurse Immigration and the Nursing Shortage." *Nursing and Health Policy Review* 2(1): 45–54.

Jensen, Joan M. 1988. *Passage from India: Asian Indian Immigrants in North America*. New Haven: Yale University Press.

Kalm, Sara. 2005. "Towards Global Migration Management? A Biopolitical Approach." Paper presented at the Annual Meeting of the International Studies Association, Honolulu, Hawaii. March 1–5.

Kandiyoti, Deniz. 1988. "Bargaining with Patriarchy." Special Issue to Honor Jessie Bernard, *Gender & Society* 2(3): 274–90.

Kanjanapan, Wilawan. 1995. "The Immigration of Asian Professionals to the United States: 1988–1990." Special Issue: Diversity and Comparability: International Migrants in Host Countries on Four Continents, *International Migration Review* 29(1): 7–32.

Kanter, Rosabeth. M. 2008. *Men and Women of the Corporation:* New ed. New York: Basic Books.

Kaushal, Neeraj, and Michael Fix. 2006. *The Contributions of High Skilled Immigrants.* Insight Policy Briefs. Washington, DC: Migration Policy Institute. www.migrationpolicy.org.

Kavada, Anastasia. 2015. "Creating the Collective: Social Media, the Occupy Movement and Its Constitution as a Collective Actor." *Information Communication and Society* 18(8): 872–86. doi:10.1080/1369118X.2015.1043318.

Kelkar, Govind. 2011. "MGNREGA: Change and Continuity in Gender Relations." *Journal of Economic and Social Development* 7(2): 11–24.

Kellner, Douglas. 2002. "Theorizing Globalization." *Sociological Theory* 20(3): 285–305.

Khadria, Binod. 2002. "Skilled Labour Migration from Developing Countries: Study on India." International Migration Papers No. 49, International Labour Organization, Geneva, Switzerland. www.ilo.org.

———. 2007. "International Nurse Recruitment in India." *Health Services Research* 42(3p2): 1429–36.

Khondker, Habibul H. 2011. "Role of the New Media in the Arab Spring." *Globalizations* 8(5): 675–79. doi:10.1080/14747731.2011.621287.

Kibria, Nazli. 1990. "Power, Patriarchy, and Gender Conflict in the Vietnamese Immigrant Community." *Gender & Society* 4(1): 9–24.

Kim, Minjeong. 2006. "Forced into Unpaid Carework: International Students' Wives in the United States." Pp. 162–75 in *Global Dimensions of Gender and Carework*, edited by M. K. Zommerman, J. S. Litt, and C. E. Bose. Palo Alto: Stanford University Press.

Kirkegaard, Jacob Funk. 2019. "The US H-1B Visa: A Boon for High-Skilled Immigrants from India." *Peterson Institute for International Economics (PIIE) Blogs.* www.piie.com.

Kofman, Eleonore, and Parvati Raghuram. 2006. "Gender and Global Labour Migrations: Incorporating Skilled Workers." *Antipode* 38(2): 282–303.

Koslowski, Rey. 2004. "International Cooperation on Electronic Advanced Passenger Information Transfer and Passport Biometrics." Paper presented at the International Studies Association Meeting, March 17–20, Montreal.

———. 2006. "Global Mobility and the Quest for an International Migration Regime." *Center for Migration Studies Special Issues* 21(1): 103–43.

Kumar, Radha. 1993. *The History of Doing: An Illustrated Account of Movements for Women's Rights and Feminism in India, 1800–1990*. New Delhi: Zubaan.

Kurien, Prema. 1999. "Gendered Ethnicity: Creating a Hindu Indian Identity in the United States." *American Behavioral Scientist* 42(4): 648–70.

———. 2001. "'We Are Better Hindus Here': Religion and Ethnicity among Indian Americans." Pp. 99–120 in *Religions in Asian America: Building Faith Communities*, edited by P. G. Min and J. H. Kim. Walnut Creek, CA: AltaMira Press.

———. 2002. *Kaleidoscopic Ethnicity: International Migration and the Reconstruction of Community Identities in India*. New Brunswick, NJ: Rutgers University Press.

Lan, Pei-Chia. 2018. *Raising Global Families Parenting, Immigration, and Class in Taiwan and the US*. Palo Alto: Stanford University Press.

Lareau, Annette. 2003. *Unequal Childhoods: Class, Race, and Family Life*. Berkeley: University of California Press.

———. 2011. *Unequal Childhoods: Class, Race, and Family Life*. 2nd ed. Berkeley: University of California Press.

Larner, Wendy. 2000. "Neo-Liberalism: Policy, Ideology, Governmentality." *Studies in Political Economy* 63(1): 5–25.

Lazzarato, Maurizio. 2000. "From Biopower to Biopolitics." *Multitudes* 1(1): 45–57.

Lee, Jennifer, and Min Zhou. 2004. *Asian American Youth: Culture, Identity and Ethnicity*. New York: Routledge.

———. 2007. "An Indigestible Meal? Foucault, Governmentality and State Theory." *Distinktion: Scandinavian Journal of Social Theory* 8(2): 43–64.

———. 2015. *The Asian American Achievement Paradox*. New York: Russell Sage Foundation.

Lemke, Thomas. 2002. "Foucault, Governmentality, and Critique." *Rethinking Marxism* 14(3): 49–64.

Leonard, Karen I. 1997. *The South Asian Americans*. Westport, CT: Greenwood Press.

Lind, Dara. 2014. "Everything You Need to Know about Obama's Executive Action on Immigration." *Vox*. www.vox.com.

Loewen, James W. 1988. *The Mississippi Chinese: Between Black and White*. 2nd ed. Long Grove, IL: Waveland Press.

Lopez, Nancy. 2003. *Hopeful Girls, Troubled Boys: Race and Gender Disparity in Urban Education*. New York: Routledge.

Lorber, Judith. 1994. *Paradoxes of Gender*. New Haven: Yale University Press.

Lorde, Audre. 2007. "The Master's Tools Will Never Dismantle the Master's House." Pp. 110–14 in *Sister Outsider: Essays and Speeches*. Berkeley: Crossing Press.

Lovejoy, Meg, and Pamela Stone. 2012. "Opting Back In: The Influence of Time at Home on Professional Women's Career Redirection after Opting Out." *Gender, Work & Organization* 19(6): 631–53. doi:10.1111/j.1468-0432.2010.00550.x.

Lowe, Lisa. 1996. *Immigrant Acts: On Asian American Cultural Politics*. Durham: Duke University Press.

Lowell, B. L. 2000. "H-1B Temporary Workers: Estimating the Population." Working Paper No. 12. La Jolla: Center for Comparative Immigration Studies, University of California, San Diego.

Luibhéid, Eithne. 2008. "Queer/Migration: An Unruly Body of Scholarship." *GLQ: A Journal of Lesbian and Gay Studies* 14(2): 169–90.

———. 2018. "Heteronormativity: A Bridge between Queer Migration and Critical Trafficking Studies." *Women's Studies in Communication* 41(4): 305–09.

Mahalingam, Ramaswami, and Janxin Leu. 2005. "Culture, Essentialism, Immigration and Representations of Gender." *Theory & Psychology* 15(6): 839–60.

Mahalingam, Ramaswami, and S. Ramakrishnan. 2002. "A Framework for a Course on Training Engineers for a Global Multicultural Professional Environment." Paper presented at the Fifth UICEE Annual Conference on Engineering and Education, February 6–9, Chennai.

Mahmood, Saba. 2005. *Politics of Piety: The Islamic Revival and the Feminist Subject.* Princeton: Princeton University Press.

Manalansan IV, Martin F. 2003. *Global Divas: Filipino Gay Men in the Diaspora.* Durham: Duke University Press.

———. 2006. "Queer Intersections: Sexuality and Gender in Migration Studies." *International Migration Review* 40(1): 224–49.

Manohar, Namita N. 2008. "Gender and Ethnicity in Union Formation: The Case of Second-Generation Patels." *International Journal of Sociology of the Family* 34(2): 209–34.

———. 2009. "Memoirs of Bharitya Naris (Indian Women): Gender, Work and Family in Transnational Migration." PhD diss., University of Florida.

Manohar, Namita. N. 2013. "Mothering for Class and Ethnicity: The Case of Indian Professional Immigrants in the United States." Pp. 159–85 in *Advances in Gender Research.* Vol 17, *Notions of Family: Intersectional Perspectives*, edited by Marla H. Kohlman, Dana B. Krieg, and Bette J. Dickerson. Bingley, UK: Emerald Group Publishing Limited.

———. 2019. "Gendered Agency in Skilled Migration: The Case of Indian Women in the United States." *Gender & Society* 33(6): 935–60.

Manohar, Namita N., and Pallavi Banerjee. 2016. "H-1B Visas," Pp. 161–68 in *Contemporary Issues of People of Color: Surviving and Thriving in the U.S. Today.* Santa Barbara, CA: ABC-CLIO.

Martin, Patricia Yancey. 2001. "'Mobilizing Masculinities': Women's Experiences of Men at Work." *Organization* 8(4): 587–618.

———. 2004. "Gender as Social Institution." *Social Forces* 82(4): 1249–73.

Martin, Philip, Manolo Abella, and Christiane Kuptsch. 2006. *Managing Labor Migration in the Twenty-First Century.* New Haven: Yale University Press.

Masselink, Leah E., and Cheryl B. Jones. 2014. "Immigration Policy and Internationally Educated Nurses in the United States: A Brief History." *Nursing Outlook* 62(1): 39–45.

McElmurry, Beverly J., Karen Solheim, Rieko Kishi, Marcia A. Coffia, Wendy Woith, and Poolsuk Janepanish. 2006. "Ethical Concerns in Nurse Migration." *Journal of Professional Nursing* 22(4): 226–35.

McKee, Kim. 2009. "Post-Foucauldian Governmentality: What Does It Offer Critical Social Policy Analysis?" *Critical Social Policy* 29(3): 465–86.

Mead, George Herbert. 1934. *Mind, Self, and Society from the Standpoint of a Social Behaviorist*. Chicago: University of Chicago Press.

Meares, Carina. 2010. "A Fine Balance: Women, Work and Skilled Migration." *Women's Studies International Forum* 33(5): 473–81.

Mehrotra, Meeta. 1999. "The Social Construction of Wife Abuse: Experiences of Asian Indian Women in the United States." *Violence Against Women* 5(6): 619–40.

Menkel-Meadow, Carrie. 2019. "The Culture of Negotiation: Trumpian Imprints on the Future?" *Negotiation Journal* 35(1): 221–25.

Menjívar, Cecilia. 1998. "The Intersection of Work and Gender: Central American Immigrant Women and Employment in California." Pp. 101–26 in *Gender and U.S. Immigration: Contemporary Trends*, edited by H. Pierrette. Berkeley: University of California Press.

———. 2006. "Liminal Legality: Salvadoran and Guatemalan Immigrants' Lives in the United States." *American Journal of Sociology* 111(4): 999–1037.

Messner, Michael A., and Jeffrey Montez de Oca. 2005. "The Male Consumer as Loser: Beer and Liquor Ads in Mega Sports Media Events." *Signs: Journal of Women in Culture and Society* 30(3): 1879–1909. doi:10.1086/427523.

Milkie, Melissa, and Pia Peltola. 1999. "Playing All the Roles: Gender and the Work-Family Balancing Act." *Journal of Marriage and the Family* 61: 476–90.

Min, Pyong G. 1998. *Changes and Conflicts: Korean Immigrant Families in New York*. Boston: Allyn and Bacon.

———. 2003. "Korean 'Comfort Women' the Intersection of Colonial Power, Gender, and Class." *Gender & Society* 17(6): 938–57.

Misra, Joya, Jonathan Woodring, and Sabine N. Merz. 2006. "The Globalization of Care Work: Neoliberal Economic Restructuring and Migration Policy." *Globalizations* 3(3): 317–32.

Mitra, Aparna, and Pooja Singh. 2007. "Human Capital Attainment and Gender Empowerment: The Kerala Paradox." *Social Science Quarterly* 88(5): 1227–42.

Mohanty, Chandra. 1988. "Under Western Eyes: Feminist Scholarship and Colonial Discourses." *Feminist Review* 30(1): 61–88.

———. 2003a. *Feminism without Borders: Decolonizing Theory, Practicing Solidarity*. Durham: Duke University Press.

———. 2003b. "'Under Western Eyes' Revisited: Feminist Solidarity through Anticapitalist Struggles." *Signs: Journal of Women in Culture and Society* 28(2): 499–535.

———. 2006. "US Empire and the Project of Women's Studies: Stories of Citizenship, Complicity and Dissent." *Gender, Place & Culture* 13(1): 7–20.

———. 2009. "Social Justice and Politics of Identity." Pp. 529–40 in *The Sage Handbook of Identities*, edited by C. T. Mohanty and M. Wetherell. London: Sage.

Mohanty, Chandra Talpade, Ann Russo, and Lourdes Torres, eds. 1991. *Third World Women and the Politics of Feminism*. Bloomington: Indiana University Press.

Montes, Veronica. 2013. "The Role of Emotions in The Construction of Masculinity: Guatemalan Migrant Men, Transnational Migration, and Family Relations." *Gender & Society* 27(4): 469–90.

Moon, Seungsook. 2003. "Immigration and Mothering: Case Studies from Two Generations of Korean Immigrant Women." *Gender & Society* 17(6): 840–60.

Moore, Mignon. 2011. *Invisible Families: Gay Identities, Relationships, and Motherhood among Black Women*. Berkeley: University of California Press.

Munoz, Cecilia, and Jeffery Zients. 2016. "The President's Actions to Promote High-Skill Immigration." White House Blog. https://obamawhitehouse.archives.gov.

Nair, Sreelekha, and Marie Percot. 2007. "Transcending Boundaries: Indian Nurses in Internal and International Migration." Occasional Paper No. 49, Center for Women's Development Studies, New Delhi. www.cwds.ac.in.

National Council of State Boards of Nursing. 2016. *NCLEX Pass Rates*. www.ncsbn.org.

Naujoks, Daniel. 2009. "Emigration, Immigration, and Diaspora Relations in India." *Migration Information Source*. www.migrationpolicy.org.

———. 2015. "The Securitization of Dual Citizenship. National Security Concerns and the Making of The Overseas Citizenship of India." *Diaspora Studies* 8(1): 18–36. doi: 10.1080/09739572.2014.957975.

Ngai, Mae M. 2014. *Impossible Subjects: Illegal Aliens and the Making of Modern America*. Updated ed. Princeton: Princeton University Press.

Obama, Barack. 2013. Transcript. "Obama's Immigration Remarks (transcript)." *POLITICO* online. www.politico.com.

O'Connell, Julia, and Derek Layder. 1994. *Methods, Sex and Madness*. New York: Routledge.

Omi, Michael, and Howard Winant. 2014. *Racial Formation in the United States*. New York: Routledge.

Ong, Aihwa. 1999. *Flexible Citizenship: The Cultural Logics of Transnationality*. Durham: Duke University Press.

———. 2003. *Buddha Is Hiding: Refugees, Citizenship, and the New America*. Oakland: University of California Press.

———. 2006. *Neoliberalism as Exception: Mutations in Citizenship and Sovereignty*. Durham: Duke University Press.

Ong, Aihwa, and Stephen J. Collier, eds. 2005. *Global Assemblages Technology, Politics, and Ethics as Anthropological Problems*. Malden: Blackwell.

Ong, Aihwa, Virginia R. Dominguez, Jonathan Friedman, Nina G. Schiller, Verena Stolcke, David Y. Wu, and Hu Ying. 1996. "Cultural Citizenship as Subject-Making: Immigrants Negotiate Racial and Cultural Boundaries in the United States [and Comments and Reply]." *Current Anthropology* 37(5): 737–62.

Padavic, Irene, and Barbara F. Reskin. 2002. *Women and Men at Work*. Thousand Oaks, CA: Pine Forge Press.

Pande, Amrita. 2017. "Mobile Masculinities: Migrant Bangladeshi Men in South Africa." *Gender and Society* 31(3): 383–406.

Pande, Rohini P. 2003. "Selective Gender Differences in Childhood Nutrition and Immunization in Rural India: The Role of Siblings." *Demography* 40(3): 395–418.

Papa, Jeff. 2005. "Basic Options in the Non-immigrant Business Context." *Indiana International & Comparative Law Review* 15(2): 279–300.

Park, Kyeyoung. 1997. *The Korean American Dream: Immigrants and Small Business in New York City*. Ithaca: Cornell University Press.

Parreñas, Rhacel Salazar. 2001. "Mothering from a Distance: Emotions, Gender, and Intergenerational Relations in Filipino Transnational Families." *Feminist Studies* 27(2): 361–90. doi:10.2307/3178765.

———. 2015. *Servants of Globalization: Migration and Domestic Work*. Palo Alto: Stanford University Press.

Paul, Sonia. 2018. "The Children of H-1B Visa Holders Are Growing up—and Still Waiting for Green Cards." *PRI's The World*. https://interactive.pri.org.

Pedraza, Silvia. 1991. "Women and Migration: The Social Consequences of Gender." *Annual Review of Sociology* 17(1): 303–25.

Percot, Marie, and S. I. Rajan. 2007. "Female Emigration from India: Case Study of Nurses." *Economic and Political Weekly* 42(4): 318–25.

Peri, Giovanni. 2010. *The Impact of Immigrants in Recession and Economic Expansion*. Washington, DC: Migration Policy Institute. www.migrationpolicy.org.

Pessar, Patricia. 1986. "The Role of Gender in Dominican Settlement in the United States." Pp. 273–94 in *Women and Change in Latin America: New Directions in Sex and Class*, edited by J. Nash and H. Safa. South Hadley, MA: Bergin & Garvey.

Pettersen, William. 1966. "Success Story, Japanese-American Style." *New York Times Magazine*, January 9, 180. www.nytimes.com.

Pfeffer, Carla A. 2017. *Queering Families: The Postmodern Partnerships of Cisgender Women and Transgender Men*. New York: Oxford University Press.

Philip, Thomas, and Pratim Sengupta. 2021. "Theories of Learning as Theories of Society: A Contrapuntal Approach to Expanding Disciplinary Authenticity in Computing." *Journal of the Learning Sciences* 30(2): 330–49.

Pittman, Patricia M., Amanda J. Folsom, and Emily Bass. 2010. "US-Based Recruitment of Foreign-Educated Nurses: Implications of an Emerging Industry." *American Journal of Nursing* 110(6): 38–48.

Poros, Maritsa V. 2001. "The Role of Migrant Networks in Linking Local Labour Markets: The Case of Asian Indian Migration to New York and London." *Global Networks* 1(3): 243–56.

Portes, Alejandro, and Patricia Fernández-Kelly. 2008. "No Margin for Error: Educational and Occupational Achievement Among Disadvantaged Children of Immigrants." *Annals of the American Academy of Political and Social Science* 620(1): 12–36.

Poster, Winifred R., and Srirupa Prasad. 2005. "Work-Family Relations in Transnational Perspective: A View from High-Tech Firms in India and the United States." *Social Problems* 52(1): 122–46.

Prashad, Vijay. 2000. *The Karma of Brown Folk*. Minneapolis: University of Minnesota Press.

Puar, Jasbir. 2013. "Rethinking Homonationalism." *International Journal of Middle East Studies* 45(2): 336–39.

Purkayastha, Bandana. 2002. "Rules, Roles, and Realities: Indo-American Families in the United States." Pp. 212–24 in *Minority Families in the United States: A Multicultural Perspective*, edited by R. L. Taylor. 3rd ed. New York: Pearson Publishers.

———. 2005. "Skilled Migration and Cumulative Disadvantage: The Case of Highly Qualified Asian Indian Immigrant Women in the US." *Geoforum* 36(2): 181–96.

———. 2010. "Interrogating intersectionality: Contemporary Globalisation and Racialised Gendering in the Lives of Highly Educated South Asian Americans and Their Children." *Journal of Intercultural Studies* 31(1): 29–47.

———. 2018. "Migration, Migrants, and Human Security." *Current Sociology* 66(2): 167–91.

Pyke, Karen. 2000. "'The Normal American Family' as an Interpretive Structure of Family Life among Grown Children of Korean and Vietnamese Immigrants." *Journal of Marriage and Family* 62(1): 240–55.

Radhakrishnan, Smitha. 2011. *Appropriately Indian: Gender and Culture in a New Transnational Class*. Durham: Duke University Press.

Raghuram, Parvati, and Eleonore Kofman. 2004. "Out of Asia: Skilling, Re-Skilling and Deskilling of Female Migrants." *Women's Studies International Forum* 27(2): 95–100.

Rajas, Jarmila. 2015. "Disciplining the Human Rights of Immigrants: Market Veridiction and the Echoes of Eugenics in Contemporary EU Immigration Policies." *Third World Quarterly* 36(6): 1129–44.

Rangarajan, Sinduja. 2019. "The Trump Administration Is Denying H-1B Visas at a Dizzying Rate, But It's Hit a Snag." *Mother Jones*. https://motherjones.com.

Ranson, Gillian. 2010. *Against the Grain: Couples, Gender, and the Reframing of Parenting*. Toronto: University of Toronto Press.

Ray, Ranita. 2017. *The Making of a Teenage Service Class: Poverty and Mobility in an American City*. Oakland: University of California Press.

Reddy, Sujani. 2008. "Women on the Move: A History of Indian Nurse Migration to the United States." PhD diss., New York University.

Rehel, Erin M. 2014. "When Dad Stays Home Too: Paternity Leave, Gender, and Parenting." *Gender & Society* 28(1): 110–32.

Reny, Tyler T., Loren Collingwood, and Ali A Valenzuela. 2019. "Vote Switching in the 2016 Election: How Racial and Immigration Attitudes, Not Economics, Explain Shifts in White Voting." *Public Opinion Quarterly* 83(1): 91–113. doi:^#0.1093/poq/nfz011.

Reskin, Barbara F. 1988. "Bringing the Men Back In: Sex Differentiation and the Devaluation of Women's Work." *Gender & Society* 2(1): 58–81.

Rich, Adrienne. 1980. "Compulsory Heterosexuality and Lesbian Existence." *Signs: Journal of Women in Culture and Society* 5(4): 631–60.

Richwine, Jason 2009. "Indian Americans: The New Model Minority." *Forbes*. www .forbes.com.

Ridgeway, Cecilia L. 2011. *Framed by Gender: How Gender Inequality Persists in the Modern World*. New York: Oxford University Press.

Ridgeway, Cecilia L., and Shelley J. Correll. 2000. "Limiting Inequality through Interaction: The End(s) of Gender." *Contemporary Sociology* 29(1): 110–20.

———. 2004. "Unpacking the Gender System: A Theoretical Perspective on Gender Beliefs and Social Relations." *Gender & Society* 18(4): 510–31.

Risman, Barbara J. 1998. *Gender Vertigo: American Families in Transition*. New Haven: Yale University Press.

———. 2004. "Gender as a Social Structure: Theory Wrestling with Activism." *Gender & Society* 18(4): 429–50.

———. 2018. *Where the Millennials Will Take Us: A New Generation Wrestles with the Gender Structure*. New York: Oxford University Press.

Rodriguez, Robyn M. 2010. *Migrants for Export: How the Philippine State Brokers Labor to the World*. Minneapolis: University of Minnesota Press.

Roediger, David R. 2018. *Working toward Whiteness: How America's Immigrants Became White: The Strange Journey from Ellis Island to the Suburbs*. Reprint ed. New York: Basic Books.

Romero, Mary. 2011. "Constructing Mexican Immigrant Women as a Threat to American Families." *International Journal of Sociology of the Family* 37(1): 49–68.

———. 2018. "Reflections on Globalized Care Chains and Migrant Women Workers." *Critical Sociology* 44(7–8): 1179–89. doi:10.1177/0896920517748497.

Romero, Mary, and Valdez, Z. 2016. "Introduction to the Special Issue: Intersectionality and Entrepreneurship." *Ethnic and Racial Studies* 39(9): 1553–65.

Roopnarine, Jaipaul L., Ambika Krishnakumar, Aysegul Metindogan, and Melanie Evans. 2006. "Links between Parenting Styles, Parent–Child Academic Interaction, Parent–School Interaction, and Early Academic Skills and Social Behaviors in Young Children of English-Speaking Caribbean Immigrants." *Early Childhood Research Quarterly* 21(2): 238–52.

Rose, Nikolas. 1996. "Governing 'Advanced' Liberal Democracies." Pp. 37–64 in *Foucault and Political Reason: Liberalism, Neo-liberalism, and Rationalities of Government*, edited by A. Barry, T. Osborne, and N. Rose. London: UCL Press.

Rose, Nikolas, and Peter Miller. 1992. "Political Power beyond the State: Problematics of Government." *British Journal of Sociology* 43(2): 173–205.

Rose, Nikolas, Pat O'Malley, and Mariana Valverde. 2006. "Governmentality." *Annual Review of Law and Society* 2: 83–104.

Ruark, Erik A., and Matthew Graham. 2011. *Jobs Americans Can't Do? The Myth of a Skilled Worker Shortage*. Washington, DC: Federation for American Immigration Reform (FAIR). www.fairus.org.

Rudrappa, Sharmila. 2009. "Cyber-Coolies and Techno-Braceros: Race and Commodi-
fication of Indian Information Technology Guest Workers in the United States."
University of San Francisco Law Review 44(2): 353–72.

Sahoo, Ajaya K., Dave Sangha, and Melissa Kelly. 2010. "From 'Temporary Migrants'
to 'Permanent Residents': Indian H-1B Visa Holders in the United States." *Asian
Ethnicity* 11(3): 293–309.

Salter, Mark B. 2004. "Passports, Mobility, and Security: How Smart Can the Border
Be?" *International Studies Perspectives* 5(1): 71–91.

———. 2006. "The Global Visa Regime and the Political Technologies of the International Self: Borders, Bodies, Biopolitics." *Alternatives: Global, Local, Political* 31(2):
167–89.

Salzinger, Leslie. 2003. *Genders in Production: Making Workers in Mexico's Global Factories*. Berkeley: University of California Press.

Sassen, Saskia. 1996. "The State and the New Geography of Power." Pp. 1–32 in *Losing
Control? Sovereignty in the Age of Globalization*. New York: Columbia University
Press.

———. 2000. "Women's Burden: Counter-Geographies of Globalization and the Feminization of Survival." *Journal of International Affairs* 53(2): 503–24.

———. 2003. "Strategic Instantiations of Gendering in the Global Economy." Pp. 43–60
in *Gender and US Immigration: Contemporary Trends*, edited by P. Hondagneu-
Sotelo. Berkeley: University of California Press.

———. 2008. "Two Stops in Today's New Global Geographies: Shaping Novel Labor
Supplies and Employment Regimes." *American Behavioral Scientist* 52(3): 457–96.

Schmalzbauer, Leah. 2009. "Gender on a New Frontier: Mexican Migration in the
Rural Mountain West." *Gender & Society* 23(6): 747–67.

Segal, Uma A. 2002. *A Framework for Immigration: Asians in the United States*. New
York: Columbia University Press.

Segura, Denise A. 1989. "Chicana and Mexican Immigrant Women at Work: The Impact
of Class, Race, and Gender on Occupational Mobility." *Gender & Society* 3(1): 37–52.

Shah, Shivali. 2007. "Middle Class, Documented, and Helpless: The H-4 Visa Blind."
Pp. 195–210 in *Body Evidence: Intimate Violence against South Asian Women in
America*, edited by Shamita Das Dasgupta. New Brunswick, NJ: Rutgers University
Press.

Sharma, Dinesh C. 2015. *The Outsourcer: The Story of India's IT Revolution*. Cambridge,
MA: MIT Press.

Sharma, Rashmi. 2011. "Gender and International Migration: The Profile of Female
Migrants from India." *Social Scientist* 39(3/4): 37–63.

Smith, Ben. 2011. "Report: U.S. Needs Immigration Boost of High-Skilled Workers."
CNN online. https://edition.cnn.com.

Smith, Dorothy E. 2005. *Institutional Ethnography: A Sociology for People*. Oxford:
AltaMira Press.

Smith, Robert. 2006. *Mexican New York: Transnational Lives of New Immigrants*.
Berkeley: University of California Press.

Spivak, Gayatri C. 1988. "Can the Subaltern Speak?" Pp. 271–313 in *Marxism and the Interpretation of Culture*, edited by C. Nelson and L. Grossberg. Urbana: University of Illinois Press.

Sprague, Joey. 2016. *Feminist Methodologies for Critical Researchers: Bridging Differences*. Walnut Creek: AltaMira Press.

Stiglitz, Joseph E. 2003. "Globalization and Growth in Emerging Markets and the New Economy." *Journal of Policy Modeling* 25(5): 505–24. doi:10.1016/S0161–8938(03)00043–7.

Suárez-Orozco, Carola, and Marcelo M. Suárez-Orozco. 2002. *Children of Immigration*. Rev. ed. Cambridge: Harvard University Press.

Sullivan, Oriel. 2006. *Changing Gender Relations, Changing Families: Tracing the Pace of Change over Time*. Gender Lens Series. New York: Rowman & Littlefield.

Surowiecki, James. 2012. "The Track Star Economy." *The New Yorker*. www.newyorker.com.

Swartz, Teresa Toguchi. 2009. "Intergenerational Family Relations in Adulthood: Patterns, Variations, and Implications in the Contemporary United States." *Annual Review of Sociology* 35: 191–212.

Szalai, Alexander. 1972. "Design Specifications for the Surveys." Pp. 31–41 in *The Use of Time: Daily Activities of Urban and Suburban Populations in Twelve Countries*, edited by A. Szalai. The Hague: Mouton.

Takaki, Ronald. 1989. *Strangers from a Different Shore: A History of Asian Americans*. New York: Little Brown.

Thibodeau, Patrick. 2017. "Trump Reviews Right of H-1B Spouses to Work." *Computerworld*. www.computerworld.com.

Thomas, Philomena. 2006. "The International Migration of Indian Nurses." *International Nursing Review* 53(4): 277–83.

Thompson, Maddy, and Margaret Walton-Roberts. 2019. "International Nurse Migration from India and the Philippines: The Challenge of Meeting the Sustainable Development Goals in Training, Orderly Migration and Healthcare Worker Retention." *Journal of Ethnic and Migration Studies* 45(14): 2583–99. doi:10.1080/1369183X.2018.1456748.

Timmons, Stephen, Catrin Evans, and Sreelekha Nair. 2016. "The Development of the Nursing Profession in a Globalised Context: A Qualitative Case Study in Kerala, India." *Social Science & Medicine* 166: 41–48.

Toro-Morn, Maura I. 1995. "Gender, Class, Family, and Migration: Puerto Rican Women in Chicago." *Gender & Society* 9(6): 712–26.

Turner, Joe, and Marcia Vera Espinoza. 2021. "The Affective and Intimate Life of the Family Migration Visa: Knowing, Feeling and Encountering the Heteronormative State." *Geopolitics* 26(2): 357–77.

U.S. Census Bureau. 2011. "DP03: Selected Economic Characteristics, 2006–2010 American Community Survey 5-Year Estimates." https://ocgov.net.

U.S. Citizenship and Immigration Services. 2018. *Characteristics of H-1B Specialty Occupation Workers, Fiscal Year 2017 Annual Report to Congress*. Washington, DC: U.S. Department of Homeland Security. www.uscis.gov.

U.S. Congress. House of Representatives. *Fairness for High-Skilled Immigrants Act of 2011.* H.R. 3012. 112th Cong., 2nd sess., 2011. www.congress.gov.

U.S. Department of Homeland Security. 2012. "DHS Reforms to Attract and Retain Highly Skilled Immigrants." www.dhs.gov.

———. A Rule of February 25, 2015. "Employment Authorization for Certain H-4 Dependent Spouses." *Federal Register* 80(37): 10284–312. Codified at 8 C.F.R. §§ 214 and 274. www.federalregister.gov.

———. N.d. "Lawful Permanent Residents (LPR)." www.dhs.gov.

———. N.d. "Nonimmigrant Admissions." www.dhs.gov.

U.S. Department of Homeland Security, Office of Immigration Statistics. 2008. "Table 3: Persons Obtaining Legal Permanent Resident Status by Region and Country of Birth: Fiscal Years 1998 to 2007." P. 12 in *Yearbook of Immigration Statistics: 2007.* Washington, DC: Department of Homeland Security. www.dhs.gov.

———. 2018. *Annual Flow Report, Nonimmigrant Admissions.* Washington, DC: Department of Homeland Security. www.dhs.gov.

U.S. General Accounting Office (GAO). 2000. *H-1B Foreign Workers: Better Controls Needed to Help Employers and Protect Workers. GAO Report No. HEHS-00–157.* Washington, DC: U.S. Government Printing Office. www.gao.go.

U.S. President. Proclamation 10052 of June 22, 2020. "Suspending Entry of Aliens Who Present a Risk to the U.S. Labor Market Following the Coronavirus Outbreak." *Federal Register* 85(123): 38263–67. www.federalregister.gov.

Urry, John. 2000. "Mobile Sociology." *British Journal of Sociology* 51(1): 185–203.

Vargas, Jose Antonio. 2014. "Why I Made 'Documented.'" *CNN* online. www.cnn.com.

Wade, Lisa. 2013. "The Growing Cost of Having Kids Is Tipping More Women Towards Ambivalence about Motherhood." *AlterNet.* www.alternet.org.

———. 2016. "The Invisible Workload That Drags Women Down." *Money.* https://money.com.

Walani, Salimah R. 2015. "Global Migration of Internationally Educated Nurses: Experiences of Employment Discrimination." *International Journal of Africa Nursing Sciences* 3: 65–70.

Wall, Glenda, and Stephanie Arnold. 2007. "How Involved Is Involved Fathering? An Exploration of the Contemporary Culture of Fatherhood." *Gender & Society* 21(4): 508–27.

Walsh, James P. 2014. "Watchful Citizens: Immigration Control, Surveillance and Societal Participation." *Social and Legal Studies* 23(2): 237–59.

Walton-Roberts, Margaret. 2012. "Contextualizing the Global Nursing Care Chain: International Migration and the Status of Nursing in Kerala, India." *Global Networks* 12(2): 175–94.

———. 2015. "International Migration of Health Professionals and the Marketization and Privatization of Health Education in India: From Push–Pull to Global Political Economy." *Social Science & Medicine* 124: 374–82. doi:10.1016/j.socscimed.2014.10.004.

Walton-Roberts, Margaret, Smita Bhutani, and Amandeep Kaur. 2017. "Care and Global Migration in the Nursing Profession: A North Indian Perspective." *Australian Geographer* 48(1): 59–77. doi:10.1080/00049182.2016.1266633.

Ward, Jane, and Beth Schneider. 2009. "The Reaches of Heteronormativity: An Introduction." *Gender & Society* 23(4): 433–39.

Warner, R. Stephen. 2005. *A Church of Our Own: Disestablishment and Diversity in American Religion*. Newark, NJ: Rutgers University Press.

Warner, R. Stephen., and Judith G. Wittner, eds. 1998. *Gatherings in Diaspora: Religious Communities and the New Immigration*. Philadelphia: Temple University Press.

Warren, Jonathan. W., and France Winddance Twine. 1997. "White Americans, the New Minority? Non-Blacks and the Ever-Expanding Boundaries of Whiteness." *Journal of Black Studies* 28(2): 200–18.

Wasem, Ruth Ellen. 2006. "H-1B Visas: Legislative History, Trends over Time, and Pathways to Permanent Residence." Memorandum, Congressional Research Service, Washington, DC. www.fosterglobal.com.

Webster, Juliet. 2014. *Shaping Women's Work: Gender, Employment and Information Technology*. New York: Routledge.

Weisshaar, Katherine. 2018. "From Opt Out to Blocked Out: The Challenges for Labor Market Re-Entry after Family-Related Employment Lapses." *American Sociological Review* 83(1): 34–60. doi:10.1177/0003122417752355.

Wells, Munira. 2013. "The Experiences of Indian Nurses in America." *Seton Hall University Dissertations and Theses* (ETDs). 1844. https://scholarship.shu.edu.

West, Candace, and Don H. Zimmerman. 1987. "Doing Gender." *Gender & Society* 1(2): 125–51.

Whatley, Monica, and Jeanne Batalova. 2013. "Limited English Proficient Population of the United States." *Migration Information Source*. www.migrationpolicy.org.

The White House, Obama Administration. 2014. "Remarks by the President in Address to the Nation on Immigration." Washington, DC: The White House. https://obamawhitehouse.archives.gov.

———. N.d. "Tell Us What You Think about We the People and the Petition Response 'Allowing Employment Authorization for H-4 Dependent Spouses.'" Washington, DC: The White House. https://obamawhitehouse.archives.gov.

Williams, Joan. 2000. *Unbending Gender: Why Family and Work Conflict and What to Do about It*. New York: Oxford University Press.

Williams, Raymond B. 1996. *Cambridge Studies in Religious Traditions*. Vol. 9, *Christian Pluralism in the United States: The Indian Immigrant Experience*. Cambridge: Cambridge University Press.

Wingfield, Adia H. 2009. "Racializing the Glass Escalator: Reconsidering Men's Experiences with Women's Work." *Gender & Society* 23(1): 5–26.

———. 2019. *Flatlining: Race, Work, and Health Care in the New Economy*. Oakland: University of California Press.

Wolf, Diane L. 1996. *Feminist Dilemmas in Fieldwork*. Boulder: Westview Press.

Wooten, Melissa E., and Enobong H. Branch. 2012. "Defining Appropriate Labor: Race, Gender, and Idealization of Black Women in Domestic Service." *Race, Gender & Class* 19(3–4): 292–308.

The World Bank. 2019. "Record High Remittances Sent Globally in 2018." www.world bank.org.

Wu, Frank H. 2003. *Yellow: Race in America Beyond Black and White*. New York: Basic Books.

Xiang, Biao. 2005. "Gender, Dowry and the Migration System of Indian Information Technology Professionals." *Indian Journal of Gender Studies* 12(2–3): 357–80.

———. 2007. *Global "Body Shopping": An Indian Labor System in the Information Technology Industry*. Princeton: Princeton University Press.

———. 2011. "A Ritual Economy of 'Talent': China and Overseas Chinese Professionals." *Journal of Ethnic and Migration Studies* 37(5): 821–38.

Young, Marisa., Jean E. Wallace, and Alicia J. Polachek. 2015. "Gender Differences in Perceived Domestic Task Equity: A Study of Professionals." *Journal of Family Issues* 36(13): 1751–81.

Zavella, Patricia. 1997. "Feminist Insider Dilemmas: Constructing Ethnic Identity with 'Chicana' Informants." Pp. 42–61 in *Situated Lives: Gender and Culture in Everyday Life*, edited by L. Lamphere, H. Ragoné, and P. Zavella. New York: Routledge.

Zhou, Min. 2009. "Conflict, Coping and Reconciliation: Intergenerational Relations in Chinese Immigrant Families." Pp. 21–47 in *Across Generations: Immigrant Families in America*, edited by Nancy Foner. New York: New York University Press.

Zinn, Maxine B. 1979. "Field Research in Minority Communities: Ethical, Methodological and Political Observations by an Insider." *Social Problems* 27(2): 209–19.

Zong, Jie, and Jeanne Batalova. 2017. "Indian Immigrants in the United States in 2015." *Migration Information Source*. www.migrationpolicy.org.

Zong, Jie, Jeanne Batalova, and Micayla Burrows. 2019. "Frequently Requested Statistics on Immigrants and Immigration in the United States in 2018." *Migration Information Source*. www.migrationpolicy.org.

INDEX

Page numbers in *italics* refer to Figures and Tables

ABOUT THE AUTHOR

PALLAVI BANERJEE is Associate Professor in the Department of Sociology at the University of Calgary. Her research interests are situated at the intersections of sociology of immigration, refugee studies, gender, unpaid and paid labor, intersectionality, transnationalism, minority families, and the Global South. She directs the Critical Gender, Intersectionality and Migration Research Group at the University of Calgary, and her research is supported by Social Sciences and Humanities Research Council, Canada, and Immigration, Refugees and Citizenship Canada.